Highly Favored of the Lord

Volume IV

Mike Stroud

Copyright *Highly Favored of the Lord*

Copyright © 2017 by Mike Stroud. All rights reserved.
cimprint@live.com

No part of this publication may be reproduced, stored in a retrieval system or transmitted in any way by any means, electronic, mechanical, photocopy, recording or otherwise without the prior permission of the author except as provided by USA copyright law.

This book is designed to provide accurate and authoritative information with regard to the subject matter covered.
Copyright © 2017 Mike Stroud
All rights reserved.

ISBN-13:978-1982093167
ISBN-10:1982093161
© 2017 Mike Stroud

DEDICATION

I would like to dedicate this book to Heidi, Scott, Orin, Heather, Becky, Adam, Clark, Jennifer, Janalee, Darren, Stacey, Brandon, and to my grandchildren, and great-grandchildren. May they all have the desire to draw near unto their Lord and Savior, Jesus Christ.

Mike & Margie Stroud

CONTENTS

	Acknowledgements	i
37	Gentiles	3
38	The Virtue of the Word of God	28
39	Secret Combinations	48
40	Trust in the Lord	79
41	Entering into The Rest of The Lord	111
42	Peace and Safety	131
43	Will Ye Also Go Away	158
44	From Eternity to Eternity	179
45	Baptism of Fire, Precursor to the Second Coming	210
46	Atonement: The Law of the Celestial Kingdom	241
47	From Within the Veil	259

ACKNOWLEDGMENTS

Thank you to Shelle McDermott, author of the "NoFearPreps.com" site for her help in encouraging, organizing, and bringing this all to fruition. Nothing would have happened without her.

I would also like to express gratitude to my two editors, Ann and Elizabeth. They have tirelessly given over a year's worth of their time and effort to convert my podcasts into readable books. They are blessing many through their talents and sacrifice of time. God bless you, dear sisters.

Editors
Phillis Ann Postak
Elizabeth Postak

Transcribers
Carol Crisp
Pat Crisp

Chapter Thirty-Seven
Podcast 037 Gentiles

Well, we're glad to have you here tonight. I was sitting in a Sunday School Gospel Doctrine class today, and the lesson was on 3 Nephi, chapter 16. A good portion of the lesson was centered around the term *Gentiles*. As I listened to the lesson, it became clear that this is a confusing concept, at least in this class. And it is my experience that it's confusing to a lot of the members of the Church, and rightly so, because there are several different meanings and understandings of the term *Gentile*. Now, the last couple of lessons that we had centered around *the Remnant of Jacob*, *the Remnant*, and other things that we've talked about that have to do with the latter-day fulfillment of prophecy that is taking place right now in our day; the *Gentiles* play a major role in all of that. In fact, in our lesson on *the Remnant of Jacob* that centered on 3 Nephi 20 and 21, *Gentiles* were mentioned prominently over and over. So, I would like to take some time tonight and let's just discuss this concept of *Gentiles*. We could ask a couple of questions on this as we go into it. One that pertains to us is: Are Latter-day Saints in any way considered *Gentiles*? And if we are, then it behooves us to look a little bit differently at some scriptures, especially those in the *Book of Mormon*. When we read about *Gentiles* doing despicable things, our tendency is to point to people outside of the Latter-day Saint community, and I think that's unhealthy. So, we're going to look at that a little bit differently. In particular, there are two *Book of Mormon* scriptures that we're going to want to break down in detail tonight. One is 2 Nephi chapter 28, and the other one is 3 Nephi chapter 16. If I present this right, I hope it will help us discern things that are taking place around us, because truly we are living in a day when these prophecies are being fulfilled or are in the process of fulfillment. We need to have a good clear look at all of this just to give you an idea about the word *Gentile* and to show you where this is mentioned the most. The term *Gentile* is mentioned 30 times in the Old Testament, 93 times in the *New Testament,* and 30 times in the *Doctrine and Covenants*. It's not mentioned at all in the *Pearl of Great Price*, but it's mentioned 112 times in the *Book of Mormon*. That right there ought to give us pause to ask ourselves why there are so many references to the term *Gentile* in the *Book of Mormon*. That will get us going in a direction that is worthwhile.

The first mention of *Gentiles* comes in the *Old Testament* over in Genesis chapter 10 where it talks about the sons of Noah. When they come out of the ark, there are three sons and their families; Shem, Japheth, and Ham. Japheth is considered the father of the *Gentile* nations; Shem is considered the father of the covenant, chosen-seed line; and Ham is considered the father of a restriction-people, or people who are under some restrictions. It actually goes back to Adam, but in the three sons of Noah, you can see groups of people who populate the earth and inherit blessings, rights, and privileges. In large measure, this goes back to what is called *the doctrine of election* and has to do with the pre-mortal world. For example, go to the *Bible* dictionary (which, by the way, is one of the great mysteries, one of the great secrets of the Church) and look under *election*. You will find all of this on page 662. You can read the whole thing, but I'm going to read just a portion of this. It's about halfway through the paragraph on *election* and says:

> An "election of grace"...has reference to one's situation in mortality; that is, being born at a time, at a place, and in circumstances where one will come in favorable contact with the gospel.

This election took place in the premortal existence.

So, what we are enjoying in this life, by way of blessings, privileges, and rights, has to do directly with who you were and what you did before you came here. So much of what we are enjoying in this life, and are considered blessings, are rewards for faithfulness that was exhibited in the premortal life. This is called *the doctrine of election.* Now, by extension, what you will enjoy in the next world, by way of blessings, rights, and privileges is a direct result of your faithfulness in this world. So, when we see people grouped into three categories, in this case, the children of Noah—Shem, Japheth, and Ham—it has as much to do with who they were before they were born in the premortal life, as what their actions were while they were in mortality. So, according to the *Old Testament* scripture, the word *Gentile* has its origin with the son of Noah named Japheth, and he becomes the father of the *Gentile* nations.

Now, this term *Gentile* has so many different meanings. If we're going to determine what *Gentile* means, we're going to have to look at three different things. You need to look at birth, you need to look at religion, and you need to look at citizenship. So, those three things can help us determine what we're talking about when we see the word, *Gentile*. In our day, virtually all meaning has been lost outside of the Latter-day Saint community for all things pertaining to the *house of Israel.* You can't understand the term *Gentile* unless you have a feeling for the term *house of Israel.* And that really makes it difficult and confusing because, again, outside of Latter-day Saint restoration doctrine, the concept of the *house of Israel* has been almost completely lost. I will tell you a little experience I had. I was in a chat room once, and I was listening to a Jewish chat that originated in Jerusalem. I was interested because I had been to Jerusalem a couple of times, to the Middle East, to Israel, and I was listening to what they were talking about. It became obvious to me that they had no concept of the term *Israelite.* They knew what an Israeli was, but they had no concept of an *Israelite.* These were Jews from all over the world. Some rabbis were online also, and while I was listening, I decided I would type in a little something and just see what would happen. I wasn't trying to be an annoyer or a disturber, but I was curious to see what their knowledge was of the concept of the *house of Israel*. And again, if we understand the term the *house of Israel*, then we can begin to get a clearer idea of what *Gentile* means. So, I told them what my name was and said, "I am an Israelite from the house of Joseph through the loins of Ephraim." Now, that's pure Latter-day Saint *restoration doctrine*. The minute I put send on that, the chat line just went crazy. It lit up like a Christmas tree, and the chat text just started to roll, and it was all negative. It was all negative; there was nothing positive, and I found myself being accused; a Christian who was trying to disturb a private Jewish chat line. All kind of anger was coming through the chat. And finally, a Rabbi from over in Norway, I believe it was in Scandinavia, came on and they apparently respected him, and he got them all settled down in the chat. My chat name was Bear Tooth. This man came back and said, "Bear Tooth, what do you mean you are an Israelite through the loins of Joseph? How do you know that?" And I told him that a holy man laid his hands on my head, gave me a blessing, and through revelation declared that lineage. And again, this chat line just went crazy. They had no idea what I was talking about, but this Rabbi had a feeling for it. See, their whole concept was that only Jews could use the word *Israel*, let alone *Israelite*. So, the concept of there being anybody else in the world, who wasn't a Jew, having any claim on the term *Israel* infuriated them. It quickly became obvious to me that the Jewish people that I was talking to have lost all knowledge concerning the term *house of Israel*, that there were twelve tribes, and that Judah was just one of those twelve, the fourth son of Jacob. It was very interesting to me that the whole concept of *Gentile* and *house of Israel* have been completely lost, outside of the Latter-day Saint community. Christianity thinks they have a pretty good feel for it, but without *restoration doctrine*, they can't discern much more than the rest of the world. So, it is really an interesting concept.

 Here are some ideas on the definition of *Gentile*. The word *Gentile* taken from the ancient texts means *nations*. In the ancient Jewish texts, the word *Gentile* in Hebrew is *goy*, which is singular; and *goyim* is plural, and it means *nation* or *nations*. Also, another definition of *Gentile* from the scriptures would be *strangers* or *sojourners*, in other words, persons who live outside the existing community—foreign nations or sojourners from another country. So, that gets down to the feeling of the word *Gentile*. Now, in modern times, as the Jewish people came home from their Diaspora and started to gather to Israel in May 1948, *Gentile* is somebody that is not a Jew. And yet, Jews don't even understand what Jews are. Jews in Israel today look more on a citizenship definition of *Jew* than they do on any blood lineage. So again, when the Lord says that part of the *restoration principle* is to restore the *house of Israel* to the true doctrine, to the true points of the doctrine of Christ, just in this one area, there is a huge need to be restored to a knowledge of the truth. They have no idea of who they are. And if you have no idea of who you are, then by inference you can't understand what rights, privileges, blessings, and covenants belong to you because of who you are in a particular lineage. And it applies the same to the Latter-day Saints. This is why we receive patriarchal blessings because in declaring lineage, it identifies not only rights and privileges that are ours, but future missions and ministries that are going to be performed because of your lineage.

And so, in ancient times, a *Gentile* was simply someone who did not belong, in citizenship or by religion—forget blood—but citizenship, religion, or by blood to the house of Judah. So, today they have no concept of Joseph. There are a few isolated rabbis who understand that there is something about Joseph that they need to understand, but it's very confusing to them. So, anytime the word *Gentile* is used in the way of religion, it is used to refer to those whose religion you don't particularly espouse. For example, Latter-day Saints, in the early days of the Church, referred to everybody that wasn't a Latter-day Saint as a *Gentile*. Jews refer to everybody that is not a Jew as a *Gentile*, and so on. So, we come into this question now, are the Latter-day Saints *Gentiles,* or are they of the *house of Israel*? Well, when you receive a patriarchal blessing, you're going to be identified, more than likely, with one of the twelve tribes of Israel. Every once in awhile, you will have a blessing that will come out, like a little gal I knew in Mongolia who received her patriarchal blessing, which said she was a daughter of Abraham. What we're finding out is that there are very few *Gentiles* who are joining the Church, pure *Gentile* as far as blood; meaning that there is no blood of the *house of Israel* in their veins. That is so rare because we live in a day where lineages and nationalities are so intermingled through marriage, that it's very difficult to find a pure *Israelite* or a pure *Gentile* these days. So, we need to look at it a little bit differently in our day.

Let's come to the Latter-day Saints for just a minute. Go to your title page in the *Book of Mormon* and let me share with you some interesting things that we've read many, many times, but we haven't really stopped to look at them. If you look right at the very first sentence it says:

> *Wherefore, it is an abridgment of the record of the people of Nephi, and also of the Lamanites—Written to the Lamanites, who are a remnant of the house of Israel; and also to Jew and* **Gentile**—

The *Book of Mormon* is written to three peoples. Now, ask yourself a question, out of those three categories—Lamanites, Jew, and *Gentile*—which one do the Latter-day Saints fit into?

Student 2: *Gentile.*

Mike: Yes. It's obvious right there. So, there on the title page, we can see that the *Book of Mormon* is written to these three groups of people and it's obvious which one the Latter-day Saints fit into. Now, going on down to the rest of that first paragraph, we skip down about four lines, it says:

> *To come forth by the gift and power of God unto the interpretation thereof—Sealed by the hand of Moroni, and hid up unto the Lord, to come forth in due time* **by way of the Gentile**—

So, how did the *Book of Mormon* come forth to us? Who was it that took it out of the hill?

Student 3: Joseph Smith.

Mike: Joseph Smith and here in the *Book of Mormon* record title page refers to the person that it's to come forth by as a *Gentile*. So, Joseph Smith who said in his own words, that he was a pure Ephraimite, is also considered a *Gentile*. Isn't that interesting? So, right on the title page, we get a little clue as to where we, as members of the Church of Jesus Christ of Latter-day Saints, fit into this whole thought of *Gentiles* and the *house of Israel*. The interesting thing is that you can be a member of the *house of Israel* by blood and also be considered a *Gentile*. We will talk about that a little bit more in a minute.

Let's go to *Doctrine and Covenants* 109. This is the great prayer revelation, the dedicatory prayer of the Kirtland Temple. It says in the section heading:

> *According to the Prophet's written statement, this prayer was given to him by revelation.*

We want to go to verse 60 now. This is Joseph's prayer:

> *Now these words, O Lord, we have spoken before thee, concerning the revelations and commandments which thou hast given unto us* [the Latter-day Saints], **who are identified with the Gentiles**.

You see that?

Student 4: Yeah, that's good!

Mike: Now, that's the obvious answer to the first question we asked at the beginning of the class: are the Latter-day Saints considered *Gentiles*? And they are. How? The great *Gentile* nation, which is referred to in the *Book of Mormon* is what we refer to as the United States of America. It's also interesting that the people who settled here in the United States from its inception all the way through the forming of the nation, the Declaration of Independence, the War of Independence, right up until today, immigrated from Eastern and Western Europe, which are the *Gentile* nations in the world today. Eastern and Western Europe, and especially Western Europe in England, Ireland, Scotland, and Germany, are populated by the descendants of Joseph and his two sons Ephraim and Manasseh. So, when Joseph Smith sends Heber C. Kimball to go to England and open-up a mission in England, what he's doing is going into the great *Gentile* nations of Western Europe and beginning a process that gathers the children of Joseph into America, the great *Gentile* nation of the last days. All of the Latter-day Saints can be considered *Gentiles* even though you have the blood of Israel flowing through your veins, and you do. There is very little adoption going on of pure *Gentiles*. That means persons who have zero blood of Israel or any of the tribes of Israel in their body. That's not happening. And if it does happen, Joseph Smith says, they are adopted into the *house of Israel* and that there is a physical transformation that takes place with these *Gentiles*, even to the changing out of their blood through the Spirit of the Holy Ghost. That's not happening. What's happening is that we have people being gathered from the *Gentile* nations of the world to the United States, the great *Gentile* nation, who have the blood of Israel mixed with *Gentile* nations in their blood. So, the fact is that you are declared an *Israelite* through your patriarchal blessing, but can also be a *Gentile* in two ways: the first is that your ancestors intermarried with the *Gentile* nations and now that blood has become mixed up in those nations through intermarriage; and the other way is through citizenship. You have citizenship in the United States of America. That's another way that you can be considered a *Gentile*. So, it's no wonder that this can be confusing.

Student 4: You mentioned adoption, and for a short time, my grandfather was adopted by Brigham Young. How does that play in what you're talking about?

Mike: Well that is a different adoption. That doesn't play into this at all. This is people who have no blood of Israel flowing in their veins, and yet accept the Gospel of Jesus Christ, are baptized and receive the gift of the Holy Ghost; they are spiritually adopted into the *house of Israel* and become members of the *house of Israel* through that adoption. The adoption that you're talking about is not a part of this at all. It is a different concept altogether.

Student 6: So, Mike, the *Gentiles*, those that would be adopted in, would be of the house of Ishmael, no?

Mike: Those that what?

Student 6: If adoption were to occur into the *house of Israel*, that would be coming from the Arab nations, like Ishmael.

Mike: You know it's difficult to say. Anciently, it may have been that way, but even though you may not be an Israelite, you can still be a part of that promised lineage that comes down through Shem, Abraham, Isaac, and Jacob. The *house of Israel* originates obviously with Jacob, but the covenant of lineage, of priesthood, temple blessings, revelation, and everything goes right on back through Isaac, and on through into Abraham, and back through Melchizedek, Shem, and Noah, etc. So, if we talk about *Israelite*, we have to bring Jacob into it, and you can't leave out Isaac and Abraham. So, for example, Moses receives the priesthood, not through an Israelite lineage. Moses was a Levite, but he receives the Melchizedek priesthood through a non-Israelite line that goes back to Abraham's third wife Keturah, which is a Melchizedek Priesthood line that was acceptable to God, but it did not come down through Abraham, Isaac, and Jacob. So, here is Moses, who is a descendant of the third son of Jacob, an Israelite/Levite, and yet he received the priesthood from a non-Israelite priesthood line, but still goes back to Abraham and is a part of the covenant of Abraham. Does that make sense? You can read about that in section 84 the *Doctrine and Covenants*.

Student 6: So, the *house of Israel* really is not temporal. It existed before this temporal sphere.

Mike: Yes, I believe that *Israel* is an eternal theme that exists in eternity and can be found on all worlds where there is a covenant line. I believe it is an eternal theme like Zion, and it did not originate in this key telestial world and will continue to resonate throughout worlds without number. It's an eternal concept that applies to a covenant people coming up and then obtaining all that the Father has—that kind of thing.

Student 6: Mike, this is a little bit of a diversion, but something I've wanted to ask you for a while.

Mike: Okay.

Student 6: Okay. Today, there are people who are called Zionists, but it's more of a—well, I think what I am referring to is a secret combination. So, is it Satan using that term?

Mike: Zionism is a term that goes back just before the establishment of Israel as a state in 1948. It goes back to a group of people who wanted to get the Jewish people into a national homeland. Their movement to do that, prior to the establishment of the state of Israel in 1948 was called the Zionist movement. And so that's a whole different ballgame. That's not the true concept of Zion that we're learning about in the Latter-day *restoration doctrine*. It is something that originates with the Jewish people prior to the founding of Israel as a homeland.

Student 6: Okay, thanks!

Mike: Good question. So, brothers and sisters, what can we derive from all of this? The point I wanted to make tonight for you to take home is this: when we read the *Book of Mormon*, that has 112 different entries about *Gentile* in there, we tend to think it's referring to somebody other than the Latter-day Saints. I think that can cause some problems in identifying what's taking place around us, as far as the fulfillment of prophecy. The Latter-day Saints are identified **among** the *Gentiles*. And so, when we read about *Gentile* prophecy, especially when it's upsetting, or it's distasteful to us, we may want to be looking to see if we fit into that category the Lord is talking about. This is the purpose of the lesson tonight. You can go online and find an endless amount of information on *Gentile*; we just hit a little thumbnail.

What I would like to do in the remaining time is take us into two scriptures and show that it's not only talking about people who are not members of the Church of Jesus Christ of Latter-day Saints, who are referred to as *Gentiles*. It's also referring to **members** as *Gentiles*, and that's where we need to receive a heads up. Let's go to 2 Nephi chapter 28, and look at a couple of scriptures here. Again, this is just kind of to get us to maybe change our thinking a little bit on things here, and see what's going on. I refer to 2 Nephi chapter 28 as the "**wo**" chapter in the *Book of Mormon*. There are so many **woes** in this chapter, and whenever the Lord uses the word *wo* we should pay attention. For example, verse 15 is a three-**wo**er. There are three **wo**es, and whenever you see three, that's a heads up! We need to pay attention. But, go to verse 32. The whole 28th chapter ends with a **wo**:

Wo be unto the Gentiles,

And so this whole section, the whole 28th chapter is talking about the *Gentiles* in the latter-days. I'm not going to go through the whole thing, but let's just take a look at verse 12:

*Because of pride, and because of false teachers, and false doctrine, **their** churches have become corrupted, and **their** churches are lifted up; because of pride they are puffed up.*

*[13] **They** rob the poor because of **their** fine sanctuaries; **they** rob the poor because of **their** fine clothing; and **they** persecute the meek and the*

*poor in heart, because in **their** pride **they** are puffed up.*

Now, for the majority of my life, I've always read those verses as non-Latter-day Saints—people living in America and other *Gentile* nations—but I never identified **them** with the Latter-day Saints. What I'm saying is, we need to read these a little closer now that we clearly discovered that the Latter-day Saints are identified as *Gentiles*. Here's another thing you need to ask yourselves: who has access to these writings here? Who is reading these words? Is it those people out there or we in here? What good would all of these things be to people who are never going to have access to these words? Who has access to all of the words in 2 Nephi chapter 28? The Latter-day Saints and those investigating the doctrines of the *Restoration*. So, that is another thing to consider. Verse 14:

They wear stiff necks and high heads; yea, and because of pride, and wickedness, and abominations, and whoredoms,

You see, before, I would read that and say, "Definitely not a Latter-day Saint!" Yet, go ask a Bishop what he deals with every day of the week.

Student 6: Where is the reference that talks about daughters of Zion mincing and tinkling as they walk?

Mike: Now, that is over in Isaiah, and it's also included in the *Book of Mormon* Isaiah chapters. And the fact that it's talking about the daughters of Zion is an indicator that we are not talking about people outside of the covenant relationship. But, if you look at the list in verse 14 that is talking about the *Gentiles*; these are the sins of the *Gentiles*: wickedness, abominations, and whoredoms. Look at this:

they have all gone astray save it be a few, who are the humble followers of Christ; nevertheless, they are led, that in many instances they do err because they are taught by the precepts of men.

See, I'm not so sure this is talking about people outside of our community. I know that it fits with the *Gentiles* that are not Latter-day Saints. I know that it fits, but keep in mind that Latter-day Saints are numbered among the *Gentiles*. That has clearly been established tonight. So, what I'm saying is that we need to read with the spirit of revelation and start to look at this and ask if this applies to me. Do we have wickedness, abominations, and whoredoms among the Latter-day Saints? Now, go over to verse 20 and watch this:

> *For behold, at that day shall he* [Satan] *rage in the hearts of the children of men, and stir them up to anger against that which is good.*
> *[21] And **others** he will pacify,*

See, you've got two groups. A group that is being torn up, stirred up and raging, and you have another group that is pacified:

> *and lull them away into carnal security, that they will say:* ***All is well in Zion;***

Now, I have no doubt in my mind that if the previous verses weren't referring to us, this one for sure is:

> *All is well in Zion; yea, Zion prospereth, all is well—and thus the devil cheateth their souls,*

And I firmly believe that this is the Latter-day Saints:

> *and thus the devil cheateth their souls, and leadeth them away carefully down to hell.*
> *[22] And behold, others he flattereth away, and telleth them there is no hell; and he saith unto them: I am no devil, for there is none—*

Etc., etc. You can read the rest of it. In verse 24, *"Therefore"* means *because of what is written in verses 20, 21, 22, and 23*:

> *[24] Therefore, wo be unto him that is at ease in Zion!*
> *[25] Wo be unto him that crieth: All is well!*

So, I believe that in chapter 28 we are talking to the *Gentiles* in general, but within that group, we are also talking about Latter-day Saints, specifically. Does that make sense, what we're trying to do here tonight?

Student 6: Absolutely!

Mike: I'm trying to take a little bit of a different twist because, again, if you are like me, I've read these things and all my life I've said, "Well that certainly is describing them over there. That is a perfect description of those people out there." And I've just come to feel that maybe we need not do that. We'll look at another one. These are just two chapters, and all through the

Book of Mormon, we have these kinds of things. Now, in 3 Nephi 16, we have a fulfillment of John 10:16, which says:

> *And other sheep I have, which are not of this fold: them also I must bring, and they shall hear my voice; and there shall be one fold, and one shepherd.*

Here He fulfills that scripture in John chapter 10. Then in 3 Nephi 16:4, this is the Savior speaking to the Nephites as He appears there:

> *And I command you that ye shall write these sayings after I am gone, that if it so be that my people at Jerusalem, they who have seen me and been with me in my ministry* [that's the Jews], *do not ask the Father in my name, that they may receive a knowledge of you by the Holy Ghost, and also of the other tribes whom they know not of, that these sayings* [the record of Joseph, the Book of Mormon] *which ye shall write shall be kept and shall be manifested unto the Gentiles, that through the fulness of the Gentiles, the remnant of their seed, who shall be scattered forth upon the face of the earth because of their unbelief, may be brought in, or may be brought to a knowledge of me, their Redeemer.*

It's my belief, as I read the scriptures that the *Dispensation of the Fullness of Times* begins with the vision that Joseph had in the Sacred Grove. And that the *Dispensation of the Fullness of Times* will go forth from that point all the way through to the Second Coming of the Lord Jesus Christ in glory; that's the *Dispensation of the Fullness of Times*. But, it's my feeling as I study the scriptures, that we can divide that dispensation into at least two main categories. The first category is known as the *Day of the Gentile*, and the second category of that *Dispensation of the Fullness of Times* is the *Day of Israel*. It's my feeling that we are coming to the end of the *Day of the Gentile*, which is also called the *Fullness of the Gentile*. That's a term that is used—the *Fullness* or the *Times of the Gentile*—meaning that that segment of the *Dispensation of the Fullness of Times* ends, and the second segment begins, which is the *house of Israel*. The *Gentiles* are fulfilling a mission in the *Day of the Gentile*, and the *Book of Mormon* just explains that very well. In some cases, the *Gentiles* are acting as a scourge to drive and scatter remnant parts of the *house of Israel*, in particular, the seed of Joseph, and the remnant of Israel; Jacob that is found here, the Lamanites. And there's a prophecy about that taking place. But the other side of it is that they fulfill a mission not only in their scourging but also in helping them come to a knowledge of their true Redeemer, which has been lost through unbelief and apostasy; and the *Gentiles* fulfill these roles. So, go down to verse 5:

And then will I gather them

This is the scattered remnants of Israel. I think that we're coming into that. You're going to see this second part of the *Dispensation of the Fullness of Times*, the restoration of the *house of Israel* to the true knowledge of their Redeemer and Savior. By the way, that's going to include the Jewish people. That's going to include the Jews.

Okay, now put your finger in 3 Nephi 16 and let's go over to *Doctrine and Covenants* 133. This talks about the return of the ten lost tribes out of the North country in verse 32; I want to go there. We can spend some more detail on this, but in verse 32, they come down out of the North. It's a miraculous restoration. They come down and look what it says:

[32] And there shall they fall down and be crowned with glory, even in Zion [the New Jerusalem], *by the hands of the servants of the Lord, even the children of Ephraim.*

These children of Ephraim, brothers and sisters, are identified among the *Gentiles*. This is us, the children of Israel that will be in Zion. This is a remnant of the house of Joseph that has their lineage in Joseph and will be there when the ten tribes come through. They have gone through all the tribulations and all the trials. These men and women have come up to a state, almost and including translation, so that they can rescue scattered Israel in their hopeless and enslaved state in pockets of nations throughout the world, and bring them to Zion. Look at verse 33:

And they shall be filled with songs of everlasting joy.

I hope to shout! To even get to Zion and receive these blessings will require a miraculous rescue that can only be done through the power of God and control of the elements with no thought of time or space. Now watch:

> *[34] Behold, this is the blessing of the everlasting God upon the tribes of Israel, and the richer blessing upon the head of Ephraim and his fellows.*

The richer blessing is that Ephraim has enjoyed the blessings of the fullness of the priesthood and the blessings of the temple. Wilford Woodruff says that these ten tribes of Israel that come down out of the North have not received their temple endowment blessings. They have prophets and the Melchizedek Priesthood, but they have not received the blessings of the temple that the children of Ephraim, the Latter-day Saints, have in our day. They receive their blessings from under the hands of Ephraim. All the sealing blessings and the endowment privileges will be administered by the children of Ephraim, who are identified among the *Gentiles*. In other words, those *Gentile* members of the Church, who are faithful enough to get through the tribulations of the coming day, will be numbered among the *house of Israel* during the second phase of the *Dispensation of the Fullness of Times*. Look at verse 35:

> *And they also of the tribe of Judah, after their pain,*

Now, that's the pain they've gone through, through their whole existence, but particularly something called Armageddon:

> *shall be sanctified in holiness before the Lord, to dwell in his presence day and night, forever and ever.*

Let's go back to 3 Nephi 16, and let me show you something. Go down to verse 6:

> *And blessed are the Gentiles, because of their belief in me, **in and of the Holy Ghost**, which witnesses unto them of me and of the Father.*

To me, that's talking about members of the Church. We have the gift of the Holy Ghost. So again, to me, that verse 6 is talking about the *Gentile* members of the Church, who have the blood of Israel flowing in their veins, but are numbered among the

Gentiles (as Joseph Smith said in section 109), and have the Holy Ghost witness to them and of the Father.

You can look at this a little bit further; this whole 16th chapter is remarkable. But, let's skip down to verse 10:

> *[10] And thus commandeth the Father that I [Jesus] should say unto you: At that day when the Gentiles shall sin against my gospel,*

What the heck is that? Here's the way I taught it for years; I taught it to mean that we as missionaries are taking the gospel out to the people, presenting it to them in discussion form, and they reject it, meaning they sin against it. I'm not so sure that's what that means. I'm wondering if this isn't talking about the Latter-day Saints. In fact, <u>I lean heavily toward the idea</u> that it has nothing to do with preaching the gospel to investigators, and it has everything to do with members of the Church, who are now sinning against the covenants they have made. Look at this, brothers and sisters; we have about 70% of the membership of the Church that does not attend any church—about 70%! I gave you the statistics once before. In Utah, Idaho, and Arizona, along the Wasatch front where we have multi-generational Latter-day Saints, the percentages are obviously higher. If you go down to Mesa, Arizona and even up here in Eagar, the activity rate among the Latter-day Saints is higher than when you get out of one of those three states. In the Philippines, it is 12%. After fifty years there are only 12% of the members of the Church that attend any church, and church activity is measured on a quarterly basis by attending one sacrament meeting every three months. So, now let's go back down to verse 10:

> *At that day when the Gentiles shall sin against my gospel, and shall reject the fulness of my gospel,*

People outside the Church do not have access to that:

> *and shall be lifted up in the pride of their hearts above all nations, and above all the people of the whole earth, and shall be filled with all manner of lyings, and of deceits, and of mischiefs, and all manner of hypocrisy, and murders, and priestcrafts, and whoredoms, and of secret abominations; and if they shall do all those things, and shall reject the fulness of my gospel,*

> *behold, saith the Father, I will bring the fulness of*
> *my gospel from among them.*

Now, when He brings the *"fulness of my gospel from among them,"* brothers and sisters, that is the end of the *Day of the Gentiles*. Now, it's going to go somewhere else.

> *[11]* **And then** *will I remember my covenant*
> *which I have made unto my people, O house of*
> *Israel, and I will bring my gospel unto them.*

So, at the bottom of verse 10, the *Gentiles* have fulfilled their ministry and assignment, and they've done what the Lord said they would do through prophecy and revelation. But, there are a few who will not sin against the gospel and the fullness of the gospel. And look at what it said in verse 11:

> *And then will I remember my covenant...and I will*
> *bring my gospel unto them* [the house of Israel].
> *[12] And I will show unto thee, O house of Israel,*
> *that the Gentiles shall not have power over you;*
> *but I will remember my covenant unto you.*

Now, here we go in verse 13:

> *[13]* **But** *if the Gentiles will repent and* **return**
> *unto me,*

How can you return to somebody that you haven't been to already? How can you return to a covenant that you haven't previously made? How can you return to membership if you haven't previously been a member?

> *[13] But if the Gentiles will repent and return*
> *unto me, saith the Father, behold* **they shall be**
> **numbered among my people, O house of Israel***.*

Now, brothers and sisters, we are *Gentiles*, and we want to be in this group that's numbered among the *house of Israel* as we make the transition from the *Fullness of the Gentiles* into the *Day of Israel*.

Remember our lesson, *The Remnant of Jacob*? Verses 14 and 15 are referring to that remnant of Jacob, the lion that goes through the sheep, and if we repent and are numbered from the *house of Israel*:

> *[14] And I will not suffer my people, who are the*
> *house of Israel, to go through among them, and*
> *tread them down, saith the Father.*

That is a direct reference to 3 Nephi 21 that the Savior is going to talk to them about in a minute, and that we already had a lesson on. That's the remnant of Jacob:

> [15] But if they will not turn unto me, and hearken unto my voice, I will suffer them, yea, I will suffer my people, O house of Israel, that they shall go through among them, and shall tread them down, and they shall be as salt that hath lost its savor,

I guess what I'm trying to say here is that maybe we've been looking at these things a little too casually and a little too naïvely.

Let me just show you a couple of other things, and we will end our discussion. Go to *Doctrine and Covenants* 84:54 for just a minute. Remember that there is a **wo** pronounced upon the members of the Church that say, *"All is well in Zion; yea, Zion prospereth, all is well."* Section 84 was given in Kirtland, Ohio in 1832, and the Church is not even two years old yet. Something has happened here, and in verse 54, He says this to the members of the Church:

> And your minds in times past have been darkened because of unbelief, and because you have treated lightly the things you have received—
> [55] Which vanity and unbelief have brought the whole church under condemnation.

That was in 1832:

> [56] And this condemnation resteth upon the children of Zion, even all.
> [57] And they shall remain under this condemnation until they repent and remember the new covenant, even the Book of Mormon and the former commandments which I have given them, not only to say, but to do according to that which I have written—
> [58] That they may bring forth fruit meet for their Father's kingdom; otherwise...

Now, watch. Think about what we've talked about tonight and the remnant: if you don't repent and are numbered among the *house of Israel*:

> *...there remaineth a scourge and judgment to be poured out upon the children of Zion*
> *[59] For shall the children of the kingdom pollute my holy land? Verily, I say unto you, Nay.*

Now, we read back in 3 Nephi 16 about secret combinations, murders, whoredoms, and abominations, etc. among the *Gentiles*. And I asked myself the question: has that ever been found among the members of the Church? Is it still found among the members of the Church? And the answer is, yes. In the Nauvoo period, there were murders; there were secret combinations, there were all kinds whoredoms, adulteries, and all kinds of stuff. Joseph Smith found himself up to his eyeballs as the mayor of Nauvoo, and Lieutenant General of the Nauvoo Legion, constantly trying to keep the society of Latter-day Saints clean. It was infiltrated with all kinds of garbage.

Now, I want you to go to *Doctrine and Covenants* 124:27, and let me show you something that is interesting. Here is an example of the *Gentiles*/members of the Church that maybe fits into these prophecies. This is a commandment for members of the Church to build the Nauvoo temple:

> *[27] And with iron, with copper, and with brass, and with zinc, and with all your precious things of the earth; and build a house to my name, for the Most High to dwell therein.*

That's the commandment to build the Nauvoo temple:

> *[28] For there is not a place found on earth that he* [Christ] *may come to and restore again that which was lost unto you, or which he hath taken away,*

Two things, He's going to restore something either that was lost or that he took away:

> *even the fulness of the priesthood.*

We've talked a lot about that. Now, skip to verse 31 where he talks about baptism for the dead, and they must build a house that is built for that ordinance. They were performing them in the midst of the Mississippi River, and it was acceptable up to a certain point, but the Lord said, "We need to have a house built unto Me to do this":

> *[31] But I command you, all ye my saints, to build a house unto me; and I grant unto you a sufficient time to build a house unto me; and during this time your baptisms shall be acceptable unto me.*

Meaning, while you build the temple, I will let you continue to do your baptisms in the Mississippi River:

> *[32] But behold, at the end of this appointment*

The appointment is that the Lord gave them a certain appointed time to build that temple. It was spelled out, and then He says that at the end of that appointment:

> *your baptisms for your dead shall not be acceptable unto me;*

In other words, if you don't get this building built, I'm not going to accept anything from you. Look what else He says:

> *and if you do not these things at the end of the appointment* ***ye shall be rejected as a church***, *with your dead, saith the Lord your God.*

How are we to understand that? So, did they get it built? Here's the question. Now, go over to verse 44:

> *If ye labor with all your might, I will consecrate that spot* [Nauvoo Temple location] *that it shall be made holy.*
>
> *[45] And if my people will hearken unto my voice, and unto the voice of my servants whom I have appointed to lead my people, behold, verily I say unto you,*

Catch this right here:

> ***they shall not be moved out of their place.***
>
> *[46] But if they will not hearken to my voice, nor unto the voice of these men whom I have appointed, they shall not be blest, because they pollute mine holy grounds, and mine holy ordinances, and charters, and my holy words which I give unto them.*

These are the members of the church:

> *[47] And it shall come to pass that if you build a house unto my name, and do not do the things that I say, I will not perform the oath which I*

> *make unto you, neither fulfill the promises which ye expect at my hands, saith the Lord.*
> *[48] For instead of blessings, ye, by your own works, bring cursings, wrath, indignation, and judgments upon your own heads, by your follies, and by all your abominations, which you practice before me, saith the Lord.*

So, are the *Gentile* members of the Church guilty of any of the things that we read about in 2 Nephi 28 and 3 Nephi 16? That's the question we need to consider. I don't know if you remember this or not, but President Benson's main message and ministry were built around *Doctrine and Covenants* 84, and he talked about bringing the Church out from under condemnation. He moved forward mightily with the *Book of Mormon* and said, "We have got to do more with the *Book of Mormon!*" And because we've treated that record with vanity and unbelief, the Lord placed us under condemnation.

So, those are some things that took place in the early days of the history of the Church which caused me to take a look at the prophecies in the *Book of Mormon* and ask, "Is this really talking only about "them" out there?" Again, brothers and sisters, they don't have access to this information. What good is it to condemn people that never read these words? What good is it? How can you be condemned if you have no access to the truth? Well, it's something to think about.

So, what's the purpose of tonight's lesson? The purpose of tonight's lesson was to help us understand that as Latter-day Saints who have the blood of Israel flowing in our veins (even though it's mixed up because of intermarriage), we are still numbered among the *Gentiles*. Our ancestry, by and large, puts us into the *Gentile nations* of the earth, which are mainly Eastern and Western Europe. Almost all the Latter-day Saints, at least original ones that came to Utah that were in the original part of the Church, can track back to Europe, but we're finding the blood of Israel is scattered all over.

Let me just close by saying one thing. When we went to Mongolia, I remember that one of the stories we heard was that they had people there who received their patriarchal blessings and all of the tribes of the *house of Israel* were represented in the patriarchal blessings of the Mongolian members. I thought it was remarkable because up to that point, we had only heard about scattered instances. Every once in awhile, we hear the story of somebody who has a patriarchal blessing that says they're from Levi, or they're from Asher, but mostly it's Joseph, through Ephraim and Manasseh. So, Margie and I were given an assignment by the mission president to work with the Young Single Adults in the country of Mongolia. One of the first things that we did was to put a countrywide YSA conference together and wanted to see all the young single adults, especially the return missionaries because at that time Mongolia, per population capita was sending more missionaries into the world that even Orem, Utah! This is why so many people would say, "Oh you went on a mission to Mongolia? Wow, we knew this Mongolian elder," or "We knew this Mongolian sister." We've heard that hundreds of times. And so, there were Mongolian brothers and sisters that had served missions throughout the world. There were no patriarchs in Mongolia, so missionaries would receive their patriarchal blessings in the countries where they went to serve. They were authorized to get a blessing when they went into the United States, Australia, East Germany or wherever they went. But, we pulled all of these people together, and I got permission from the mission president to put a big whiteboard out by the entrance where all of these young men and women were coming in. These are all Mongolians; this is Asia, Middle Asia, right? What I did was list all twelve tribes of Israel, including Dinah. I put Dinah, which is the only daughter of Jacob, up there just in case. And then in Mongolian and English, I wrote on the board, "Without putting your name, if you've received your patriarchal blessing, put a check next to the tribe of Israel that you're identified with through your blessing." We only had a small group of 80 people there. Out of 80 returned missionaries, every tribe of the *house of Israel* was identified. The majority, of course, was from Ephraim and Manasseh, but every tribe was there. I just found that remarkable and what that did is show me how mixed up the blood of Israel is in all the nations of the world. And it truly takes a patriarch, operating under a prophetic revelatory power, to declare a lineage by the power of the Holy Ghost.

Well, I hope that helps tonight. I hope that helps us, as members of the Church, to gird up our loins and not be found among those *Gentiles*, who are members of the Church, who are going to be cut off in a coming day because of vanity and unbelief. We want to make sure that we're among those *Gentiles* who are numbered with the *house of Israel,* who will take part in the mighty acts of the establishment of Zion, the building of the New Jerusalem, and the blessings of the tribes of Israel when they come out of the North. That's our heritage. I testified to that in the name of Jesus Christ, amen.

Student 4: I have a question.

Mike: Go ahead.

Student 4: In section 105, this is a section where they were encamped on Fishing River, and he receives this revelation, and the Lord says that the Church is under condemnation because of the transgressions of the people, speaking concerning the church and not individuals.

Mike: What verse are you reading in section 105?

Student 4: Verse 2:

> *[2] Behold, I say unto you, were it not for the transgressions of my people, speaking concerning the church and not individuals, they might have been redeemed even now.*
>
> *[3] But behold, they have not learned to be obedient to the things which I required at their hands, but are full of all manner of evil, and do not impart of their substance, as becometh saints, to the poor and afflicted among them;*
>
> *[4] And are not united according to the union required by the law of the celestial kingdom;*
>
> *[5] And Zion cannot be built up unless it is by the principles of the law of the celestial kingdom; otherwise I cannot receive her unto myself.*

The three laws are obedience, giving to the poor and needy, and being united in the laws of the Celestial Kingdom.

Mike: Now, read verse 6 too, because it is also important.

Student 4: Okay:

[6] And my people must needs be chastened until they learn obedience, if it needs be, by the things which they suffer.

By the way, this is the third or fourth section that talks about condemnation. And we had a temple talk one morning over in Snowflake, where the temple president told us that we were still under condemnation and we're not out of that because of the things you've talked about tonight. And it's us, both Jew and *Gentile*, and everything. So, thank you for a great talk.

Mike: And one more thing, it ties in perfectly with what we're talking about. I'm not saying whether the Church is under condemnation or not. I believe the Church is led by revelation and we have apostles and prophets. Individually in our day, you can be condemned, and individually in our day, you can come out from underneath that condemnation. It doesn't matter what's going on around you. What matters is where you are in your relationship with your Redeemer. Where are you? It doesn't matter as a community because the whole gospel of Jesus Christ is built individually, one-on-one; and Zion will be established that very way. It's not going to be a whole group of people that come together all of a sudden, and you've got this Zion people. It's one woman and one man at a time, coming up and obtaining these blessings from the Lord, to where they become Zion in stature. You get enough of those individual people together, and at that point, you begin to form a society. So, if you are operating under the Spirit of the Holy Ghost, if you have revelations that are coming to you, and if you are guided by the Spirit, you can know that you are not under condemnation. If you continue that, then the day will come when you will be numbered among the *house of Israel* and participate in all those blessings. But, I will tell you that the message is that number-wise, among the members of the Church, those who will be numbered among the *house of Israel* are relatively small, compared to the total number.

Student 4: Alright, thank you.

Mike: I just pray that we can access that blessing, that we're wise, walk by the Spirit, and be obedient, humble, and submissive.

References:
Bible dictionary: election
Book of Mormon title page
D&C 109 section heading
D&C 109:60
2 Nephi 10:8 refers to a great Gentile nation
D&C 84:6-16 priesthood lineage of Moses
2 Nephi 28:12-
Isaiah 3:16; 2 Nephi 13:16 "...daughters of Zion...mincing as they go, and making a tinkling with their feet:"
John 10:16
3 Nephi 16:4
D&C 133:32-35
3 Nephi 16:10
3 Nephi 16
D&C 84:54-59
D&C 124:27-32, 44-48
D&C 105:2-6

Chapter Thirty-Eight
Podcast 038 The Virtue of the Word of God

Something I would like to mention tonight is that nobody should believe anything I say on these podcasts. I want that to be understood; you should not believe anything I say. What we are doing here is gathering information. All of us are truth seekers and once we gather this information, we should take it to our Heavenly Father, in the name of His Son, and let the Holy Ghost confirm or deny what we hear. It's up to each one of us, who are seeking after truth, to let the Holy Ghost confirm that it is truth or it is error, and we each have the franchise to do that. The only difference is that I've been teaching for a while and with my employment, I'm exposed to Church doctrine. Other than that, I am nobody special, so I just don't want anybody to take face value in anything that I say. I have some people calling me and asking, "Who are you anyway?" And I tell them, "Basically nobody. I just live over in Eagar, Arizona." And then I give them a little bit of background and move on from right there, just so that people can get a feel for that kind of thing.

As I had been pondering and seeking the Lord and His Spirit on what we could talk about, there were two or three things that came to mind, but this is one I'd like to chat with you about. It's in Alma 31:5. What's happening here is that Alma is giving up the judgment seat to a Nephite judge, so he doesn't have to belong or be involved with the political, day-in and day-out proceedings of the Nephite government. He wants to take upon himself the full-time ministry of preaching the gospel to the Nephite people. In verse 5, we have a little key here, something that will set the stage for what I'd like to talk about. I hope the Lord will bless us with His Spirit, so it comes out okay. Let's go to verse 5. Alma said:

> *And now, as the preaching of the word had a great tendency to lead the people to do that which is just—yea, it* [the preaching of the word of God] *had had more powerful effect upon the minds of the people than the sword, or anything else, which had happened unto them—therefore* **Alma thought it was expedient that they should try the virtue of the word of God.**

So, Alma is going on a mission, and his main thrust on this mission is to preach the revealed word of God to the people, knowing that it has a more powerful effect on them than anything else. A synonym for *virtue* that is used in the scriptures is *power*. So, he is saying, "Let's try the *virtue,* or the *power,* of the word of God." With that, I would like to read to you a little statement by Brother Boyd K. Packer that ties in with that, and we have referred to this several times on these podcasts. Elder Packer said this:

> *True doctrine, understood, changes attitudes and behavior.*
> *The study of the doctrines of the gospel will improve behavior quicker than a study of behavior will improve behavior.*

The part we never quote is this part:

> *Preoccupation with unworthy behavior can lead to unworthy behavior. That is why we stress so forcefully the study of the doctrines of the gospel.*

I've had some people who have contacted me in the last few weeks that are struggling with some of their children, and some of their children are still living in the home, and some have moved out of the home. They listened to the podcast on devils and unclean spirits, and the information in those two podcasts painted an all too familiar picture of what they are seeing in their families. These moms and dads are frustrated, frightened, and worried for their children. They've observed a downward spiral in their kids and have tried everything they know how, to little, if any, avail. If there has been success, it has been short-lived, and then the behavioral problems simply come back. It's been my observation that what we do in the Church councils is, basically, talk about behavior. We talk about the behavior of the members of the Church: whether they are not paying enough tithing or not paying any tithing; they are not attending their meetings, not accepting calls, don't have a temple recommend, not saying their prayers, not reading their scriptures, not doing their home teaching, etc. So, a good portion of our time in Church councils revolves around talking about the behavior of the Latter-day Saints and trying to come up with a plan on how to turn that around. I remember sitting in the mission president's office with President Evan Schmutz, president of the Cebu Mission. He had just gotten there maybe 30 days ahead of us. I remember sitting in his office, and he was just super concerned, and he said, "Elder Stroud, how do we stop the hemorrhage that's going on in the Church?" What he was referring to was the 88% less-active rate among members of the Church in the Philippines. We had only 12% that were attending church and found that almost as quickly as they came in, they go right out the back door. So, we talked back and forth about this. Since that talk, I found out, as Alma did, that *"the preaching of the word had a great tendency to lead the people to do that which is just."* Brother Packer says, *"True doctrine understood, changes attitudes and behaviors."* So, for those children whose parents are concerned that they are in a state of rebellion and their behavior is less than desirable, they need to be able to be taught true doctrine and understand it! The problem is that they are in a state where they don't want to talk about the Church or doctrine or anything to do with spirituality. They turned their moms and dads off, and you just can't approach them. How do we get to a point where we can teach true doctrine and testify of it to people who are hard-hearted? Well, we have to do something different than we have been doing before. The frustration comes when you see no progress, in that we continue to do the things that we have done before and don't see any success at it. We think that if we just keep doing these same things long enough, it's going to resolve the situation. I heard somebody say that that's a definition of insanity, doing the same thing over and over and over again expecting different results. So, what we need to do now is identify the behavior. If a parent thinks that a child is being afflicted with an unclean spirit (which is what these parents were talking to me about), and won't listen to any kind of information, then you as a parent have to do something different so that the Lord will favor you and soften your child's heart. There has to be some kind of a change in the thinking and the feeling of that child, in order for you to be able to approach them.

So, here is what I'd like to recommend. In the scriptures, it talks about different orders of prayer. Now, it doesn't use that word *order*, except in one place, but I can identify three different orders of prayer in the scriptures. This is the conversation I had with these moms and dads, and I have done this myself, so I am giving some personal experience on what has helped in my own personal situation with children who have walked away from activity and didn't want to have anything to do with the gospel.

The first order of prayer is what I call *primary prayer*, and that's the prayer we are taught by the missionaries: you bow your head, fold your arms, and close your eyes. The reason I call it *primary prayer* is because that is the first prayer that an investigator, a primary child, or a child in the home is taught by the parents. You take that posture, close your eyes, fold your arms, bow your head, and kneel or sit and then the prayer goes like this:

> You address Heavenly Father, thank Him for what you have, ask Him for what you need, and close your prayer in the name of Jesus Christ.

That's the prayer that we teach every investigator that comes into the Church, and it's a good prayer. It's primary and foundational. Like everything else in the gospel, there are higher steps, and in this case, it's different orders of prayer. Just like there are different orders of priesthood, there are different orders of prayer. Our problem is that we stay in the primary mode of prayer throughout our membership in the Church, and then we wonder why we get bored, why the gospel does not hold the same fascination or the same excitement that it did when we first came into contact with it, and we start finding fault. The problem is that you need to graduate from that foundational level of prayer into the next order of prayer that the scriptures call *mighty prayer*. So, for these parents who are struggling with this, I would recommend that you take a look at this order of prayer. Let me give you an example. It is all over the place once you start to recognize it. Let's go to the book of Enos in the *Book of Mormon* where we have a good example of *mighty prayer*. It starts in verses 2 and 3, but I want to go to 4. You can look at all the characteristics of this, but in verse 4 we start to receive some identifiers that we are talking about a higher order of prayer. In the scriptures, the *primary prayer* is usually identified using words like, "prayed unto the Lord; praying unto the Lord; a prayer unto the Lord," etc. When you read phrases like that you're talking about something foundational. Now, look at verse 4 in Enos:

> *And my soul hungered; and I kneeled down before my Maker, and I cried unto him in **mighty prayer** and supplication for mine own soul;*

The keywords that identify *mighty prayer here* are, *"I cried unto him."* Now, in the temple, I can see that every time we use the words *"cry unto the Lord"* instead of *"pray unto the Lord,"* we are talking about something higher, something that has greater results. You're now using knowledge that you have gained from the scriptures or personal revelation or another source to apply something different in your life that you haven't done before, expecting bigger, better, greater, more profound results. Every time we move up into something of a higher order or a step up in our gospel progress, we should expect and receive better results. In this case, we want our prayers to be heard and answered. One of the things you are looking for when you see *"cry unto the Lord,"* is this higher order of prayer. In 3 Nephi 19, we find some other things that have to do with *mighty prayer*. In verse 24, the Savior comes back at the beginning of the second day. His disciples already have a huge congregation of thousands of people broken into twelve different groups/congregations, and the disciples are teaching them what Jesus taught yesterday, and they are all involved in prayer when the Savior comes:

> *[24] And it came to pass that when Jesus had thus prayed unto the Father, he came to his disciples,*

> *and behold, they did still continue, without ceasing, to pray unto him;*

Now, that's not the main key. Here's why they prayed without ceasing:

> *and they did not multiply many words, **for it** [whatever they are saying in their prayer] **was given unto them what they should pray**, and they were filled with desire.*

That's your key! They were given what they should pray. When you get into *mighty prayer*, you start praying in a revelatory way where the Holy Spirit and the Holy Ghost give you the words to say in the prayer. It becomes almost poetic. It becomes scriptural, and you'll find yourself saying things that are above and beyond what you normally would say in your prayers. You find out that as you are speaking one sentence, in the back of your mind the Holy Ghost has already placed the next sentence, just waiting for your lips to finish speaking, so it can come and take the next sentence's place. I'll also mention that in *primary prayer* when you bow your head, fold your arms, and close your eyes, in body language, that is a closed position; you're closing everything out. When you pray in *mighty prayer*, you want to open yourself up. You want to get into an open, receiving posture.

Let me show you what that is. Let's go to *Doctrine and Covenants 88* and you can read about why prayer posture is important. Prayer posture is an important thing. It never dawned on me how important it was until I was on my mission in New Jersey when I experimented around with some things that I had never done before. Let's go to verse 120, and look at what the Lord says here:

> *[120] That your incomings may be in the name of the Lord; that your outgoings may be in the name of the Lord; that all your salutations may be in the name of the Lord, **with uplifted hands** unto the Most High.*

You can read about the *School of the Prophets* starting in verse 127 going through the end of section 88. Look at verse 132 when they entered the *School of the Prophets* and when they prayed:

*[132 And when any shall come in after him, let the teacher arise, and, **with uplifted hands to heaven**, yea, even directly, salute his brother or brethren with these words:*

When they prayed in the *School of the Prophets*, they knelt in a circle, and they raised their hands toward heaven. This is before you have Elijah and Moses and all these people appearing. That prayer on the upper floor of the Newel K. Whitney Store where the *School of the Prophets* was held, whatever they did there in that group was enough to bring Jesus Christ Himself into the room; they saw Him. And the Holy Father came into the room; they saw Him. You can read that account by a man named Zebedee Coltrin. These men were involved in a higher level of prayer, *mighty prayer*. If you were to be standing behind the person who was praying with uplifted hands, you would see that they form a V. That V form creates a compass posture. I'm not talking about a compass that goes North, East, South, and West. I'm talking about the architect's compass. It also forms a mark that we have in the garment. The purpose of that compass is to circumscribe a circle, to draw a perfect circle, which is the geometric symbol for eternity. When a person prays with uplifted hands, they form that mark, that symbolic mark of the architect's compass. You notice that the compasses on the earth that are used are with the open point down. It's the compass we use in mathematics and architecture to draw circles and to trace lines on maps, and the inversion is down. The Godly compass we're talking about that is represented in the temple is pointed up, and it circumscribes or forms a circle heavenward. It also conveys that all truth can be found within that circle. So, what I am presenting to you here today is that postures symbolically open up power sources for us. In the *Bible dictionary* under *prayer*, if you look at the postures mentioned, you'll see that never in ancient time did we ever hear of any records with people praying with their arms folded, their eyes closed, and their heads bowed. It just didn't happen. I have a hunch that the reason we have that in in the Church today was when the first Primaries, whenever they came into place, were trying to teach little kids how to pray so they can focus: fold your arms, bow your head, close your eyes, and be able to focus. I wonder.

Nonetheless, if you want something more, if you want God to touch the heart of your child, then we need to do something differently.

I remember when we were in New Jersey; I saw that our Christian friends in the Christian world have a touch for this. If you've ever been in an evangelical meeting, you'll see that when they pray they'll have at least one hand stretched heavenward, sometimes they'll stretch both. That is an open receiving posture; you're seeking something from heaven, and you're opening yourself up to receive it. You may find also that the posture will make a difference in the words that you speak. I remember the time when I first did this was in New Jersey. I'd read this, I'd studied this, and I knew that they did it in the *School of the Prophets*. I could see it in lots of different Christian churches, and I knew that it was something Joseph did in sacred circles. So, I thought, "I'm gonna try this!" I went out one morning as the sun was coming up. I was in a park and I looked around like Joseph did in the Sacred Grove. This was a park that had a walking path of about a mile. Margie and I would exercise by walking this path, and it was a beautiful hardwood forest park that was just gorgeous. So, I looked around to make sure that nobody could see me. I didn't want to be interrupted; I didn't want to be sidetracked. As I came around the corner there was a shaft of sunlight that was coming down through this grove of trees that was just beautiful and I said, "That's my place." I had visions in my mind of the Sacred Grove with Joseph praying; you know that picture we see with that shaft of light coming down? If you've ever noticed, most of the First Vision pictures also picture Joseph with his hands stretched towards heaven. I don't know if he knew anything at that time, but I think it's interesting that they portray it that way. You never see a picture of Joseph during that vision when the light is coming down, with his arms folded, his head bowed, and his eyes closed. He may have started out that way, I don't know, but nonetheless. So, I went and stood in that light. The reason I stood in the light is because I understand that the SUN is symbolic of the SON. I wanted to be facing and bask in the source of all light. So, after I had looked around to make sure no one was going to bother me, I went and stood in that light, closed my eyes, looked up to where the sun was just bathing my face, stretched my hands up heavenward, and started to talk to Heavenly Father. It was such a sweet experience. It was just so different. It was so focused. I could feel that heat, I could sense all of that light, and it was truly a prayer that was given to me. The only reason I didn't keep it up for quite awhile was because I got nervous that someone was going to come walking down that path and see this guy standing in the path doing that.

So, brothers and sisters, try something different. Start to seek for the Holy Spirit to guide you. Another ancient way they prayed was prostrate. It was not uncommon for a person to prostrate themselves right on the ground, symbolic of the desire to be meek, humble, and lowly of heart, to be in a state of grace, having a broken heart and a contrite spirit. So, posture is something you may want to try.

Here's another thing: *mighty prayer* is almost always accompanied with fasting. If you look at the sons of Mosiah and Alma, they involved themselves and they fasted and prayed oft. I understand that praying oft is daily and if you really want to do it the way scripture says, you want to start something different now than what you've done before. Remember, if you always do what you have always done, you're always going to get what you've always had. So, if you're looking for something different to touch your children so that you can have an opportunity to teach them true doctrine that will change their behavior, you've got to do something different. You've got to do something different and let the Spirit be your guide. So, when it says, "they fasted oft," in my mind fasting oft isn't once a month. I think once a month is primary and preparatory and foundational. So, if praying oft, according to the scriptures, is three times a day, and President Benson said we need to associate ourselves, in the coming days (talking about the difficult days that are coming), with men who, like Daniel, prayed three times a day. Alma 34 says pray three times a day. So, if we are looking for a way to do things differently, maybe we need to try that.

Fasting once a month is not oft. I just can't see any way that it fits the bill of what the scripture calls *"oft."* So, Margie and I talked about that while we were in the Philippines, and we've been fasters; we fasted every fast Sunday, we do that. But, in the

Philippines, we started to tap into something more and we just decided that wasn't enough. So, we decided that we were going too fast every week. Now, this is a personal thing, some people can't do it physically. I understand that, but for us, we could do it and we decided to do that. We fasted every week for about eight months. I want to testify to you of the increase of dreams, and visions, and on-going revelatory flow through the Holy Ghost, that we have never felt ever before. And we knew that it was a true principle, and the interesting thing was that the first time we did it, it was hard. But I read Brother John Pontius's books and he had some things to say about fasting. One of the things he said was to begin your fast twenty-four hours before you actually fast. In other words, start to prepare for it, make it a spiritual experience. So, twenty-four hours before you actually begin the fast, you've given thought and go into the fast with a purpose. The next thing brother Pontius taught was that the ultimate form of fasting is to not fast until the Holy Spirit tells you too. Now, if you are going to fast once a week or often, then a set time is okay, but the step above that is to not fast until you've received a revelation from God that He wants you to fast and do it now. Well, we got away from that. We went to New Jersey and in the year since we got home from our mission, we've found ourselves just kind of stagnate.

We came into the office one day and Margie said to me, "I feel stuck!"

I said, "Me too! What are we going to do about it?"
And so, we talked back and forth as husband and wife, and we decided that we were going to do two things; we were for sure going to attend the temple every week and not let anything get in the way of weekly temple attendance, and we were going to go back to fasting every week. I can tell you that in the eight months we had done that in the Philippines, within the second week after starting, we looked forward to it, we longed for it, and it was an excitement to be able to fast that coming week. It was something we just anticipated and looked forward to. Well, we've been doing this again now for about two and a half months, fasting every week, and I'll tell you that it is a great source of power, and it's always accompanied with a higher level of prayer called *mighty prayer*.

I just give that to you to think about because what you want to do is get your loved ones to where you can talk to them. And they're already probably turned off because you've talked to them before saying, "Why aren't you going to church? How come you don't say the prayer? What's the matter with you? You know better than this!" I know all these things because I've done all this. When I stopped talking to my kids about why they weren't going to church, they started opening up to me and let me start talking to them about other things. They already knew what they should be doing. They didn't need to have me come in and rehearse the whole thing to them one more time. It just drove them further away. So, <u>this is me now</u>, on purpose, I stopped all talk about church activity and I just prayed to the Lord, "Let me take my kids where they are and love them and see them the way You see them. Let me have that charity so I can interact with them in a way that will bless their lives." My son drives a semi-pump truck, a big Peterbilt, and I had stopped talking to him about the Church and we started to have a relationship again. He wasn't doing what he should, and he knew what my values were, and I didn't stop doing what I was doing, but we were able to meet on common ground. I remember one night we went out in his Peterbilt truck and I spent all night with him at work helping him clean out sewer lines and pumping out traps. I'd been praying for him, that this would open up. And very naturally, a conversation opened up to how he had been feeling so discouraged and so depressed. He had even had the thought while he was going down the road in his tanker truck, "Why don't I just crank the wheel to one side and drive this rig over the edge and end it all?!"

I had no idea he was having those kinds of despondent thoughts and I said, "Scott, can I share something with you that I have learned that I didn't know until just a little while ago?"

He said, "Sure dad, what is it?"

And I told him that there is, in the world, light and darkness, good and evil and that the evil is organized intelligence, and I went into a little bit about devils and unclean spirits. And I said, "You are being victimized and afflicted by persons behind the veil who seek your misery, and you don't even know it. You are not the originator of this depression and discouragement. This is coming from evil influences, and you're picking up on their emotions." And guess what we started to do? I started to teach him true doctrine.

Do you know what he said? He kept looking over at me as he was driving down the road and he said, "You mean, Dad, I'm not crazy?" That was his comment, "You mean I'm not crazy?"

I said, "No son, you are not crazy." And that led from one thing to another, and in time, I was able to put my hands on his head and give him a blessing and start the process for him to be healed from these afflictions and attachments that were going on.

Brothers and sisters, here's the point; we've got to be able to get to a point where our kids will let us talk to them about this; that they'll even open up. When they open up, I have found that the best way to do this is, "Can I share something with you that I've learned that I've never known before?" That's the way I did it. There was nothing about the Church, there was nothing about priesthood, there was nothing about prophets or apostles, nothing about temples, nothing. It was just, "I've learned something that's really been a blessing to me in my life. Can I share it with you?"

And he said, "Yes." And I've done that with others the same way. So, I recommend that and share that with you, but go into *mighty prayer* and ask the Lord for a favor.

Now, go with me over to *Doctrine and Covenants* 50 and let me show you another thing. This is the power of *the word*. All of this is coming out of the scriptures. Verse 10 is another key that we learn in the scriptures:

> *[10] And now come, saith the Lord, by the Spirit, unto the elders of his church, and let **us** reason together, that **you** may understand;*

"*Let **us**.*" You see this is the Lord and Mike. This is the Lord and yourself. "*Let **us** [the two of **us**] reason together, that **you** may understand.*" We are going to reason together, you and I, but the result of this reasoning is that **you** understand something. It's not that the Lord understands, but that you understand something as a result of this interaction. So, in your prayers, in *mighty prayer*, brothers and sisters, what you want to do is reason with the Lord. I have found out, through personal experience, that God, our Father, and His Son, Jesus Christ, love to reason with us. Now, the question is, what is He saying?

> *[11] Let us reason even as a man **reasoneth** one with another face to face.*
>
> *[12] Now, when a man **reasoneth**, he is understood of man, because he **reasoneth** as a man; even so will I, the Lord, reason with you **that you may understand**.*

Now, go back to this principle of Brother Packer, *"True doctrine **understood** changes behavior."* So, what you can do is *reason* with the Lord so He can help you understand something. You are going to *reason* with your children so that they can understand something. *Reasoning* with each other is one of the keys to understanding, and understanding leads to improved, healed behavior. I remember when I was thinking, "What does this mean, to *reason* with the Lord? What does that mean?" Here's one of those mysteries that is hidden in plain sight. Here's one of those things that, until the Spirit shows it to you, you'll never see it. I love the way God hides things in plain sight. So, what does it mean to *reason* with one another? Here's what it means; you give the Lord your *reason* for approaching Him and asking what you're asking. *Reasoning* with the Lord means you're giving the *reasons* for what you are doing. Why are you doing what you are doing? "I'm approaching You in this prayer and the purpose for this, the *reason* for this is, I have children who won't listen to me, and I don't know what to do. I know that their hearts need to be softened, but I can't do that, but I know You can. So, the *reason* I am coming to You is so that You touch their hearts, so that I can come in and teach them the doctrine of Christ." So, *reasoning* with the Lord simply means you state the *reason* for the purpose you're approaching Him. Isn't that so simple?

Let me give you an example of *reasoning* with the Lord. Let's go over to Ether 3, in the *Book of Mormon*. I'm going to show you one of the magic stories in the *Book of Mormon* and the power of scriptures. You see, everything that we are talking about—how we can do this, how we can get to a point where we can talk to our children, and they'll listen to us—it's all in the scriptures. Here's an example, and you know the story: the brother of Jared has built the barges, they're dark, and there is no

light. So in verse 1, the brother of Jared comes up with this idea to:
> ...*molten out of a rock sixteen small stones; and they were white and clear, even as transparent glass;*

He comes upon the mount, and I'm sure there was an altar there. It doesn't say so, but I am sure there was an altar there because these people worshiped at altars. I can see him take these sixteen stones and place them upon the altar and in verse 3:
> ...*but behold these things which I have molten out of the rock.*

We'll come back to this in a minute, but I want you to ask yourself this question: where in heaven's name does Mahonri Moriancumer, the brother of Jared, come up with the idea for these sixteen stones? I mean, that isn't what I would have done. Now, go with me and let me show you how he *reasons*. Prior to the Lord touching these stones with His finger, the key that opens the veil so the finger can come out is *reasoning* with the Lord. So, go back to verse 2. Here is the brother of Jared *reasoning* with the Lord:
> *O Lord, thou hast said that we must be encompassed about by the floods.*

Another thing God said was, "You can't have windows and I won't let you have fire." So, automatically at 2,000 years before the birth of Christ, 2,200 B.C., the Lord just removed any alternatives for light within a darkened barge. You can't have fire, and you can't have a window. What else is there? In that day, what else is there? The brother of Jared says, "Well, I've got these sixteen stones, which by the way, are not lit." We may want to pattern our approach to the Lord, in *reasoning* with Him, somewhat after what the brother of Jared does because the results of his *reasoning*, brothers and sisters, were magnificent. Wouldn't you agree? So, now he says:
> *Now behold, O, Lord, and do not be angry with thy servant because of his weakness before thee; for we know that thou art holy and dwellest in the heavens, and that we are unworthy before thee; because of the fall our natures have become evil continually; nevertheless, O Lord, thou hast given*

> *us a commandment that we must call upon thee, that from thee we may receive according to our desires.*

This is what you call *reasoning with the Lord*. Look at the next verse:

> *[3] Behold, O Lord, thou has smitten us because of our iniquity, and hast driven us forth, and for these many years we have been in the wilderness; nevertheless, thou hast been merciful unto us. O Lord, look upon me in pity, and turn away thine anger from this thy people, and suffer not that they shall go forth across this raging deep in darkness; but behold these things which I have molten out of the rock.*

Now, that's an example of *reasoning with the Lord*. You take that example of this magnificent prophet and the unparalleled results and ask yourself the question: what kind of a pattern can I use in my circumstances, similar to this, that would bring about different results than I've been having in the past?

Let me show you one last thing before we run out of time. Remember our message tonight is try *the virtue of the word of God*. Every morning, I look forward so much to my scripture study. The first thing I do when I get out of bed is come down into my office and talk to Margie. She has usually beat me up a little bit, not physically, but beats me up out of bed. So, she'll be in her office already studying, and I'll go in and say, "What did you learn this morning?" And we'll talk about it, "What did you learn and what have you been taught?" etc. Then I'll go down into my office, shut the door, kneel down, and I just talk to my Heavenly Father and tell Him how grateful I am to be able to study His holy word. I tell him I understand what a difficult challenge it's been to preserve these records so that I can have them in 2016. I don't know if I've shared this story with you, but I will. During one of these mornings, I was just thanking the Lord and asking Him as I began my scripture study, to open up my mind, to enlighten my mind, to quicken my intellect, and to broaden my understanding. I think about the initiatory blessings that are pronounced upon the head, the ears, and the eyes. Think back on that; remember the wording on the head, the ears, and the eyes, and then apply that as you approach the Lord. Apply those words. In other words, as part of your *reasoning*, as you are learning things, learning new doctrine that the Lord is teaching you, involve that information, involve that verbiage, involve those words in your prayers and watch what a difference it makes because now you're growing in Christ. Well, as I was kneeling down and thanking Him for this, I had a little vision come into my mind:

> I saw a man running through a forested area, and I couldn't tell if he had anything in his hands. It just lasted for a split second, but in that split second that I had this little mini vision, I knew that this man was trying to protect holy records and that he was being hunted because he was a caretaker of sacred writ. I knew that. It was in something like a hardwood forest, it wasn't in a jungle situation, and he was running. I can't remember what clothes he had on, but I remember the thought, "He's being hunted." And then the thought was followed up with, "He was killed." It has changed forever how I approach the Lord and express my gratitude for the scriptures. The thought I was left with was this, "There have been people give up their lives so that you and I could have these records." And that has made a difference in how I approached the Lord.

So, in closing, let me show you another magnificent thing about the scriptures. Where did the brother of Jared ever get this idea of sixteen stones? In pondering this, you might want to ask, did the brother of Jared come before or after the flood? And you'll discover that he came after the flood. So the brother of Jared is probably a descendent of Shem since he has a favored status with the Lord. But he is a descendent of the family of Noah. Now, let's go to the *Bible* for just a minute. I want you to go to Genesis and see how everything in the scriptures has been preserved in such a remarkable way. It's just so fun to look at this! Let's go to Genesis 6:14. Now, these are the instructions on building the ark. Keep in mind that the brother of Jared follows Noah. Do you think that Noah had any scriptures on-board the ark? What do you think? Do you think Noah had scriptures? Well, if you want to answer that question, you have to look at the pattern. Did all of the holy patriarchs, coming down through time, have scriptures? Did Adam keep a record of his dealings? Were there scriptures in his day, and did his posterity have those? The answer is, yes! The scriptures are referred to as a *book of remembrance*, and they were carried on down. So, every patriarch had the scriptures of the prophets that preceded them, plus the revelations God gives them to add to that. By the time we get down to Noah's ark, he should have a pretty good library of the scriptural record of the patriarchs, from Adam all the way down to the seven patriarchal heads, to Noah. So, he's got scriptures on board the ark. That's the pattern. Look at Genesis 6:14 where the Lord says:

> *[14] Make thee an ark of gopher wood; rooms shalt thou make in the ark, and shalt pitch it within and without with pitch.*
> *[15] And this is the fashion which thou shalt make it of: The length of the ark shall be three hundred cubits, the breadth of it fifty cubits, and the height of it thirty cubits.*
> *[16] A window shalt thou make to the ark, and in a cubit shalt thou finish it above; and the door of the ark shalt thou set in the side thereof; with lower, second, and third stories shalt thou make it.*

Now, every picture that you've probably seen of an ark had a door and a window in it; at least the door, and I've seen some with windows. It comes from Genesis 6. Look at your footnote on Genesis 6:16a:

> *HEB tsohar; some rabbis believed it was a precious stone that shone in the ark. Ether 2:23 (23-24)*

The word *window* is a mistranslation. The translation in Hebrew is *tsohar*. Notice that your cross reference there is Ether 2:23-24 where it talks about how dark it is in that barge. So, now watch what happens. The question comes up, where did the brother of Jared get the idea for sixteen stones? Well, he had the scriptural record of Noah, and he knew that inside the ark there was a stone that glowed in the dark. I bet you that if we had that record of that stone in Noah's ark, you would find that God's finger came through the veil and touched that stone. Go back to Ether 3, verse 4 and look at this. It all starts to come together; this is the fun of the scriptures, this is where it gets so exciting:

> *[4] And I know, O Lord, that thou hast all power, and can do whatsoever thou wilt for the benefit of man;*

How does he know that? Well, he has scripture records that go all the way back to Adam that show God's dealings with His children. Now, watch this:

> *therefore touch these stones, O Lord, with thy finger,*

Now, where in heaven's name did he get that idea? If we had the record, I know that Noah's record, his scriptures, would talk about that stone being touched by the finger of God to give light in that darkened ark. There wasn't a window in that ark at all:

> *and prepare them that they may shine forth in darkness; and they shall shine forth unto us in the vessels which we have prepared, that we may have light while we shall cross the sea.*

Here are some other fun things. You want to get into this where the scriptures really become magnificent. They have two stones per barge; eight barges, two stones. Where did they place them? Well, with the brother of Jared, the book of Ether tells us they put stones at either end. Why not both of them in the middle? And he also says that these barges were peaked. They were peaked and the stones went in either end. If you were to get a description of the *Urim and Thummim*, you would see that there are two stones fastened in a bow. So, the barges are representative of ancient tools that God has used all through time, called *Urim and Thummim*. Two stones: Urim means *lights*, and Thummim means *perfections*. Joseph Smith says that they were triangular shaped stones, one with the apex up and one with the apex down, fastened in a silver bow, which looked somewhat like ancient spectacles, so that a person fastening the breastplate could have these spectacles in front of his eyes to look through them and have his hands free to do whatever needed to be done. Now, you take these two triangular stones and lay one across the other, and you have the Star of David or the Seal of Solomon, and that gets into a whole different thing. The point is, the *Urim and Thummim* and the barges are fashioned in a similar way; peaked at both ends with a stone in both ends to give light to the barges. At any rate, it is just a marvelous thing!

So, what's the lesson to be learned from this? How can we benefit from this story from Mahonri Moriancumer? Here's the lesson: don't expect angels to come and give you information; don't expect God to come and give you information; don't expect the Holy Ghost to reveal to you information that is already available in the written word of God. Let me say that again. If you're looking for angels, the *spirits of just men*, if you're looking for revelations through the Holy Spirit and the Holy Ghost about doctrines, and you want to get it from God's mouth, you're going to be slow to get that revelation if it's already available to you in His canonized, written, scriptural word. So, what does this behoove us then, brothers and sisters? It behooves us to become scripturally literate and to know what He has already given us. If you have an angel come to you and he brings you information concerning life and salvation, you can bet he is going to give you something that you don't already have available in the written word of God. What's the greatest source of revelation for us that we have right now? It's the written word of God. In particular, that unadulterated, non-prostituted record called *The Book of Mormon*. No wonder Joseph said:

A man [or woman] *would get nearer to God by abiding by its precepts, than by any other book.*

That's a good gospel principle that God will not reveal to you, personally, what He has already previously revealed and is available to you, if you will simply awake and arise and pay the price to access what's right in front of you. Satan knows that, brothers and sisters. That's why his thrust is to keep you out of that *word*. So, Alma is right: the *word* of God, *"had had more powerful effect upon the minds of the people than the sword, or anything else, which had happened unto them—therefore Alma thought it was expedient..."* Do you know what that word means? It means absolutely, critically necessary. *"...expedient that they should try the virtue of the word of God."* And, *"True doctrine, understood, changes...behavior."* Comments or thoughts? Does that make sense?

Student 3: Yes!

Mike: I love the scriptures. I look forward, with great anticipation, to my hour to two hours every morning of scripture reading, meditation, prayer, praise, and seeking the Lord in *mighty prayer*. I have a two-hour devotional that I try to spend every day with my Father in Heaven. I can do that because I'm retired. I couldn't always do it, but I am now. And I just have to tell you that I love that time with my Savior and my Father. They are so gracious to me. There is not a day goes by when I open the scriptures, but what He doesn't reveal something to me that I have not seen or understood before. But I ask for it, "Enlighten my mind, quicken my intellect, and enlarge and broaden my understanding so that I can see and understand Thy holy mysteries." And He answers that prayer! And it's so gracious, and it's so kind. Well, that's it. That's it for tonight. Do you have any comments or anything you want to add to that?

Student 6: So, we'll get to the third prayer next week?

Mike: The third prayer you'll have to discover. The third prayer is a higher order of prayer and that's only taught in the temple. You need to become proficient in *mighty prayer*, and then the Lord will guide you to something higher and more profound.

References:
Alma 31:5
Little Children by Boyd K. Packer Ensign, November 1986, 17
Enos 1:4
3 Nephi 19:24
D&C 88:120, 132
Zebedee Coltrin's account of seeing Jesus Christ and God: "House of Revelation" Ensign, Jan 1993
Bible Dictionary: prayer; 5th paragraph discusses postures
Alma 6:6; Helaman 3:35; 4 Nephi 1:12- fasting oft
Alma 34:21- pray three times a day
John Pontius books referencing fasting oft and fasting when prompted by the Spirit:, *Following the Light of Christ into His Presence* page 64-66; *Journey to the Veil* chapter 5-The Miracle of Obedience; chapter 5-Matriculation into Eternity; chapter 9-Doing Less, Being More; chapter 9-Holy and Without Spot.
D&C 50:10-12
Ether 3:1-3
Genesis 6:14-16
Ether 3:4
History of the Church, 4:461, "...a man would get nearer to God by abiding by its precepts, than by any other book."

Chapter Thirty-Nine
Podcast 039 Secret Combinations

Tonight, I'd like to take our time and spend it on discussing a pure *Book of Mormon* doctrine. It's not mentioned in the *Bible*, only once in the *Doctrine and Covenants*, once in the *Pearl of Great Price*, but it's mentioned seventeen times in the *Book of Mormon*. It is the doctrine of *secret combinations*. I'd like to spend a little time on that tonight, especially with the current political atmosphere, and what's going on in our country and throughout the world. I think that the primary purpose the *Book of Mormon* was given to us was so that we could recognize what's going on around us and have some power to confront it. It's not going away. It's something that comes from the pre-mortal life. The war in heaven was a *combined* war. The enemy *combined* against the Father and the Savior. To start out tonight, I'd like to go to *Doctrine and Covenants* 38. Then I want to look into the history of things a bit. The whole idea is to kind of bring us up to date on what the Lord has said about this. This section is one that is little studied and little talked about. It was given in January 1831, so we are in the early history of the Church:

> *[11] For all flesh is corrupted before me; and the powers of darkness prevail upon the earth, among the children of men, in the presence of all the hosts of heaven—*

And these powers of darkness and corruption:

> *[12] ... causeth silence to reign,* **and all eternity is pained***,*

Isn't that an interesting statement?

> *and the angels are waiting the great command to reap down the earth, to gather the tares that they may be burned;*

Now, those angels had been praying day and night for the Lord to set them loose, to separate the wheat from the tares, and bind the tares in bundles and burn them. And according to Wilford Woodruff, in 1896 those angels had been set loose and are now working upon the face of the earth. But, I want you to look at the last part of verse 12:

> *and, behold,* **the enemy is combined.**

There is where we get that word, *combined*. And then, look at verse 13:

> *[13] And now I show unto you a mystery, a thing which is had in secret chambers, to bring to pass even your destruction in process of time, and ye knew it not;*
>
> *[14] But now I tell it unto you, and ye are blessed, not because of your iniquity, neither your hearts of unbelief; for verily some of you are guilty before me, but I will be merciful unto your weakness.*
>
> *[15] Therefore, be ye strong from henceforth; fear not, for the kingdom is yours.*

I would say there has probably never been a time in the history of the world where we are going to need to be stronger and more courageous than we are right now and even more so in the days that are coming. Back up in verse 13, the Lord said, *"I show unto you a mystery."*

Keep in mind now, in these verses we're talking about a *combined* enemy which seeks the destruction of the Saints. Now, skip over to verse 28:

> *And again, I say unto you that the enemy in the* **secret chambers** *seeketh your lives.*

The key here is that the enemy is not in the open. The enemy is in *secret chambers*. So, now we have these two words back in verse 12; the enemy is *"combined"* and they operate in *"secret,"* and this is where you get the phrase *secret combinations*. When the enemy is combined, it means there are groups of people, operating under the direction of Satan, the devil, to overthrow all people. The purpose of devils is to captivate and enslave. Devils are interested in one thing. They're interested in power and enslaving God's children. It's my opinion that because they have not had bodies that they are not interested so much in the physicalness of the telestial world, i.e., sexual sins and those kinds of things. Unclean spirits are, but devils are interested in captivating, enslaving people, and obtaining power over them. Go to verse 29:

> *[29] Ye hear of wars in far countries, and you say that there will soon be great wars in far countries, but ye know not the hearts of men* **in your own land**.

That's speaking of America. This is in 1831:

> *[30] I tell you these things because of your prayers; wherefore, treasure up wisdom in your bosoms, lest the wickedness of men reveal these things unto you by their wickedness, in a manner which shall speak in your ears with a voice louder than that which shall shake the earth;*

In other words, you're going to find out about these combinations. You're going to learn about them. You can learn about them before they are on you, or you can learn about them while you're under attack and there's little hope of deliverance. But you **are** going to learn about them. And then notice the last part, which is really famous among the Latter-day Saints:

> *but if ye are prepared ye shall not fear.*

Well, the preparation is to learn about these *combinations*. They operate in the dark, they operate in secret places, they seek to enslave all of God's children, and they've done a pretty dang good job of it throughout the history of the world. Let's go over to Moses in the *Pearl of Great Price,* and let's look at where the first *secret combination* comes from. This is the account of the first one in **this** world. We see that it has to do with Cain. Go to Moses 5:16:

> *And Adam and Eve, his wife, ceased not to call upon God. And Adam knew Eve his wife, and she conceived and bare Cain,*

Now, it's interesting that if you go back to verse 12 it says:

> *[12] And Adam and Eve blessed the name of God, and they made all things known unto their sons and their daughters.*

They had many sons and daughters before Cain. You can't get that so much out of the Bible. So, one of the great Bible/Christian mysteries is: Where did Cain come from? Who did he marry? There were all kinds of posterity of Adam and Eve before Cain comes on the scene. Then, why is Cain mentioned? Look at what Eve says, verse 16:

> *and said: I have gotten a man from the Lord; wherefore he may not reject his* [the Lord's] *words.*

What is Eve saying here?

> *But behold, Cain hearkened not, saying: Who is the Lord that I should know him?*
>
> *[17] And she again conceived and bare his brother Abel. And Abel hearkened unto the voice of the Lord. And Abel was a keeper of sheep, but Cain was a tiller of the ground.*

What Eve is looking for here is a priesthood heir. They understood the *Patriarchal Order* of the priesthood at this point. Adam's whole emphasis throughout his life is to bring his posterity, his children, and their children, and their children, unto many generations, up through the priesthood, through ordinances, through a knowledge of the gospel, into the presence of Christ. He wants them to have a face-to-face encounter with Jesus Christ, and through that, become redeemed from the *Fall*. Most of Adam and Eve's children reject that invitation. We don't have the full background or record here, but Eve was hoping that this son, over other sons and daughters, would be the priesthood heir, in the patriarchal order, to all that Adam had. That is a likeness or a type of all of us becoming heirs with Christ, in all that the Father has. That's the *Patriarchal Order*. That's where this whole system of becoming joint heirs with Jesus Christ comes in. In the *Patriarchal Order*, there's only one legal heir in a generation, and it appears that Eve hoped that that heir would be Cain. Look at verse 18:

> *[18] And Cain loved Satan more than God. And Satan commanded him, saying: Make an offering unto the Lord.*

We know the whole story that his offering was rejected, and the Lord tries to reason with him. Let's go down to verse 23. Here's the Lord speaking to Cain, who is upset because his offering was rejected and Abel's was accepted. We won't go into the reason for that. But, the Lord is reasoning with Cain and says:

> *[23] If thou doest well, thou shalt be accepted. And if thou doest not well, sin lieth at the door, and Satan desireth to have thee; and except thou shalt hearken unto **my** [the Lord's] commandments, I will deliver **thee** [Cain] up, and it shall be unto thee according to his desire.*

In other words, Satan desired this and was the architect behind this rebellion that was taking place in their family. But, the last sentence in verse 23 is interesting. The Lord is speaking to Cain and says:

> *And thou [Cain] shalt rule over him [Satan];*

That's an interesting little statement. Remember we've said several times throughout our podcasts, and this comes from the Prophet Joseph Smith:

> *All beings who have bodies have power over those who have not.*

Possessing a physical body is a powerful edge in spiritual things. One of the reasons that Cain would rule over Satan is the fact that he has this physical body. Look at verse 24:

> *[24] For from this time forth thou shalt be the father of **his** lies;*

You, Cain, will be the father of Satan's lies:

> *thou shalt be called Perdition; for thou wast also before the world.*

This is an interesting little statement because it shows that Cain comes into this world with a predisposition toward things that would allow him to be captivated like he's about to be here.

In the book *Jesus the Christ,* James Talmage, in talking about *perdition* and what it took for a person to qualify to have a body in the telestial world, versus the third part who were cast out never to have that birth, said that those who did not come out in active warfare against the Father and the Son obtained a physical body. I assume that Cain would fall into that category, along with some other characters that we see that are born into this world, that have physical bodies, and yet end up being abjectly evil.

I want to skip down to a little thing in verse 29. Cain takes his posterity and others that will follow them, and he has them enter into an agreement with him. This is the beginning of your *secret combinations*. You can't have a *combination* unless you have more than one person involved. You've got to have at least two persons that *combine* together for the same purpose, in this case, it is how to murder and get gain, and keep it a secret. This was the great *combination* in the early days of the history of the world, and it is the great *combination* still in our day. But, look at this interesting thing that they do here:

> *[29] And Satan said unto Cain: Swear unto me by thy throat, and if thou tell it thou shalt die;*

We'll come back to that throat thing in just a minute:

> *and swear thy brethren by their heads, and by the living God, that they tell it not; for if they tell it* [this combination/secret, these great plans of darkness], *they shall surely die; and this that thy father may not know it; and this day I will deliver thy brother Abel into thine hands.*

Now, that's Satan speaking to Cain. In other words, we're entering into a covenant here, of darkness, which is what a *secret combination* is. It's a covenant. The master of the covenant invites someone of a lesser standing to enter in, and that person either chooses in or out, accepts the covenant or says no. There are two sides. This is the dark counterfeit of the covenant relationship that we have with the Father and the Son. They invite us to enter in, and we choose either to accept the conditions and enter in or to reject them. If you accept the conditions of a covenant with the Father and the Son, the by-product of that is that you are now able to tap into power and knowledge that you otherwise would not have. These are called the *mysteries of Godliness*. You have access to those *mysteries* when you accept the covenant from God. Now, here is the anti-god, Satan, who is now inviting Cain to enter into a covenant, and Cain accepts that. It's interesting, and we miss this, but look at verse 30:

> *[30] And Satan sware unto Cain that he* [Satan] *would do according to his* [Cain's] *commands.*

Did you catch that?

> *And all these things were done **in secret**.*

Let me back up again. Up in verse 29, Cain says, "Sware unto me...this and this and this..." and in verse 30, Satan swears to Cain that he (Satan) would do according to Cain's commands. You've got a two-way partnership here. Satan realizes that he needs to have mortal counterparts in the telestial world in order to fully captivate, enslave, and destroy God's children. He understands he needs to have mortal counterparts, and I'll tell you, brothers and sisters, that today, those mortal counterparts are every bit alive as they ever were. As a matter of fact, one of the interesting things about Cain is that we have no record that he dies in the scriptures. It just simply says that he will be a vagabond on the earth.

I want to share with you a little story here. This comes out of President Kimball's book, *The Miracle of Forgiveness*. President Kimball said this:

> *On the sad character of Cain, an interesting story comes to us from Lycurgus A. Wilson's book on the life of David W. Patten.*

David W. Patten was the first apostolic martyr in this dispensation. He was shot to death at the Battle of Crooked River:

> *From the book I quote an extract from a letter by Abraham O. Smoot* [a member of the Quorum of the Twelve] *giving his recollection of David Patten's account of meeting "a very remarkable person who had represented himself as being Cain."*

Here is the quote from David Patton's account:

> *As I was riding along the road on my mule, I suddenly noticed a very strange person walking*

> *beside me.... His head was about even with my shoulders as I sat in my saddle.*

Now, I'm a horseman, and I can tell you that when you are sitting on a mule, they are taller than most horses. So, if you're a six-foot person sitting on a mule, and his head is about even with your shoulders, the person you're talking to standing next to the mule, is pretty good-sized.

> *He wore no clothing but was covered with hair. His skin was very dark. I asked him where he dwelt and he replied that he had no home, that he was a wanderer in the earth and traveled to and fro. He said he was a very miserable creature, that he had earnestly sought death during his sojourn upon the earth, but that he could not die, and his mission was to destroy the souls of men. About the time he expressed himself thus, I rebuked him in the name of the Lord Jesus Christ and by virtue of the Holy Priesthood and commanded him to go hence, and he immediately departed out of my sight....*

What we have with Cain, and then later on with his descendants, are these *secret combinations*, and again, the purpose of the *secret combinations* is how to murder to get gain, make money at it, and keep it a secret. You can tell when a *secret combination,* then and now, is working at its peak; it's when people think there is no such thing. You can tell when it's operating at its greatest performance because when you try to expose them, the majority of the people will say that there is no such thing. That's when it's working very well.

I find it very interesting that the word *conspiracy* is also tied in with *secret combinations*. There's something about us, as men and women in this world, and as Latter-day Saints (we're not immune from it), that we get very upset to think that there is any kind of a power that we're not aware of that is operational and controlling our lives, day in and day out. Our independence just struggles with that, and we want to discard the idea that, "I'm being manipulated, or I'm being controlled in any way, especially when I don't know about it." But, that's the definition of a conspiracy and a *secret combination*. Let's go to section 89, and let me just show you a couple of things here that are kind of interesting in the scriptures. Latter-day Saints, above all people, should understand that there is conspiracy in the world. You cannot believe in a devil and reject the idea of conspiracy. You can't do it because, by his very nature, the devil is a conspirator. His plans are conspiratory. Section 89 is the Word of Wisdom. We've read it over and over, but I want to go down to verse 4; it's the verse we don't talk about very much:

> [4] Behold, verily, thus saith the Lord unto you: In consequence of **evils and designs** which do and will exist in the hearts of **conspiring men in the last days**, I have warned you, and forewarn you, by giving unto you this word of wisdom by revelation—

Did you ever stop to think that the purpose of the Word of Wisdom was to counteract a satanic conspiracy that's operational in our day? How many of us have thought about that? The Lord gives it to us because there's a conspiracy to destroy God's children by working through the things they take into their body; the elements of food, water, and sustenance, etc.

Doctrine and Covenants 123:11 is another one of these things that we're talking about. The Lord is warning us about these things that are taking place in secret chambers. The Lord says:

> [11] And also it is an imperative duty that we owe to all the rising generation [this was given in 1839], and to all the pure in heart—
> [12] For there are many yet on the earth among all sects, parties, and denominations, who are blinded by the subtle craftiness of men, whereby they lie in wait to deceive [that's a definition of a secret combination], and who are only kept from the truth because they know not where to find it—

In other words, there's a conspiracy to keep people from coming into contact with revealed, Restoration truth. Look at this one:

> [13] Therefore [because of this—because of the subtleness and craftiness that people are blinded by], that we should waste and wear out our lives in bringing to light all the hidden things of

> *darkness, wherein we know them; and they are truly manifest from heaven—*

Look at footnote 13b, where it says, *"bringing to light all the hidden things of darkness."* What does it say at the bottom of the page? *"Secret Combinations."*

> *[14] These* [hidden things] *should then be attended to with great earnestness.*

We're going to find out why, because people are being destroyed by a power that is organized and *combined*, and they are kept from a knowledge of it *"because they know not where to find [the truth.]"* Look at what it says in 15:

> *[15] Let no man count them as small things; for there is much which lieth in futurity* [this is in the future, from 1839 to our day], *pertaining to the saints, which depends upon these things.*

So, here we have various scripture references where the Lord is talking to us. We need to be aware of what's going on. Let me tell you what President Benson said in his next to last general conference talk. His last talk was in April 1989, and it was a little address given to children. The last talk before that was in October 1988, and you can look it up, is called *I Testify*. I just want to pull out a couple of things from this talk. He said:

> *I testify that wickedness is rapidly expanding in every segment of our society.* [This was in 1988!]
> *It is more highly organized, more cleverly disguised, and more powerfully promoted than ever before. Secret combinations lusting for power, gain, and glory are flourishing. A secret combination...*

He was talking about multiple, and now he's talking about one. A specific *secret combination*:

> *that seeks to overthrow the freedom of all lands, nations, and countries is increasing its evil influence and control over America and the entire world.*

Let's take just a minute and go over to Ether 8 in the *Book of Mormon*. Of any place in the *Book of Mormon*, the Book of Ether probably gives us the most definitive information on *secret combinations*. Moroni is speaking here in the Book of Ether. Let's go to verse 18. Here is a great warning for us:

> *[18] And it came to pass that they formed a secret combination,*

This is talking about some of the Jaredites, a person by the name of Akish, and some of that family:

> *even as they of old;*

Which means going back before the flood. The Jaredites are after the flood. It's interesting that the records of these *secret combinations* were on the Ark. They came across the flood with Noah and his family, these same *combinations* that were had in the days of Cain and Lamech, and every one of the great *Master Mahans* that came up through the *Patriarchal Order*, all the way through to Noah. They had a record of these things:

> *which combination is most abominable and wicked above all, in the sight of God;*
>
> *[19] For the Lord worketh not in secret combinations, neither doth he will that man should shed blood, but in all things hath forbidden it, from the beginning of man.*
>
> *[20] And now I, Moroni, do not write the **manner** of their oaths and combinations,*

I'm going to take you over in a minute and show you that Alma gave a commandment to one of his sons concerning these secret oaths, and he said the same thing. Notice that they don't write the **manner** of these oaths:

> *for it hath been made known unto me that they are had among **all** people, and they are had among the Lamanites.*

These same ancient *combinations* that we're reading about here, in this book, are alive and well in our day, probably operating more successfully now than they have in the history of the world. And there are probably more involved and enrolled in these now, numerically, than ever before. Moroni says in verse 21:

> *[21] And they have caused the destruction of this people* [the Jaredites] *of whom I am now speaking, and also the destruction of the people of Nephi.*

You see, Moroni is warning us here. He is saying, "You latter-day Gentiles," (and we've given a lesson on that; members of the Church who have these records) "You members of the Church, you need to pay attention because there have already been several large civilizations living on the very same soil that we're living on, that are no more because of these *combinations*." This is the warning:

> *[22] And whatsoever nation shall uphold such secret combinations,*

Isn't that interesting that the goal of the *secret combination* is to take over the government and to have its headquarters and its seat within governmental power? When it gets to a governmental level, then it's in a position to enslave the whole national population, which is what it desires to do. That's the purpose. In some of his talks, President Benson said that we, in the United States, need to pay attention to this because the government of the United States is guilty of "upholding these *secret combinations*." Back to verse 22:

> *to get power and gain, until they shall spread over the nation, behold, they shall be destroyed; for the Lord will not suffer that the blood of his saints, which shall be shed by them, shall always cry unto him from the ground for vengeance upon them and yet he avenge them not.*

I remember when I first read that, I thought, "Wait a minute; this *combination* isn't killing Latter-day Saints. There are no Latter-day Saints that are being murdered and butchered because of this." But there have been. It didn't say, "The saints of the last days." Notice what it does say:

> *for the Lord will not suffer that the blood of **his saints**, which shall be shed by them, shall always cry unto him from the ground*

The saints have always been murdered by these *combinations*. According to John, in the Book of Revelation, we, as members of the Church, are going to go into a persecution time in the future, when many will lose their lives by beheading—which is interesting, and I will talk about that in a minute—because of these *combinations*.

> *[23] Wherefore, O ye Gentiles,*

Now, we, as members of the Church, need to perk up when we hear that because **we are Gentiles!** The Church of Jesus Christ of Latter-day Saints is a Gentile organization, and the United States of America is the great Gentile country of the latter-days:

> *[23] Wherefore, O ye Gentiles, it is wisdom in God that **these things should be shown unto you**,*

Remember that I said that there are **seventeen** references to *secret combinations* in the *Book of Mormon*, none in the *Bible*, one in the *Doctrine and Covenants*, and one in the *Pearl of Great Price*. This is one of the purposes of the *Book of Mormon*, to warn us **right now**:

> *that thereby ye may repent of your sins, and suffer not that these murderous combinations **shall get above you**,*

Look at that wording; it is government! If this combination controls the government, and gets above us as citizens:

> *which are built up to get power and gain—and the work, yea, even the work of destruction come upon you, yea, even the sword of the justice of the Eternal God shall fall upon you, to your overthrow and destruction if ye shall suffer these things to be.*

Last two verses, now watch:

> *[24] Wherefore, the Lord commandeth you, when ye shall see these things come among you that ye shall awake to a sense of your awful situation, because of this secret combination which shall be among you; or woe be unto it, because of the blood of them who have been slain; for they cry from the dust for vengeance upon it, and also upon those who built it up.*
>
> *[25] For it cometh to pass that whoso buildeth it* [the combination] *up seeketh to overthrow the freedom of all lands, nations, and countries; and it bringeth to pass the destruction of all people,*

We need to be aware that these things are here. Going back to another statement by President Benson:

> *I testify that as the forces of evil increase under Lucifer's leadership, and as the forces of good*

> *increase under the leadership of Jesus Christ, there will be growing battles between the two until the final confrontation. As the issues become clearer and more obvious...*

I've been politically involved all of my life. There has never been a presidential election that I have not voted in. I have studied these *secret combinations* for almost 40 years. I've been heavily involved in working with congressmen and senators and writing presidents to a point where I just decided it was futile, and refused to do it any longer. But, I've been following this, and I noticed what President Benson said here, *"...there will be growing battles between the two. As the issues become clearer and more obvious..."* In my lifetime, I have never seen issues clearer and more obvious than they are right now in United States politics. Back to President Benson:

> *...all mankind will eventually be required to align themselves either for the kingdom of God or for the kingdom of the devil. As these conflicts rage, either secretly or openly, the righteous will be tested. God's wrath will soon shake the nations of the earth and will be poured out on the wicked without measure.*

Are we there yet? Not yet, but we're getting close. Let's go to Ether 2. Let me show you something. This is a warning to us. This is all toward us. This is the United States of America. Brothers and sisters, the United State of America is the *Book of Mormon* Promised Land. It's not Canada, it's not Mexico, and it's not South America. It is the place where the New Jerusalem will be built, and you can expect that Satan's headquarters will also be here. You can say what you want about the New World Order being headquartered in Brussels, Belgium and in Europe, but I think those headquarters are right here in the United States. Now, let's look at the warning in Ether chapter 2, starting in verse 7. He is talking about the Jaredites:

> *[7] And the Lord would not suffer that they should stop beyond the sea in the wilderness, but he would that they should come forth even unto **the land of promise**, which was choice above all*

> other lands, which the Lord God had preserved for **a righteous people**.
>
> [8] And he had sworn in his wrath unto the brother of Jared, that whoso should possess this land of promise [that's you and I right now], *from that time henceforth and forever, should serve him, the true and only God, or they should be* **swept off** *when the* **fullness of his wrath** *should come upon them.*

You've got two terms here. This is a warning to us. President Benson said:

> *Too often we bask in our comfortable complacency and rationalize that the ravages of war, economic disaster, famine, and earthquake cannot happen here* [America]. *Those who believe this are either not acquainted with the revelations of the Lord, or they do not believe them. Those who smugly think these calamities will not happen, that they somehow will be set aside because of the righteousness of the Saints, are deceived and will rue the day they harbored such a delusion.*

That's pretty bold and was said in a general conference talk! So, two statements: *"swept off"* and *"the fulness of his wrath."* I think I understand *swept off* because we have a record here of two civilizations that were wiped out in genocidal war, down to the last man. Verse 9:

> [9] *And now, we can behold the decrees of God concerning this land, that it is a land of promise; and whatsoever nation shall possess it shall serve God* [now that is the United States of America], *or they shall be* **swept off** *when the* **fulness of his wrath** *shall come upon them. And the* **fulness of his wrath** *cometh upon them when they are ripened in iniquity.*

So, there are two times in two verses that we're told that if we don't worship the God of the land and keep His commandments, **we** will be swept off. We have no guarantee that that won't happen:

> *[10] For behold, this is a land which is choice above all other lands; wherefore he that doth possess it shall serve God or shall be **swept off**; for it is the everlasting decree of God. And it is not until the fulness of iniquity among the children of the land, that they are **swept off**.*

Four times in three verses he used that term. In verse 11, Moroni is speaking to **us**. I believe that this is us, members of the Church because the Gentiles that are not members of the Church don't have this record. They're not reading these words, so there is no value to those Gentiles. But, to the Gentiles who are numbered among the Church, it says:

> *[11] And this cometh unto you, O ye Gentiles, that ye may know the decrees of God—that ye may repent, and not continue in your iniquities until the fulness come, that ye may not bring down the fullness of the wrath of God upon you as the inhabitants of the land have hitherto done.*
>
> *[12] Behold, this is a choice land* [and it is the United States of America], *and whatsoever nation shall possess it shall be free from bondage, and from captivity, and from all other nations under heaven, if they will but serve the God of the land, who is Jesus Christ,*

Now, go over to Ether 15:19 and let me show you what it means when it says, *"the fulness of the wrath of God,"* and when whole civilizations are *"swept off."* The Lord said at this time that there were no civilizations that were larger or more populous than the Jaredite civilization. In a very short period of time, it came down to two men, Coriantumr and Shiz. Millions of men, women, and children were wiped out in genocidal war because of the *secret combination* that was amongst them. Moroni says this *secret combination* caused this destruction of the Jaredites. Here is a definition of *"the fulness of the wrath of God."* Watch:

> *[19] But behold, the Spirit of the Lord had **ceased striving** with them, and Satan had full power over the hearts of the people; for they were given up unto the hardness of their hearts, and the*

> *blindness of their minds that they might be destroyed; wherefore they went again to battle.*

All God has to do for the fullness of His wrath to be poured out is to withdraw His Spirit. This is why He comes out and says that His Spirit shall not always strive with man. You can get to a point where He withdraws His Spirit, and at that point, *"the fulness of the wrath of God"* comes upon you. In the *Doctrine and Covenants* section 19, He talks to Martin Harris about this. Martin felt this just a little bit with the loss of 116 pages:

> *[20] Wherefore, I command you again to repent, lest I humble you with my almighty power; and that you confess your sins, lest you suffer these punishments of which I have spoken, of which in the smallest, yea, even in the least degree you have tasted at the time **I withdrew my Spirit**.*

When the Lord withdrew His Spirit, even a small little withdrawal with the loss of the 116 pages, Joseph and his whole household went into the darkest time that they'd ever experienced. Martin Harris said:

> *I have lost my soul, I have lost my soul.*

It led Joseph to say:

> *Oh, my God, my God, all is lost!*

That's what it means to have *"the fulness of the wrath of God"* poured out.

Now, I'd like to read you some statements by general authorities on *secret combinations*. We'll put all these up for you to look at (see reference section at the end of this chapter). Here's J. Reuben Clark, Oct. 1941:

> *We are in the midst of the greatest exhibition of propaganda that the world has ever seen. Just do not believe all you read and hear.*

Do you think that has value today? One of the tactics of the *secret combinations*, brothers and sisters, is disinformation. We have to be so practiced and become as perfect as we possibly can in taking the Holy Spirit for our guide. This is why *Doctrine and Covenants* 45:57 says that you won't make it through the Second Coming and the leading up events unless you have learned how to take the Holy Spirit as your guide. It's the only way. And He comes out and says that these are the only ones who will stand

and be there when He comes. Here's another one by President Clark, from 1944. Notice that these are during the war:
> *If the conspiracy comes here it will probably come in its full vigor and there will be a lot of vacant places among those who guide and direct, not only this government but also this Church of ours.*

How's that for a statement? Let me give you another one. This one is by Ezra Taft Benson:
> *Concerning the United States, the Lord revealed to his prophets that its greatest threat would be a vast, worldwide 'secret combination' which would not only threaten the United States but also seek to 'overthrow the freedom of all lands, nations, and people.'*

Another one by J. Reuben Clark, given in 1949, after the war:
> *Do not think that these usurpations, intimidations, and impositions are being done to us through inadvertence or mistake; The whole course is deliberately planned and carried out; its purpose is to destroy the Constitution and our constitutional government; then to bring chaos, out of which the new Statism with its slavery is to arise, with a cruel, relentless, selfish, ambitious crew in the saddle, riding hard with whip and spur, a red-shrouded band of night riders for despotism.*

Of course, he's talking about Red Communism. I once heard the definition of the difference between communism and socialism. I like this definition: "Communism is enforced with a bayonet; Socialism is enforced at a ballot box." President Benson:
> *This most correct book on earth states that the downfall of two great American civilizations came as a result of secret conspiracies whose desire was to overthrow the freedom of the people. "And they have caused the destruction of this people of whom I am now speaking," says Moroni, "and also the destruction of the people of Nephi." (Ether 8:21.) Now undoubtedly Moroni could*

> *have pointed out many factors that led to the destruction of the people, but notice how he singled out the secret combinations, just as the Church today could point out many threats to peace, prosperity, and the spread of God's work, but it has singled out the greatest threat as the godless conspiracy.* **There is no conspiracy theory in the Book of Mormon —it is a conspiracy fact.**

Well, brothers and sisters, we're living in historic times. I don't know what the Lord's strange act is. In the *Doctrine and Covenants*, He talks about His strange act, His strange work when He will gather together His jewels, but there are some strange things going on. It's been interesting to watch the presidential politics that have unfolded over the last year and a half, and here we are forty-eight hours from the election. I chose this lesson tonight because I think that never before have we had exposed a global conspiracy and a *secret combination* than we have right now, that's going on in our very current history. I'd like to go to one more scripture here. Let's go to Mosiah 29. I think it's giving us some information. We've had judges that were assassinated in the *Book of Mormon*. <u>I feel</u> that we've had a Supreme Court Judge that was assassinated here recently. Time will tell. Let's go to verse 25. This is kind of a form; it's called the system of the judges. It's a form that points to a future time when a constitutional republic will be brought forth in the Promised Land. So here, King Mosiah says:

> *[25] Therefore, choose you by the voice of this people, judges, that ye may be judged according to the laws which have been given you by our fathers, which are correct, and which were given them by the hand of the Lord.*

Here is a truth; this is a gospel truth:

> *[26] Now it is not common that the voice of the people* [majority] *desireth anything contrary to that which is right;*

In any given circumstance in the telestial world, where God's children have a right to govern themselves, it is not common that the majority choose wrong:

> *but it is common for the **lesser part** of the people to desire that which is not right; therefore this shall ye observe and make it your law—to do your business **by the voice of the people**.*

That's describing the Constitutional Republican form of government, which we have. Now, look at verse 27, here's the warning:

> *[27] And if the time comes that the voice of the people* [the majority] *doth choose iniquity,*

I worry about that. I think that in the next short period of time, we're going to see where we stand as a people in the Promised Land:

> *then is the time that the judgments of God will come upon you; yea, then is the time he will visit you with great destruction even as he has hitherto visited this land.*

Any comments on that?

Student 4: We're in trouble!

Mike: Yep. I think we've been in trouble for quite awhile. What we see boiling up now has been coming on for a very long time! But, I don't ever remember seeing evil as in-your-face, as it is in our day, right now. It's like President Benson said in the *I Testify* quote. He said:

> *As the issues become clearer and more obvious, all mankind will eventually be required to align themselves either for the kingdom of God or for the kingdom of the devil.*

I want to read the end of that quote:

> *But God will provide strength for the righteous **and the means of escape**; and eventually and finally truth will triumph.*

President Benson said:

> *I testify that it is time for every man to set in order his own house both temporally and spiritually. It is time for the unbeliever to learn for himself that the work is true... It is time for us, as members of the Church, to walk in **all** the ways of the Lord, to use our influence to make popular that which is sound and make unpopular that which is unsound.*

> *We have the scriptures, the prophets, and the gift of the Holy Ghost. Now we need eyes that will see, ears that will hear, and hearts that will hearken to God's direction.*

Let me say something interesting; <u>and this is my feeling,</u> that in our day Satan counterfeits as close as he can what God reveals. In the counterfeit is a mixture of truth with error, and there is power. Not only does he do it to deceive, but the fact that there is truth, mixed with error, gives the error power. Anciently, what these people would do is that they swore oaths by their heads. Now, we've seen anciently with Laban; you saw it with Goliath; you saw Coriantumr take off the head of Shiz; you see all this beheading. John the Revelator talks about beheadings taking place, yet in the future, for those who will not give up their witness of Christ; they will not align themselves with the *beast* and the *whore of Babylon*. They die by beheading. Have you ever wondered what that was? Taking off a head, symbolically, destroys the identity of the person in eternity. Everything from the neck up controls everything from the neck down. You remove the head, and you've not only killed the person for sure, but you take away their identity, their very awareness, that part of them that is their individual "I Am." Taking off the head, anciently, was a symbol that you've obliterated that person, not only in this life, but you did not have to worry about them in eternity. So, ancient oaths were made with penalties, where they swore by their throats that they would lose their head. They cut off the head if they violated these ancient oaths. Another thing they did was to take out the heart. You can see that down through all time. It becomes symbolic of losing the thing that's closest to you in your heart. For a man, that's his wife. Removing the heart is symbolic of losing your wife. Disemboweling is symbolic of losing your seed, your family, and your children. So, these ancient things that we looked at as ways that life can be taken, and literally talked about the loss of everything in eternity: your identity, your wife or husband, and your family. Great symbolism involved, and you can see it in all ancient cultures.

Well, just some interesting thoughts, brothers and sisters. God bless us and our great land. I can tell you that I'm on the phone weekly with various places throughout the world, and I want you to know that the whole world is watching us right now. It's almost like they've all taken in a collective deep breath, and they're holding their breath to see what's going to happen with America because, with all of our faults, America is that light upon a hill. It is the shining beacon. It'll be interesting to see what we do with what we've got, and what the consequences are for those choices. I pray that God will bless us, that we'll exercise our franchise as citizens of this great country, and that we'll do our part individually, to see that everything that was laid for the foundations of this great land, scripturally, is preserved and maintained now and in the future.

References:
D&C 38:11-15, 28-30
Wilford Woodruff, "But I want to tell you now, that those angels have left the portals of heaven, and they stand over this people and this nation now and are hovering over the earth waiting to pour out the judgments." *Doctrine and Covenants Institute Manual*, 190-1
Moses 5:12, 16-18, 23
"All beings who have bodies have power over those who have not." Joseph Smith, "Extracts from William Clayton's Private Book," pp. 7–8, Journals of L. John Nuttall, 1857–1904
Moses 5:24,
Jesus the Christ, James Talmage "...the majority either fought with Michael or at least refrained from active opposition, thus accomplishing the purpose of their "first estate…"
Moses 5:29-30
Miracle of Forgiveness, David W. Patten and "Cain" Spencer W. Kimball, (SLC: Bookcraft, 1969), 127–128.
D&C 89:4
D&C 123:11-15
"I Testify" by Ezra Taft Benson, October 1988
Ether 8:18-25
Ether 2:7-8
"Prepare for the Days of Tribulation" by Ezra Taft Benson, October 1980 General Conference.
Ether 2:9-12
Ether 15:19
D&C 19:20
Martin Harris and Joseph Smith quotes on losing the 116 pages: Lucy Mack Smith, History, 1844–1845, book 7, pages 2–7
J. Reuben Clark, Conference Report, October 1941
D&C 45:57 "...[take] the Holy Spirit for [your] guide…"

J. Reuben Clark, Conference Report, April 1944
Ezra Taft Benson, Conference, October 1961
J. Reuben Clark, jr.,*Church News,* September 25, 1949
Ezra Taft Benson, General Conference, April 1972
"Strange act" D&C 95:4; D&C 101:95
"...when I shall make up my jewels..." D&C 60:4; 101:3
Mosiah 29:25-27
Ezra Taft Benson "I Testify" Oct. 1988 (provide means for escape)

David W. Patten and "Cain" Spencer W. Kimball, Miracle of Forgiveness, (SLC: Bookcraft, 1969), 127–128.

On the sad character of Cain, an interesting story comes to us from Lycurgus A. Wilson's book on the life of David W. Patten. From the book, I quote an extract from a letter by Abraham O. Smoot giving his recollection of David Patten's account of meeting "a very remarkable person who had represented himself as being Cain."

As I was riding along the road on my mule I suddenly noticed a very strange person walking beside me.... His head was about even with my shoulders as I sat in my saddle. He wore no clothing but was covered with hair. His skin was very dark. I asked him where he dwelt and he replied that he had no home, that he was a wanderer in the earth and traveled to and fro. He said he was a very miserable creature, that he had earnestly sought death during his sojourn upon the earth, but that he could not die, and his mission was to destroy the souls of men. About the time he expressed himself thus, I rebuked him in the name of the Lord Jesus Christ
and by virtue of the Holy Priesthood, and commanded him to go hence, and he immediately departed out of my sight....

President Ezra Taft Benson October 1988

I testify that wickedness is rapidly expanding in every segment of our society. (See D&C 1:14–16; D&C 84:49–53.) It is more highly organized, more cleverly disguised, and more powerfully promoted than ever before. Secret combinations lusting for power, gain, and glory are flourishing. A secret combination that seeks to overthrow the freedom of all lands, nations, and countries is increasing its evil influence and control over America and the entire world. (See Ether 8:18–25.)

I testify that as the forces of evil increase under Lucifer's leadership and as the forces of good increase under the leadership of Jesus Christ, there will be growing battles between the two until the final confrontation. As the issues become clearer and more obvious, all mankind will eventually be required to align themselves either for the kingdom of God or for the kingdom of the devil. As these conflicts rage, either secretly or openly, the righteous will be tested. God's wrath will soon shake the nations of the earth and will be poured out on the wicked without measure. (See JS—H 1:45; D&C 1:9.) **But God** will provide strength for the righteous and the <u>means of escape</u>; and eventually and finally truth will triumph. (See 1 Ne. 22:15–23.)

I testify that it is time for every man to set in order his own house both temporally and spiritually. It is time for the unbeliever to learn for himself that this work is true, that The Church of Jesus Christ of Latter-day Saints is the kingdom which Daniel prophesied God would set up in the latter days, never to be destroyed, a stone that would eventually fill the whole earth and stand forever. (See Dan. 2:34–45; D&C 65:2.) It is time for us, as members of the Church, to walk in all the ways of the Lord, to use our influence to make popular that which is sound and to make unpopular that which is unsound. We have the scriptures, the prophets, and the gift of the Holy Ghost. Now we need eyes that will see, ears that will hear, and hearts that will hearken to God's direction.

Waking Up to Secret Combinations: An LDS Perspective on Conspiracy

Most of us seem content to accept the world largely in the way it is presented to us by what passes as the mainstream of society. Conspiracy, despite its overwhelming historical precedence, is often dismissed as non-existent or, at best, limited to small or foreign groups [1].

Consequently, when a discussion in a Church class arises upon the subject of secret combinations, such organizations as the Mafia, Ku Klux Klan and terrorist groups often end up on the blackboard.

While it is true, no doubt, that many of these groups conspire, and some do great evil, do they actually fit the full description of what we know about secret combinations?

In trying to answer this we need to understand what the scriptures tell us about such oath-bound societies, as well as review the words of Church leaders on the issue.

What Do The Scriptures Teach Us About Secret Combinations?

Secret combinations existed both in the Old and New World in ancient times. Below is a list of some of the things we learn from the scriptures concerning the nature, purpose and methods of these secret combinations:

1. Cain founded the first secret combination and became known as Master Mahan.[2] This title and the oaths and covenants were passed down to subsequent leaders of the secret combination (<u>Moses 5: 31, 49; Helaman 6:30</u>).

2. Secret combinations are "most abominable and wicked above all" in the sight of God (see <u>Ether 8:18</u>).

3. Secret combinations are Satanic in nature, receiving revelation from, and being founded and held up by, the devil (<u>Moses 5:29–30</u>; <u>2 Nephi 26:22</u>; <u>Helaman 6:26</u>; <u>3 Nephi 6:28</u>; <u>Ether 8:16, 25</u>) who transforms himself

into an angel of light and stirs up men to contention whereby wickedness and thus secret combinations increase (2 Nephi 9:9; Helaman 6:21; 3 Nephi 7:7).

4. Secret combinations administer secret ancient oaths handed down from Cain (Ether 8:15–16), taken by swearing by the God of heaven, the heavens, the earth, the throat and the head (Moses 5:29–30; Ether 8:13–14).

5. The manner of their oaths and combinations are had among all people (Ether 8:20).

6. Secret combinations have secret signs and words (Helaman 6:22), protect one another (Helaman 6:21, 23), and mingle into society in a manner whereby they cannot be found (Helaman 1:12).

7. Members of secret combinations are punished by the combination if they reveal the wickedness of their co-conspirators (Helaman 6:24; Ether 8:14).

8. One of the purposes of secret combinations is to murder (Moses 5:31; Helaman 2:8); they also seek to murder the prophets of God (Alma 37:30). These combinations cause slaughter (3 Nephi 1:27, 2:11), war and millions of deaths; the Jaredites and Nephites being destroyed because of them (Helaman 2:13–14; Ether 8:21).

9. Secret combinations are established to rob and get gain (Moses 5:31; Helaman 2:8). The Book of Mormon refers to them as "robbers" over fifty times, which suggest that theft was their chief activity or the activity for which they were most notorious.

10. Gadianton Robbers prefer to plunder rather than working for themselves (3 Nephi 4:1–5).

11. Members of secret combinations regard each other as brethren and appear to have a communal attitude toward property (3 Nephi 3:6–7).

12. The teachings and practices of the robbers are tempting and corrupt the hearts of the people as they spread, eventually even seducing most of the righteous into believing in their works, partaking of their spoils, and even becoming involved in their secret murders and combinations (Helaman 6:38; Ether 9:6).

13. Pride, the desire for money, and seeking the praise of man make people susceptible to uniting with secret combinations; such go on to murder, plunder, and bear false witness against their neighbor (Helaman 7:21, 25–26).

14. Secret combinations help those who seek for power to gain power as well as to murder, plunder, lie and commit wickedness and whoredoms (Ether 8:16).

15. Secret combinations keep the people in darkness (Ether 8:16) and use fair promises to lead people away (Ether 8:17).

16. Secret combinations flourished first in the more settled parts of the land (Helaman 3:23) and among the wicked (Helaman 6:38; 4 Nephi 1:42).

17. One of the purposes of secret combinations is to gain power (Helaman 2:8; Ether 8:23, 11:15) by usurping power and authority over the people (Helaman 7:4). They seek to gain sole power over the government and, in the Book of Mormon, were successful in doing so (Helaman 6:39).

18. Secret combinations retain power so that they and their supporters may get gain and glory, and so that they may more easily steal, commit adultery, kill and do according to their own will (Helaman 7:5).

19. Secret combinations break the laws of God and the laws of their country (Helaman 6:23).

20. Secret combinations stir up rebellion (Ether 11:15) and dissent, and use lies and flattery to lead people to join with them (3 Nephi 1:28–29), targeting the rising generation (3 Nephi 1:29–30).

21. The members of secret combinations believe their secret works and society to be good (3 Nephi 3:9).

22. Secret combinations pretend to act on behalf of their people in reclaiming their rights (3 Nephi 3:10), believing they have been wronged and hating the righteous (3 Nephi 3:4).

23. Secret combinations seek to overthrow government (3 Nephi 7:6), establish kings – or oligarchies (see Mosiah 29:21–22) – and destroy the liberty of a republic (3 Nephi 6:30, 7:10); the king-men believe they have the blood of nobility (Alma 51:21).

24. Secret combinations, once in government, lay aside the commandments of God, corrupt righteous laws, and administer no justice to the people (Mosiah 29:22; Helaman 7:4), condemning the righteous for their righteousness, allowing the guilty to go free because of their money (Helaman 7:5).

25. Secret combinations shed the blood of the saints and oppress them (Helaman 6:39; 3 Nephi 6:29; Ether 8:22), threatening not only the rights and liberty of the people but also the Church (3 Nephi 2:12).

26. When any society has suffered such combinations to spread over them they will be destroyed (Ether 8:22).

27. One of the purposes of the Book of Mormon is to show us the work of ancient secret combination so that we may repent and suffer not that these same murderous combinations should get above us (Ether 8:23), and that we should awake to a sense of our awful situation when we see these things among us (Ether 8:24).

28. Speaking of a secret combination built up by the devil, the master of lies, in our day, the Book of Mormon tells us that those who build it up do so to overthrow the freedom of all lands, nations and countries (Ether 8:25).

29. In the last days the gentiles shall build up secret combinations which shall spill the blood of the saints and seek to destroy the people (2 Nephi 26:22; Ether 8:25; Mormon 8:27).

30. Preaching the word of God destroys secret combinations (Helaman 6:37).

What Have Church Leaders Said About Secret Combinations?

What do we know about secret combinations from latter-day prophets, seers and revelators? It's interesting in reading these how they generally give a very different view than the one commonly held by members of the Church. The following quotations are in chronological order (titles added):
- A secret band will sap the strength of America in the last days

"I have seen the end of this nation and it is terrible. I will tell you in the name of the LORD that a secret band will sap the life of this nation."(Moses Thatcher, from an address given at the Franklin Ward, Franklin, Idaho, June 16, 1882 and entered into the Historical Record thereof)
- We are in the midst of great propaganda and even the elect are being deceived

"We are in the midst of the greatest exhibition of propaganda that the world has ever seen. Just do not believe all you read or hear. The elect are being deceived." (J. Reuben Clark, Conference Report, October 1941)
- A global tyranny to be established by stealth in the last days

"Satan...[plans] to destroy liberty and freedom ~ economic, political, and religious, and to set up in place thereof the greatest, most widespread, and most complete tyranny that has ever oppressed men. He is working under such perfect disguise that many do not recognize either him or his methods." (First Presidency, General Conference, October 1942)
- Government & Church to suffer "vacant places" due to the Conspiracy

"If the conspiracy comes here it will probably come in its full vigor and there will be a lot of vacant places among those who guide and direct, not only this government, but also this Church of ours." (J. Reuben Clark, Conference Report, April 1944)
- Satan has control now and is guiding the governments of the world

"Satan has control now. No matter where you look, he is in control, even in our own land. He is guiding the governments as far as the Lord will permit him. That is why there is so much strife, turmoil, confusion all over the earth. One master mind is governing the nations. It is not the President of the United States...it is not the king or government of England or any other land; it is Satan himself." (Joseph Fielding Smith, Doctrines of Salvation, Vol. 3, pp. 314-315)
- Socialism-communism is a conspiracy

"...we should accept the command of the Lord and treat socialistic communism as the tool of Satan. We should follow the counsel of the President of the Church and resist the influence and policies of the socialist-communist conspiracy wherever they are found–in the schools, in the

churches, in governments, in unions, in businesses, in agriculture." (Ezra Taft Benson, Conference, October 1961)
- A vast, worldwide secret combination to seek to overthrow all lands

"Concerning the United States, the Lord revealed to his prophets that its greatest threat would be a vast, worldwide 'secret combination' which would not only threaten the United States but also seek to 'overthrow the freedom of all lands, nations…'(Ether 8:25)" (Ezra Taft Benson, Conference, October 1961)
- A deliberate conspiracy to destroy the U.S. Constitution exists

"And do not think that these usurpations, intimidations, and impositions are being done to us through inadvertence or mistake; The whole course is deliberately planned and carried out; its purpose is to destroy the Constitution and our constitutional government; then to bring chaos, out of which the new Statism with its slavery is to arise, with a cruel, relentless, selfish, ambitious crew in the saddle, riding hard with whip and spur, a red-shrouded band of night riders for despotism." (J. Reuben Clark, jr., *Church News,* September 25, 1949)
- Socialist-communist conspiracy at work both at home and abroad

"Our priceless heritage is threatened today as never before in our lifetime: from without by the forces of Godless Communism, and at home by our complacency and by the insidious forces of the Socialist-Communist conspiracy, with the help of those who would abandon the ancient landmarks set by our fathers and take us down the road to destruction. It was Alexander Hamilton who warned that 'nothing is more common than for a free people, in times of heat and violence, to gratify momentary passions, by letting into the government, principles and precedents which afterwards prove fatal to themselves.' (Alexander Hamilton and the Founding of the Nation, p. 462.)" (Ezra Taft Benson, General Conference, April 1968)
- There is no conspiracy theory in the Book of Mormon

"This most correct book on earth states that the downfall of two great American civilizations came as a result of secret conspiracies whose desire was to overthrow the freedom of the people. "And they have caused the destruction of this people of whom I am now speaking," says Moroni, "and also the destruction of the people of Nephi." (Eth. 8:21.) Now undoubtedly Moroni could have pointed out many factors that led to the destruction of the people, but notice how he singled out the secret combinations, just as the Church today could point out many threats to peace, prosperity, and the spread of God's work, but it has singled out the greatest threat as the great conspiracy. **There is no conspiracy theory in the Book of Mormon –it is a conspiracy fact**. And along this line I would highly recommend to you the book None Dare Call It Conspiracy by Gary Allen." (Ezra Taft Benson, General Conference, April 1972; book recommendation added by Ezra Taft Benson during talk after he discovered a Russian delegation was in attendance. Not included in the prepared or text archives of the talk).
- Modern founders of secret works arose about same time as Restoration

"It is well to ask, what system [referring to Isaiah 29:15–16] established secret works of darkness to overthrow nations by violent revolution? Who blasphemously proclaimed the atheistic doctrine that God made us not? Satan works through human agents. We need only look to some of the ignoble characters in human history who were contemporary to the restoration of the gospel to discover fulfillment of Isaiah's prophecy. I refer to the infamous founders of Communism and others who follow in their tradition…" (Ezra Taft Benson, A Witness and a Warning, Conference, October 1979)

- Gadianton robbers fills the seats in many governments

"Gadianton robbers fill the judgment seats in many nations. An evil power seeks to overthrow the freedom of all nations and countries." (Apostle Bruce R. McConkie, speaking in the April 1980 General Conference)

- We must recognize, address and quit building up secret combinations

"…the Book of Mormon exposes the enemies of Christ. It confounds false doctrines and lays down contention. (See 2 Ne. 3:12.) It fortifies the humble followers of Christ against the evil designs, strategies, and doctrines of the devil in our day. The type of apostates in the Book of Mormon are similar to the type we have today. God, with his infinite foreknowledge, so molded the Book of Mormon that we might see the error and know how to combat false educational, political, religious, and philosophical concepts of our time…Now, we have not been using the Book of Mormon as we should. Our homes are not as strong unless we are using it to bring our children to Christ. Our families may be corrupted by worldly trends and teachings unless we know how to use the book to expose and combat falsehoods in socialism, rationalism, etc…The situation in the world will continue to degenerate unless we read and heed the words of God and quit building up and upholding secret combinations, which the Book of Mormon tells us proved the downfall of ancient civilizations." (Ezra Taft Benson, First Presidency Message, Ensign, January 1988).

- A specific secret combination is increasing its global dominion

"[Wickedness] is more highly organized, more cleverly disguised, and more powerfully promoted than ever before. Secret combinations lusting for power, gain, and glory are flourishing. A secret combination that seeks to overthrow the freedom of all lands, nations, and countries is increasing its evil influence and control over America and the entire world." (Ezra Taft Benson, I Testify, Conference, October 1988).

- Modern-day Gadianton Robbers seek to bring down the Church, woo the people with sophistry and take control of society

"It is the terrorist organizations that must be ferreted out and brought down. We of this Church know something of such groups. The Book of Mormon speaks of the Gadianton robbers, a vicious, oath-bound, and secret organization bent on evil and destruction. In their day they did all in their power, by whatever means available, to bring down the Church, to woo the people with sophistry, and to take control of the society. We see the same thing in the present situation." (Gordon B. Hinckley, General Conference, October 2001)

- Evil schemers promote heavy taxation, false promises, loose morals, war

"The Book of Mormon narrative is a chronicle of nations long since gone. But in its descriptions of the problems of today's society, it is as current as the morning newspaper and much more definitive, inspired, and inspiring concerning the solutions of those problems. I know of no other writing which sets forth with such clarity the tragic consequences to societies that follow courses contrary to the commandments of God. Its pages trace the stories of two distinct civilizations that flourished on the Western Hemisphere. Each began as a small nation, its people walking in the fear of the Lord. But with prosperity came growing evils. The people succumbed to the wiles of ambitious and scheming leaders who oppressed them with burdensome taxes, who lulled them with hollow promises, who countenanced and even encouraged loose and lascivious living. These evil schemers led the people into terrible wars that resulted in the death of millions and the final and total extinction of two great civilizations in two different eras." (Gordon B. Hinckley, First Presidency Message, Ensign, August 2005)

Is History an Accident?

Accidentalism is the view of history taught today in most schools. This portrays history as largely a series of unrelated events. Another view, and one posited in this article is what has been called the conspiratorial view of history. This latter teaches that history is largely a series of related events. Today many people view conspiracy as something strange, on the fringe or to be dismissed, and that those who speak of conspiracy must be a little crazy or extreme. This is a very perplexing viewpoint because it is a matter of historical record that conspiracy has been with us from the beginning. Plots, intrigues, and secret combinations have plagued government and societies at large from the beginning of time. Small groups or families conspired in ancient Rome, they conspired among the city-states of Renaissance Italy and in the churches and towers of medieval Europe. Plays, movies, and books have been made about them. Nations, and civilizations have risen and fallen due to the events enacted by such conspiratorial groups.

As Latter-day Saints, we do not subscribe to accidentalism. We believe that the hand of Providence has helped shaped out world and that, among other things, the Lord guided the events in this world to bring about the circumstances where religious freedom was sparked leading eventually to a free nation under God wherein the Restoration could begin. However, we sometimes have a harder time believing that the non-accidental view of history also includes events inspired of the devil such as the events leading to the Great Apostasy. We should not be oblivious or stand in denial of such a view of history, or of the existence and nature of secret combinations. We need to, as Moroni put it, wake up to our awful situation.

What Now?

It has been said that the revelations of God provide the answer to all questions. We often forget this and are quick to base our views purely upon what the world teaches us about history, politics, science and other important subjects.

With this is mind, we should prayerfully ponder and read what the scriptures and Church leaders have said touching on the topics of liberty, government, agency, secret combinations, and so forth. The amount of material on these topics may surprise you if you have not looked into it before. As far as talks by leaders of the Church are concerned, you might want to start by visiting www.ldsfreedomportal.net which lists (and links to) many important addresses by Church leaders.

If you really want to look into things a bit deeper then I would recommend the following books for your primer reading list – most of which have been recommended by Church leaders:

None Dare Call It Conspiracy (Gary Allen) – recommended in Conference by Ezra Taft Benson

The Naked Communist (W. Cleon Skousen) – recommended in Conference by David O. McKay

The Naked Capitalist (W. Cleon Skousen) – important sequel to The Naked Communist

The 5000-Year Leap (W. Cleon Skousen) – perhaps the most well-read LDS work on liberty

The Elders of Israel and the Constitution (Jerome Horowitz) – Recommended in Conference by Ezra Taft Benson

The Book of Mormon and the Constitution (H. Verlan Andersen) – LDS General Authority and very close friend to Ezra Taft Benson

The Moral Basis of a Free Society (H. Verlan Andersen)

An Enemy Hath Done This (Ezra Taft Benson, compilation of political speeches)

The Law (Frederic Bastiat) – not an LDS author but quoted heavily by Ezra Taft Benson

Notes

[1] Doctrine & Covenants 38:28–29 appears to refer to this preconception.

[2] The word Mahan is of uncertain origin but the footnotes to Moses 5:31 suggest that the root of the word ("maha") can be rendered as "mind", "destroyer", or "great one". Matthew M. Brown favours the "destroyer" meaning (see "Girded about with a Lambskin", Journal of Book of Mormon Studies: Volume – 6, Issue – 2, Pages: 124-151, Provo, Utah: Maxwell Institute, 1997). Depopulation, through various means, seems to be a strong theme in conspiratorial agendas. Joseph Smith, commenting on government and tyrants, once said that "The greatest acts of the mighty men have been to depopulate nations and to overthrow kingdoms; and whilst they have exalted themselves and become glorious, it has been at the expense of the lives of the innocent, the blood of the oppressed, the moans of the widow, and the tears of the orphan." (Teachings of the Prophet Joseph Smith, Section Five 1842-43, p.248). This gives even more weight to the meaning of Mahan as "destroyer".

This article represents the views of the author. It should not be considered an explanation of the views of The Church of Jesus Christ of Latter-day Saints.

Chapter Forty
Podcast 040 Trust in the Lord

Of the forty podcasts that we have done on Sunday nights, the two that have had the most comments and have elicited the greatest response are the ones on *Devils and Unclean Spirits*. There's not a week goes by that those of you who are listening to the podcasts don't, in some way or another, comment on the information that's in these particular podcasts. And many of you are asking questions such as, "I've identified that I have had this problem either in myself, my family, or someone that I care about. Because of the information in the podcast, I believe that we're afflicted or they're afflicted, and what do we do about it?" That's the question. "What do we do about that? How do we deliver ourselves from this?" So, along with the information you already have in those two podcast, I'd like to give you a little more additional information and insight on what has already been discussed. I'd like you to go to Isaiah 5:13. This is one of my favorite scriptures, and I'll apply it to what we're talking about tonight:

*[13] Therefore **my people** are gone into captivity,*
*because **they have no knowledge**:*

This is talking about people who have made a covenant with the Lord, who are being held captive for lack of knowledge. First of all, let me just say that these devils and unclean spirits thrive on remaining in a state of anonymity. It's very important for them that they remain undisclosed, and that anytime that anyone sheds light on them, their strategies, their designs, or their combinations, it causes a stirring-up to take place among their organizations and their societies. **You want to do that!** That stirring-up is good! As the opposition increases and you experience affliction, I'd like you to take a little different look at it. This is where knowledge comes in and gives you some power. I want you to have a different view. If you feel that you are under the influence or are experiencing this opposing of the light and the Father and the Son, I want you to look at that differently. I want you to let that be an indicator of who you were before you came here, and who you are now that they know. Being within the veil now, you have been caused to forget as a result of being born into the telestial world and having your former memory erased. The fact that you're experiencing this should tell you something about yourself. If you were not a threat to them, if the knowledge that you're receiving—new knowledge concerning who they are and what their tactics are—if that didn't threaten them, then you wouldn't be experiencing the increase in opposition that you are. So, I want you to take that as a badge of honor, as it were. It should also tell you something about your destiny. They know something about you that you may not know about yourself right now. Again, *"**my people** are gone into captivity because they have no knowledge:"* Let's go back and finish that verse:

and their honourable men are famished, and their multitude dried up with thirst.

Let's go to Moroni 6 for just a moment. We have honorable men that we're talking about here. These honorable men are the priesthood. When it says they *"are famished,"* they are dying for lack of nourishment. They're starving to death spiritually. We've talked about that, how the priesthood is starving and has basically been neutralized. Go with me to Moroni 6:4:

And after they [members of the Church] *had been received unto baptism, and were wrought upon and cleansed by the power of the Holy Ghost, they were numbered among the people of the church of Christ; and their names were taken, that they might be*

And here's what happens now. Once they've joined the Church, they now are numbered in that group of members, *"their names [are] taken, that they might be"*:
> remembered and **nourished** by the good word of God,

Think about what Isaiah said again, *"my people are gone into captivity, because they have no knowledge: and their honourable men are **famished**, and their multitude dried up with **thirst**."* You're dying of starvation and a lack of spiritual water. So, back in verse 4, here's what happens if they are nourished:
> to keep them in the right way, to keep them continually watchful unto prayer, relying alone upon the merits of Christ, who was the author and the finisher of their faith.

The purpose of being nourished is first, *"to keep them in the right way,"* and second is *"to keep them continually watchful unto prayer."* If you are nourished by the good word of God, you're going to be receiving revelation that's going to tell you, "You need to up your game." Satan has increased his opposition to the Father and the Son. The Father and the Son have allowed that. That's the day we live in. In order for you to survive, you are going to have to **do** something different. It's like the hymn we sing in Church, *"Then wake up and **do** something more than dream of your mansion above."* See, we've got to be doing something more. We've got to "step up." We've got to up our game. We've got to be doing something that will elevate us and give us more power in the battle that's raging. One of the things that I'm noticing as I chat with good members of the Church that email me or call me on the phone is that the battle is combined, the enemy is raging, and families are being stirred up to anger against that which is good. Now, if you have knowledge concerning what's going on there, it gives you an edge, not only to look differently at it but to form a battle tactic to successfully engage in the conflict and come out victorious. And by the way, upping your game means you will probably need to do as Alma 34 says; you need to be praying *"morning, mid-day and evening."* You're going to need to do what Joseph Smith said and associate yourselves with good men like Daniel, who pray three times a day. Here's the bottom line, brothers and sisters: what we've done in the past will not be sufficient for the day that's here and for what's coming. It won't be sufficient. The third purpose was, *"relying alone upon the merits of Christ, who was the author and the finisher of their faith."* That's what comes if you are nourished; and if you are not nourished, according to Isaiah, you go into captivity because you have no knowledge. Look at Isaiah 5:14:

[14] Therefore hell hath enlarged herself,

I can tell you that the men and women who are dying unredeemed, without a knowledge of the redemptive power of Christ, go into the spirit world and they are classified with that group called *unclean spirits*. It's enlarging itself exponentially by the millions that are dying and becoming part of that group. *Hell hath enlarged herself,*

*and opened her mouth without measure: and **their** glory,*

Now, who are we talking about? Go back up to verse 13 where it says, *"my people."* None of this is talking about non-members; ***their*** *glory*. Think about the lesson we had on *glory*. You are a *glorious* being. You can either add to that *glory*, or it can be diminished, based on what you do. If you lack knowledge, and you go into captivity, your *glory* is diminished:

*and their **multitudes**,*

Think about posterity in eternity. Think about your posterity being as endless as the stars in the heavens or the sands of the seashores. Think about the blessings of Abraham, Isaac, and Jacob that you were promised in your temple sealing. One of those blessings is innumerable posterity. You notice what it says:

and their glory, and their multitude, and their pomp, and he that rejoiceth, shall descend into it.

We lose everything—everything—because we lack knowledge!

I want you to go over to Hosea 4:6. This is another scripture on that:

My people *are destroyed for lack of knowledge:*

In Isaiah it says you go into captivity because of no knowledge. Hosea says you *"are destroyed for lack of knowledge:"*

because thou hast rejected knowledge, I will also reject thee, that thou shalt be no priest to me:

Brethren, think about your initiatory blessings where you have the promise of being a Priest and a King, and your wife being a Priestess and a Queen. Because of a lack of knowledge, you will be no priest to Him:

> *seeing thou hast forgotten the law of thy God, I will also forget thy children.*

Sobering things.

Last week we talked about the various penalties that used to be mentioned in the temple endowment. The one penalty that represented the head is a loss of identity in eternity. You go backward in native intelligence and back into primal life. The one that represented the breast is the loss of your wife, she who is closest to your heart. The one that represented the bowel represented a loss of posterity in eternity, no posterity. So, in those three things: no wife, no children, and no identity are the penalties. Notice what the Lord says, *"seeing thou hast forgotten the law of thy God, **I will also forget thy children.**"*

> *[7] As they were increased, so they sinned against me: therefore will I change their glory into shame.*

All of this, why? *"My people are destroyed for lack of knowledge."* So, when you go into this area of not only devils and unclean spirits, but any area of the Gospel of Jesus Christ, it is knowledge that saves a person. That's what Joseph Smith said, *"A man is saved no faster than he gets knowledge."* God is who He is, among other reasons, because He possesses more knowledge than any other. That's according to the Prophet Joseph Smith. So, knowledge is an amazing thing. When you are kept from it, then you're going into captivity, or are going to be destroyed. Well, these devils and unclean spirits (especially the devils) want to keep you from gaining any knowledge about them. They don't want you to shine a light on them.

So, what are you going to be required to do? People are asking me, "I feel that I have a problem here. What do I do about it?" So, what I'd like to do is shine a light on these and give some additional information. The challenge is that there is no handbook on this. You're now moving into an area where you are going to have to rely on your personal relationship with the Lord, and revelations from Him through the Holy Ghost and the Holy Spirit, to teach you what to do. I can give you a few things that we find from the early Restoration information, but I've read the handbooks, and there is nothing in either the red one or the blue one to help. The blue one is for Priesthood Leadership, and it's not available to the general membership or the leadership of the Church. It's for stake presidents, mission presidents, general authorities, etc. The last one I read was a 2010 edition that had no information on this at all. I don't know if that's changed, but I don't think that it has, for whatever reason. I'm not finding fault. The point is that your priesthood leaders are not receiving any information through the handbooks of the Church on how to deal with devils and unclean spirits. So, we have masses of people in the Church who feel like they are chemically imbalanced, have bipolar disorders, schizophrenia, or any one of a number of, what appears to be, mental health issues. In reality, and it's my feeling, that this is all connected to organized, evil intelligence.

I heard a story today. The bishop came into our high priest group and wanted to teach the lesson. He read a story about a young man who grew up in the early sixties and made some bad choices that led into the hippie movement. He got involved in drugs and sex and everything that was going on in the mid 60's. He was just a horrible mess, and something happened in his mind where he had an experience and decided this was not the path that he wanted to travel. So, he went to see his bishop and told him that he wanted to go on a mission. The bishop had to have special clearance from the First Presidency to allow him to go because of some of the things that he'd done. Well, he was allowed to go on a mission and went to Argentina. I guess when he went to Argentina, he was so faithful that he became a leader in the mission and eventually an assistant to the president, and just did marvelous things. He performed just all kinds of miraculous things in that mission field. He came home, met a gal at BYU, got married and within a year they had a little daughter. They weren't rich but they were happy. They were working on a career and doing things like this, and a bishop offended him. He said, "As long as that man is the bishop, I'll never go back to Church." And, he didn't. When that bishop was released, this man still didn't go back to Church. One of the issues that he had, before going on the mission, was that they had diagnosed him with schizophrenia. He was hearing voices and had a multiple personality disorder, etc. That was not addressed. So, after he left the Church, it wasn't very long until one thing after another, his schizophrenia issues continued to get worse and worse until eventually, he asked for his name to be removed from the records of the Church. This true story took about twenty minutes for the bishop to tell, but long story short, the rest of their children grew up inactive. They only had one girl out of four children that stayed with the Church. The wife received a blessing that if she would pray every day and read her scriptures every day, the day would come when she and her husband would be husband and wife in eternity, and everything would work out right. For the next 34 years, he remained aloof and inactive—not just inactive, but antagonistic, an enemy. Then he had an experience with an illness, and the home teacher came and talked to him, gave him a blessing, and later on in life he came back to Church, and he is going to be re-baptized this December, after 34 years. The bishop went around the room and asked, "What did the Spirit teach you about this?" I wasn't asked, but here's the thought I had: It's good that he came back, and I'm so happy for the prodigal son and the lost sheep, and that's a great principle. But, I think about what his wife went through for 34 years. Of course, she had experiences that helped her grow, and I know all of that stuff, but his family went out and struggled. Apparently, he had quite a remarkable patriarchal blessing that had all kinds of blessings. The bishop said today, "It appears like the blessings that were mentioned in that patriarchal blessing have been voided because he had been rebelling against God." Anyway, I couldn't help thinking about a scripture in 2 Nephi 9 that says:

> *[27] But wo unto him that has the law given, yea, that has all the commandments of God, like unto us, and that transgresseth them, and that wasteth the days of his probation, for awful is his state!*

I thought, "How sad! It's good that he came back, but he lost opportunities." Here's the point: If somebody had looked at this schizophrenia early on, and had asked the question and addressed that situation as unclean spirits and/or devils that were afflicting him, perhaps at an earlier time, if we had had knowledge, then that whole thing could have been turned around, and who knows what the outcome might have been. That was the thought I had.

When we were in the Philippines I came across this information, and I began a search for it, and I just could not put it down. I was just obsessed with it. I was so obsessed with it that Margie said, "You need to leave this alone. It's now cutting into what we are supposed to be doing on our mission." I agreed. So, I left it, but I couldn't leave it alone. We never used this information to any degree in the Philippines, for whatever reason. And so, toward the end of our mission, I told Margie, "There must be something at home that we need to know this information for, for some reason." So, now I'm hearing from lots and lots of people that have listened to those two podcasts. The podcasts are a result of my search, what I've found in the early writings of the Church, and my own personal experience and revelation. Let me just say this: if you have decided that you are afflicted with this, here are some things that you may want to consider to help you start to find deliverance from this. First of all, take a different view. This is a positive view! You would not find this going on in your life if you didn't threaten those powers on the other side of the veil. Remember also this in 1 Corinthians 10:13:

> *There hath no temptation taken you but such as is common to man: but God is faithful, who will not suffer you to be tempted above that ye are able; but will with the temptation also make a way to escape, that ye may be able to bear it.*

I want you to remember that. If you are experiencing these things, it's because God knows that you can handle it and will provide the way to escape. That's what we're talking about now. For whatever reason, you need to have this experience. You probably agreed to this before you came here. I doubt that there is much that happens to us in this life that ultimately turns for our good, that we didn't plan for and agree to before we were born. That's my feeling. So, rejoice in this, and figure out a way. What's the way that God has provided for you to escape?

Very few of the people I'm talking to are what I would consider possessed. Possession is where an evil or unclean spirit goes into your body and takes over your body. Now, I have worked with people who have had possession, and it becomes very clear that the person that is inside is not the person that used to be there. That is rare. Out of my experience, more often we are dealing with unclean spirits that attach themselves to us. If you look at Velcro, you're one-half of the Velcro, and they're the other half. For whatever reason, they attach themselves to us, and they're more or less with us all the time. You feel and experience their emotions, they whisper to you, they talk to you, and your spirit-mind picks up on those messages, and you act them out. Those spirits are found in as many strategies and strata as there are in this life. So, the first thing that you want to do is to find a Melchizedek Priesthood bearer that you can trust, and who is open to learning something new. Again, there are no handbooks written on this. So, you are now going into an area of personal revelation. You need to be guided by the Lord on what to do here. Here are just some suggestions and you can fill in the blanks with the Spirit, or you can take a different approach altogether. <u>This is my experience, and I just give it to you.</u>

Find a Melchizedek Priesthood bearer that you can approach and talk to about these specific things, that we're going to talk about right now, who is open to it and is willing to learn and put into practice, in his administration, this information.* First of all, for many Melchizedek Priesthood bearers, the only experience they may have had with devils and unclean spirits may have been something that took place in their missionary days as 19-21-year-olds. Possibly they were sent to Brazil, Argentina, the Navajo Indian Reservation, or somewhere, and it usually scares the heck out of them, and they're traumatized because of it and don't want to go there. So, when you start talking to them about devils and unclean spirits, don't be surprised if you see a little resistance in them, a little unbelief, a little doubt, a little unsureness. That's normal because they've not received any instruction on this. So, just go forward with faith and be calm. They may have some feelings of, "Gosh, I wonder if she's off her medicines, or he's been smoking something, or something is going on." Just be patient. Don't worry about it. Again, you're going into an area that's uncharted as far as handbooks of instruction.

Try to find a quorum to administer to you. Ordinarily, we call for two elders. The smallest priesthood quorum is three. There is power in priesthood quorums. So, if you can find three men that are unified and can come and exercise their faith in you, that's better than one or two. That's just something to think about; a quorum is three.*

The next thing is, you need to use consecrated oil. Normally, we think that we only use consecrated oil if a person has a physical illness. My personal experience is that anointing the person with oil that you're going to administer to in this area of spiritual enemies is an important part of it. So, anoint just like you normally do in the priesthood.*

The next thing is, the more specific you can be in the words you use in the administration, the more specific the results are going to be. This is where you may have to do a little talking with the people who are going to administer to you. **We, in the priesthood, all too often pray over a person instead of pronouncing a blessing.** When a person asks for a blessing, we're more comfortable praying over them than actually pronouncing a blessing. This is what President Nelson is talking about. We, in the priesthood, need to "come up!" We need to do things differently. We need to exercise power and not be timid. We need to be bolder and more open to revelation and revelatory flow. So, the more specific you can be, the better.

Something you may want to remember is that unclean spirits can repent. Repentance is still afforded to them. My personal opinion is that for all devils—or if not all, then for most—the gift of repentance is **not** offered. Repentance is a gift. But unclean spirits are men and women that have had a mortal life and who have died without knowledge or the redeeming power of the Atonement of Christ. They are called unclean spirits because they have not been cleansed from the spots and filthiness that all of us acquire by living in this world. These unclean spirits are the same group of people that our missionaries in the spirit world are visiting and are declaring repentance, vicarious baptism for the remission of sins, and the gift of the Holy Ghost. It's the same thing. That's the group that you are more likely to be dealing with, although I have had experience with devils. It's obvious when you're dealing with a devil versus an unclean spirit. Pray for the gift of discerning of spirits, but you'll see very quickly that those are two distinct groups. You are going to invite them to leave, once you've determined and discerned who you're dealing with. If it's a devil, then the temple tells you how to deal

with them.
> "We command you to depart."
> "By what authority?"
> "In the name of Jesus Christ, our Master."

That's how you deal with devils. With others, in varying degrees and as directed by the Spirit, you invite them to leave. You just talk to them and say:

> "You're causing problems here. You are bothersome. You're causing problems in the marriage. You're causing problems in the home. You're not wanted here. You need to leave. In the name of Jesus Christ, and by the authority of the Priesthood,* we command you to depart, to stand back and off and come not back."

I'd like you to go with me for just a minute to Matthew 12. I'd like to show you something else that takes us into the next phase of what I want to talk about here. I hope these things are helpful to you. In this chapter there is this interesting little parable, starting in verse 43. The previous 42 verses are talking about something completely unrelated. Then from 46-50 is talking about something unrelated, so these three verses, 43-45, are just stuck in here, and it's interesting that they have nothing to do with what preceded or what follows. But, it teaches a principle, and I think that is why the Lord included this story here:

> *[43] When the unclean spirit is gone out of a man, he* [the spirit] *walketh through dry places, seeking rest, and findeth none.*

If you were to describe the emotion of unclean spirits, the primary emotion, among others, would be anxiety. This is the most anxious group of people that you have ever seen in your life. Now, I never heard this before five or six years ago, and I find it interesting that what we are hearing, and I hear it all the time, is, "I'm having an anxiety attack." That seems to be the buzzword everywhere. I hear it from my family, "I'm anxious," etc, etc. I just ponder that, and think, "I bet you are because the spirits that are around you are anxious by nature."

> *[44] Then he saith* [the unclean spirit], *I will return into my house from whence I came out;*

That is a mortal's physical body. That person has been possessed:

> *and when he is come, he findeth it* [the house, the body of the mortal] *empty, swept, and garnished.*

There's your kicker now; this is the key:

> *[45] Then goeth he, and taketh with himself seven other spirits more wicked than himself, and they enter in and dwell there* [they go and take possession of that man's body]*: and the last state of that man is worse than the first.*

And then this interesting statement:

> *Even so shall it be also unto this wicked generation.*

Now, he's talking to the generation of the Jews at that time, but by extension, he's speaking to us. So, here's the key: once you have opened up and expelled these unclean spirits, you need to replace that vacancy with light. You need to, as it were, pull the weeds and plant the flowers. If you just leave it open, the chances are that they are just going to come back. I can't tell you how many I've heard say, "Yeah, I received a blessing and felt relief, but it didn't last." The reason it didn't last is two-fold. Number one, the person being blessed doesn't take an active role in this whole process. They just sit back and wait for someone to take care of their problem without being actively involved, not only in resolving it in the first place but keeping it resolved thereafter. You have to be actively involved. And the second part is that we did not invite light to come in where darkness was.

Here is the next thing we need to do: Joseph Smith said that you have to understand the laws that govern these spirits. One of the laws that govern good spirits is that you need **to invite them.** The spirits of light, angels, the *spirits of just men made perfect*, the spirits of departed ancestors, especially those that are endowed, or the spirits of your progeny who are going to be born, through your children or your body depending on your age— they're all spirits of light. Here's the law: they need to have an invitation and permission to come in and have an effect in your life for good. They can see the conflict that's raging. They can see that you are afflicted. It's almost like they're standing off to the side with their arms folded and tapping their foot saying, "Make any move, whatever you can, to invite me to come in, so that I can help you. I can help you!" I'm not going to say that they can't help without being invited and without being permitted, but I will say that it's a correct principle to those who have ultimate respect and reverence for man's agency to give them permission and an invitation to come and help you. So, in that blessing, have those that perform this blessing, after they've expelled the darkness, to invite the light in. It's also good to go into this fasting. Fasting is a tremendous power source. Remember in Mark 9, where there was a child possessed with a spirit, and it was just horrible. The disciples tried to remove that spirit from this person and couldn't do it. They called on Jesus to do it, and He immediately rebuked that spirit, and it came out and the person was at peace. In verse 21, Jesus had asked the father:

> *How long is it ago since this came unto him? And he* [the father] *said, Of a child.*

Then, at the end of verse 28, the disciples came up afterward and asked:

> *Why could not we cast him out?*

The Savior taught this principle:

> *[29] ...This kind can come forth by nothing, but by prayer and fasting.*

"*This kind...*" See, you ought to ponder that. That tells us right there that you have different levels of strata in this society. They are not all the same. So, hopefully, brothers and sisters, this information will help. This is the most common question, in emails and phone calls that I receive from people who listen to these podcasts. They see that this is a problem in their life and want to do something about it.

Now, in closing this particular session, I want you to go with me to Joseph Smith-History, verse 20. This is just after the First Vision. Joseph comes in from the Sacred Grove, and he's leaning on the fireplace, and his mother asks if everything's all right. Joseph says:

> *'Never mind, all is well—I'm well enough off.' I then said to my mother, 'I have learned for myself that Presbyterianism is not true.'*

That's one of the great understatements in the history of the

Church. Now, in this next part, if you are having this opposition, I want you to remember this: the greater the opposition, the greater the blessings that are in store for you. We've talked about that. Joseph said this:

> *It seems as though the adversary was aware, at a very early period of my life, that I was destined to prove a disturber and an annoyer to his kingdom;*

That's what you want to be! Especially priesthood brethren, that's what you want to be. When you start to shed light on this darkness and expose it for what it is, you can expect the "bells of hell" to start ringing! You can expect that your name will move to the front of the agenda sheet that's discussed by devils. You want to be *"a disturber and an annoyer to his kingdom."* Then Joseph says:

> *else why should the powers of darkness combine against me?*

Some of you have asked that question and said, "I don't know why this is happening!" From Joseph:

> *else why should the powers of darkness combine against me? Why the opposition and persecution that arose against me, almost in my infancy?*

See, this is really a compliment. They know something about you that you have forgotten. When you start to expose them, then the Lord also reveals to you laws and principles that are used to govern all the spirits and gives you power over them. Enough said on that.

    I'd like to go to one last thing that I want to talk to you about tonight. I'd like to go to Proverbs in the *Old Testament*, and this is another area that in the discussions I have, a lot of people are asking me, "Can you recommend a book that I can read on this or that?" Another question is, "In your library of study, what books do you have that you absolutely use for a foundation?" And, I have some of those. I have a vast library over the years, and I've been a very good customer of Deseret Book and Seagull Book and other places. That has its place, but what I'm saying more and more to people who ask questions is something like this, "That's a great question. Why don't you take that question you just asked me, exactly the way you asked it to me, to the Lord and ask Him?" He is so anxious for us to come to Him.

Remember, brothers and sisters, the Lord Jesus Christ is the keeper of the gate, and **He employs no servant there**. That means that there should be nobody, no one, between you and the Lord.

It's okay, as part of the process of moving up, for us to rely upon the opinions and the wisdom and the knowledge of other mortals. It's okay to be there, **but it's not okay to stay there**. The problem is, we end up staying there, and we want others to tell us what to do. Or, we want others to validate the decisions we make. We are continually, consciously or subconsciously, seeking for allies to tell us that the path we're on or the things we are doing are okay. That's not a good place to be. So, what I want you to do is go to Proverbs 3:5 and look at a few scriptures, in closing this tonight. This is really the heart of tonight's discussion:

> *[5] Trust in the Lord with all thine heart; and lean not unto thine own understanding.*

And I would add to that, *"lean not unto thine own* [or anybody else's] *understanding."*

> *[6] In all thy ways acknowledge him, and **he shall direct thy paths**.*

That's where we want to be. It is such a subtle trap for us to be continually relying on other mortals for what we do, where we go, and our spiritual progression on our journey back to the Father. It has its place, but if we don't rise above that, it ends up being damning instead of exalting. Why would we want to continue to drink water down in the pasture where the cows have walked to it, where it's diluted, where it's polluted, rather than go to the source of the spring? Let me read a few quotes from some of the early Brethren of the Church. These are great quotes, and I hope that you understand what I'm saying here, and I'll try to say this in a way that there is no misunderstanding. This was written by Joseph Fielding Smith. It's in his personal journal dated December 28, 1938, so he would have been Elder Joseph Fielding Smith. He's one of the younger members of the Quorum of the Twelve. Prior to that, and during his tenure, he served as the Church Historian. So, in 1938, he had access to all the records of the Church that were in existence at that point. He said this:

> *It is a very apparent fact that we have traveled far and wide in the past 20 years. What the future will bring I do not know. But if we drift as far afield from fundamental things in the next 20 years, what will be left of the foundation laid by the Prophet Joseph Smith? It is easy for one who observes to see how the apostasy came about in the primitive church of Christ. Are we not traveling that same road?*

Here is another quote, by Brigham Young, from the *Journal of Discourses*, Volume 10, Discourse 8:32:

> *There is nothing that would so soon weaken my hope and discourage me as to see this people in full fellowship with the world, and receive no more persecution from them because they are one with them.*

That was Harold B. Lee's biggest concern, that we would be so accepted by the world and that would be an indicator that we were on the wrong path. If the world loves us, and the majority accepts us, we've left the path. That's what the Brethren are saying. President Young said:

> *In such an event, we might bid farewell to the Holy Priesthood with all of its blessings, privileges, and aids to exaltations, principalities, and powers in the eternities of the Gods.*

Another quote by Brigham Young is in *Journal of Discourses*, Volume 6 page 100, and he said:

> *The First Presidency have of right a great influence over this people; and if we should get out of the way and lead this people to destruction, what a pity it would be! How can you know whether we lead you correctly or not? Can you know by any other power than that of the Holy Ghost? I have uniformly exhorted the people to obtain this living witness each for themselves; then no man can lead them astray.*

George Q. Cannon, who was in the First Presidency, said this:

> *Do not, brethren, put your trust in man, though he be a bishop, an apostle, or a president. If you*

> *do, they will fail you at some time or place. They will do wrong or seem to, and your support will be gone. But, if we lean on God, He will never fail us. When men and women depend on God alone, and trust in Him alone, their faith will not be shaken if the highest in the Church should step aside.*

Now, we're not saying that any of the leadership of the Church have gone astray; not saying that at all. What I am saying is that as things are not going to get better because the "bells of hell" are ringing. The only sure ground is to have that relationship with the Father and the Son, through the power of the Holy Ghost and the Holy Spirit, so that you can know for yourself, under any circumstances, that whatever you hear or experience, is either from God or is in error and from the dark side.

Let me give you another one. Let's go to 2 Nephi 4. What's the message here? Trust in the Lord and no one else. It doesn't mean that you don't follow your leaders. That is not what it means at all. It doesn't mean that we don't listen to prophets, or apostles, or stake presidents, or our bishops. But what they're trying to do, brothers and sisters, is to get each man and each father to come up to a position of first, a prophet in his own home, being able to have all the revelatory power within his own home that the president of the Church has over the whole Church, or that a stake president has over his stake, or that a bishop has over his ward. All of that leadership is designed to help dads and men to come up to be first, prophets, then second, priests, and then next, kings. We sing a hymn, "I Know That My Redeemer Lives" and in the third verse, it calls Christ, *"My Prophet, Priest, and King."* That's a priesthood progression: prophet, priest, king. Joseph Smith moved through that. He was a prophet, then a priest, and then a king. The Church members got so upset because they didn't understand the doctrine that they rejected it as a whole. And Joseph mourned again because he couldn't bring the Latter-day Saints up to something higher and nobler. Well, that's what's going on. Pray for our leaders. Sustain them. Also, seek to know for yourselves, by the power of the Holy Ghost and the Holy Spirit, that they are being led by God, that they are being inspired by Him, and that their words come from Him. Otherwise, we're on shaky ground. You ought to read the whole of 2 Nephi 4. This is what scholars call the *Song of Nephi or the Psalm of Nephi*. It's wonderful. We'll start in verse 19:

> And when I desire to rejoice, my heart groaneth because of my sins; nevertheless, **I know in whom I have trusted**.

And then because of that trust, look at what Nephi experiences in verses 20 and 21:

> *My God hath been my support; he hath led me through mine afflictions in the wilderness* [preserved in the wilderness]; *and he hath preserved me upon the waters of the great deep* [protected upon the waters].
> [21] *He hath filled me with his love, even unto the consuming of my flesh.*

I've not experienced that, but I'd like to:

> [22] *He hath confounded mine enemies, unto the causing of them to quake before me.*

I think we're going to need to have that in a coming day. You're going to need to be able to have that power to either make you and your loved ones, or those you have stewardship over, invisible to your enemies or be able to call down power from heaven over the elements and protect you, and if necessary, destroy them.

> [23] *Behold, he hath heard my cry by day, and he hath given me knowledge by visions in the night-time.*

All of these things that Nephi is talking about as an old man now, probably in his late 60's or early 70's, he is saying come because *"I know in whom I have trusted."*

> [24] *And by day have I waxed bold in mighty prayer before him; yea, my voice have I sent up on high; and angels came down and ministered unto me.*
> [25] *And upon the wings of his Spirit hath my body been carried away upon exceedingly high mountains.*

Take that literally, that's not figurative. That is a physical transportation by heavenly powers, where this mortal man's physical body was lifted from point A to point B.

> *And mine eyes have beheld great things, yea, even too great for man; therefore I was bidden that I should not write them.*

So, all of these things and more come because of verse 19, *"I know in whom I have trusted."* Let's go to verse 34. Notice how many times the word *trust* is mentioned in verse 34? Five times:

> *[34] O Lord, I have **trusted** in thee, and I will **trust** in thee forever. I will not put my **trust** in the arm of flesh; for I know that **cursed is he that putteth his trust in the arm of flesh**.*

When the same thing is mentioned twice in the same scripture, pay attention! Here it is again:

> *Yea, **cursed is he that putteth his trust in man or maketh flesh his arm**.*

I think there is no mistaking the message here. What's the balance? Again, I don't want this interpreted to mean I don't listen to, follow, and sustain my leaders. The whole purpose of the Church of Jesus Christ of Latter-day Saints and all its organizations is to bring us to a point where we can be so familiar within this telestial world, within the veil, be so familiar with that voice of Christ, that we become experienced and perfected in hearing, recognizing, and heeding that voice.

Go with me to *Doctrine and Covenants* 29:7 and let me show you a little different twist to something there. We use this a lot about missionary work, but let me give you a different twist:

> *[7] And ye are called to bring to pass the gathering of mine elect; for mine elect hear my voice and harden not their hearts;*

Who are the elect? The word *elect* ties in with the word *election*. So, now we are talking about people who are advanced and have progressed in their spiritual journey. We're not talking about novices here. We are talking about people who had **stepped up** and find themselves on a higher plane and in a higher order of things than when they first joined the Church. This is the same group of people in *Doctrine and Covenants* 121:34 that says:

> *Behold, there are many called, but few are chosen.*

This group *of chosen*, and this group of *elect* have a relationship. Now, look at the rest of verse 7:

> *for mine elect hear my voice and harden not their hearts;*

Do you want to know who these *elect* are? Do you want to find out if you are one of the *elect*? *"Mine elect hear my voice and harden not their hearts."* Who is speaking here? It's Christ.

The book by Brother John Pontius, *Following the Light of Christ into His Presence,* is so exceptional, so foundational, and so enlightening. If you have not read that book, I **urgently** recommend that you purchase it and read it. Those of you that have read it before read it again! The whole premise of that book is that every step you need to be taught, every place you need to go, every blessing, every design of God for your life, everything you need to do is done by "following the voice of Christ;" that's called the Holy Spirit. That's what we're talking about. He says, *"mine elect hear my voice."* This is the voice of Him that you covenant every Sunday to remember, to keep His commandments, to take His name upon you so that you can have His Spirit to be with you. That's Christ's Spirit, His voice, that's what we're talking about in verse 7. "You can have My voice with you for the next seven days."

Hardening your heart means that you hear that voice enough and know from whence it comes, know the doctrine, you've had experiences, and you reject that voice. You go backward. That's hardening your heart. See, the definition of *"hardening your heart"* in the *Book of Mormon* is to rebel against the voice of Christ, the Holy Spirit, as it communicates with you. That is the definition of a *hard heart*.

Well, in closing, I want to take you to some statements by John Taylor. Brother Taylor talks about the days that are coming up, and you have this handout. It's on a previous podcast and is called, *The Coming Crisis and How to Meet It*. It talks about how God's power is going to be revealed as it has never been before. Because that happens, Satan's power is also going to increase like it never has before. God is going to work miracles that will eclipse anything written in the scriptures, and Satan is going to counterfeit those miracles! Brother Taylor comes out and says that:

> *The Devil in the last stage of desperation, will take such a pre-eminent lead in literature, politics, philosophy, and religion; in wars, famines, pestilences, earthquakes, thunderings and lightnings, setting cities in conflagration, etc., that mighty kings and powerful nations will be constrained to fall down and worship him. For his signs and wonders will be among all nations. Men will be raised for the express purpose of furthering the designs and marvelous works of the devil. Every description of curious and mysterious arts that penetrate beyond the common pale of human sagacity and wisdom, will be studied and practiced beyond what has been known by mere mortals. The great capabilities of the elements of fire, air, earth, and water, will be brought into requisition by cunning men under the superior cunning of the prince and the God of this world. And, inflated with the knowledge of these wonderful arts and powers, men will become boasters, heady, high-minded, proud, and despisers of that which is good.*

We've talked about that. With all that going on, how are you going to keep from being deceived? Here's another statement that Brother Taylor said:

> *God, the true and living Sovereign of Heaven and Earth, will contribute to produce the delusion. He has said that "He will send them strong delusions that they might believe a lie." He gives his reason and apology for acting after this stranger manner because, knowing the truth, they do not love it unadulterated.*

Isn't that amazing that when we have revealed, restored truth, that we prefer truth adulterated, rather than pure truth? Isn't that amazing? And we prefer the philosophies of men, mingled with scripture, rather than revelation to you personally through the power of the Holy Ghost and the Holy Spirit? We prefer that? We seek the opinions of others on what they think to direct our footsteps, and we seek their opinions to ally with us so that we can feel that what we are doing is correct? And we are slow to approach God in prayer and fasting and seek for revelation, and have a revelatory flow and become prophets and prophetesses in our own right?

> *And knowing God, they do not choose to glorify Him as God. Therefore their foolish hearts become darkened, and God suffers Satan to compound and mix up truth and error in such proportions as to be captivating and strongly delusive.*

Just a couple more statements. This one talks about the need for us to have revelation for ourselves. Without it, there is no way that you can come to it. Let me just finish up what he says here:

> *You cannot know God without present revelation. Did you ever think of this most solemn and essential truth before? You may have been accustomed to praying all of your lifetime, and as yet, even you do not know God. You may have heard many thousands of sermons with a sincere desire to both remember and practice it, and yet you do not know God. But it has been decided in the court of heaven, that no man can know the Father but the Son, and he to whom the Son REVEALETH him.*

There is your key word. Talking about the deceptions that are coming up, he says:

> *Mere flesh and blood cannot help you now. It requires an Almighty arm to effect your deliverance. Therefore, **put no more trust in man**, for a curse rests upon him that will be guided by the precepts of man. I do not ask you to be guided by what I say to you, unless the Lord from heaven shall reveal to you that I speak the truth, even as it is in Christ. Although I know that I am declaring heaven's truth to you, in all sobriety, yet, my knowing it, does not suffice for you. You also must know it for yourself, and not for another.*
>
> *This is your right and your privilege. For God has*

made this promise to you, and not to you, reader, only, but to all others whom He calls to repentance.

Final word:

Now, go and get revelation for yourself.

Brothers and sisters, we live in the time when this is what needs to be done. Again, what you have done in the past will not suffice for today's challenges and what's coming tomorrow. It won't. If you think you're going to get through what's coming by just doing what you've been doing, you are either K.I.A. or M.I.A. You will not stand in the conflict. In a battle, if a soldier is down, he's out of the fight, K.I.A. Killed in action, or missing in action, doesn't do anything to help the cause of Zion. I hope these things are helpful to you. God bless you all, and we'll see you next week.

References:
Isaiah 5:13
Moroni 6:4
"Have I Done Any Good?" *LDS Hymn Book*, #223
Alma 34:21 "[pray] morning, mid-day, and evening."
"You must make yourselves acquainted with those men who like Daniel pray three times a day toward the House of the Lord." Joseph Smith (Teachings, p. 161.)
Isaiah 5:14
Hosea 4:6-7
"A man is saved no faster than he gets knowledge." History of the Church, 4:588; from a discourse given by Joseph Smith on Apr. 10, 1842, in Nauvoo, Illinois; reported by Wilford Woodruff.
"God has more power than all other beings because He has greater knowledge;" History of the Church, 5:340; from a discourse given by Joseph Smith on Apr. 8, 1843, in Nauvoo, Illinois; reported by Willard Richards and William Clayton.2 Nephi 9:27
1 Corinthians 10:13
Matthew 12:43-45
"...having a knowledge of the laws by which spirits are governed..." History of the Church, 3:391–92; from a discourse given by Joseph Smith about July 1839 in Commerce, Illinois.
Mark 9:14-29, casting out unclean spirits with fasting and prayer
Joseph Smith-History, verse 20
Proverbs 3:5-6
Joseph Fielding Smith, personal journal dated Dec. 28, 1938.
Brigham Young, *Journal of Discourses* Vol 10, Discourse 8:32
Brigham Young is in *Journal of Discourses* JD Vol 6 pg. 100

George Q. Cannon, "Need For Personal Testimonies," (15 February 1891), Collected Discourses 2:178. See Millennial Star 53:658–659, 673–675.
"I Know That My Redeemer Lives" *LDS Hymn Book,* #136
2 Nephi 4:19-25, 34
D&C 29:7
D&C 121:34
Following the Light of Christ Into His Presence by John Pontius
John Taylor, Millennial Star, April 30, 1853—Vol. 15 Pg 273

*As Mike is constantly learning and his experience and knowledge are expanding, he gives additional, modified insight and instruction on the topic of using priesthood in later podcasts. See chapter 57- Familiar Spirits/Calling & Election and chapter 58- Weapons of Light.)

The Power of the Priesthood and/or the name of Jesus Christ always works to cast out or away evil/unclean spirits. The reason for the and/or is that **women also have power by faith and in the name of Jesus Christ to command these spirits to depart.** Many people falsely believe that only the Power of the Priesthood must be used to do the casting out. They will also depart in the name of Christ.

Samuel W Richards (Editor)
The Coming Crisis & How to Meet It
Millennial Star, 30 April 1853
A great and awful crisis is at hand — such a crisis was never known before since the foundation of the world. All nations are looking through the misty future in order to descry, if possible, what is about to happen. Many sermons have been preached, many speeches have been made, and some pamphlets have been published, with the hope of lifting up the veil of the future. Yet none but the servants of God who have the testimony of Jesus, which is the spirit of prophecy, can unfold the mysteries of the future. They can give the trump a certain sound, and their counsel will not be guess work. God will do nothing except He reveal His secrets to His servants and Prophets. God, the Lord God of Israel, will take the control of these great events which are shortly to come to pass. Not a sparrow will fall to the ground without His notice. But His servants will be fully advised to every important event that is to transpire. They will be the heralds of blessings and also of vengeance. For the Lord hath a controversy with all nations, and the hour of recompense is at hand.
But, says the reader, I would like to know of what this crisis is to consist! Who are the contesting parties? Well, reader, if you will be patient and honest-hearted, praying withal, with unceasing diligence and thanksgiving to God, you shall have the keys of such knowledge as all the sectarian priests of Christendom are by no means able to reveal, because they are only revealed to God's servants, the Prophets.
Perhaps you will be disappointed if I tell you that the time is coming, and now is, when, not only God, the Highest of all, shall be revealed in spirit and in mighty power, but the Devil or Satan also, will be revealed in signs and wonders and in mighty deeds! This, reader, is the great key to all the marvelous events that are to transpire shortly upon the earth.

Now just stop right here, and pause, and mark emphatically this key. Then you and I will proceed to unlock the mysteries and to prepare ourselves to the battle. For there will be no neutrals in the approaching controversy. I say again, that God the Highest of all will make bare His arm in the eyes of all nations. And the heavens even will be rent, and the lighting down of His power will be felt by all nations.

But this is not all. Satan also will be revealed. He has made some manifestations of his power in different periods of the world, but never before has there been such an array of numbers on his side, never before such a consolidation of armies and rulers, never before has there been such an imposing and overwhelming exhibition of miracles as Satan will shortly make manifest. Don't suppose for a moment, that I am uttering dark sayings or speaking unadvisedly upon speculation or the strength of mere human opinion. Don't tell me about Popes and Prelates sitting in the Temple of God as God. One far greater than any Pope or Prelate is soon to be revealed and he will claim to be worshipped as God. Now, remember, that it is no modern wicked man that is going to claim divine honors. No, it is that old Serpent, the Devil. He it is that will head the opposition against God and His Christ. And he, the son of perdition it is, that will be allowed a much longer chain than heretofore. And such will be the greatness of his power, that it will seem to many that he is entirely loose. He will be so far unshackled and unchained that his power will deceive all nations, even the world. And the elect will barely escape the power of his sorceries, enchantments, and miracles!

And even God, Himself, the true God, will contribute to put means and instruments in his way and at hand, for his use, so that he can have a full trial of his strength and cunning, with all deceivableness of unrighteousness in them that perish.

It is not to be expected that Satan will carry on his great warfare against Christ and his Saints by means of any one religion exclusively. It is not the Papal or Protestant religion alone that you have need to fear. But the great and abominable Church which you should expect to encounter is Anti-Christ. Whatever exalts and opposes itself to God, that is Anti-Christ, whether it is a civil or religious power. But the most formidable power that will be arrayed against Christ and his Saints in the last days, will consist of the revelations of Satan.

These revelations of Satan will come through every medium and channel by which the cunning and power of Satan can be brought to bear against the Saints and their Lord. It is a great mistake to suppose that Satan is altogether a religious personage. No, far from this. He is a politician, a philosopher, an erudite scholar, a linguist, a metaphysician, a military commander, a prince, a god, a necromancer, an enchanter, a diviner, a magician, a sorcerer, a prophet, and (if it were not railing) a clergyman and a liar from the beginning. With these universal endowments, he has never hitherto made a full and grand exhibition of himself, as it remains for him to do. But the Lord, who gave him an opportunity to try is battery upon good old Job, is fully designing to give him sufficient apparatus to deceive all the nations that love not the truth and have pleasure in unrighteousness. His signs and tokens are as ancient as the apostasy of Cain and as varied as will suit the secret designs of all ages. Through him, men learn how to become "observers of time and seasons," with great skill and astonishing accuracy. He presides over the arts of astrology, clairvoyance, mesmerism, electro-biology, and all auguries and divinations. Being Prince of the power of the air he understands aeronautic and steam navigation, and he can compose and combine the various elements, through the co-operation of them that believe in him, with far more than human skill.

Now don't doubt what I say concerning this matter, but rather read the history of his skillful exploits and his mighty power, as they are recorded in the Old and New Testaments. Take a Bible and Concordance, (if you have any Faith in the Bible left, in an age when the Bible is perverted beyond all other books), and read attentively for yourselves, and you will there learn that I am telling you the truth.

Now there is a greater destruction coming upon the wicked nations of the earth than was even experienced by Pharaoh at the Red Sea. But before that destruction can be made manifest, men's hearts will be hardened, and wickedness will rise to a more over-towering height than many bygone generations have been allowed to witness. God, through his Prophet, will roar out of Zion. His voice will be heard in spite of all the confusion and indignant opposition from many nations. After the testimony of His servants has been proclaimed to all nations, as a witness, then shall the scene of the end come. And great shall be that scene.

The Devil in the last stage of desperation, will take such a pre-eminent lead in literature, politics, philosophy, and religion; in wars, famines, pestilences, earthquakes, thunderings and lightnings, setting cities in conflagration, etc., that mighty kings and powerful nations will be constrained to fall down and worship him . And they will marvel at his great power and wonder after him with great astonishment. For his signs and wonders will be among all nations. Men will be raised for the express purpose of furthering the designs and marvelous works of the devil. Every description of curious and mysterious arts that penetrate beyond the common pale of human sagacity and wisdom will be studied and practiced beyond what has been known by mere mortals. The great capabilities of the elements of fire, air, earth, and water, will be brought into requisition by cunning men under the superior cunning of the prince and the God of this world. And, inflated with the knowledge of these wonderful arts and powers, men will become boasters, heady, high-minded, proud, and despisers of that which is good. But the God, who is above all, and over all, and who ruleth in the armies of heaven, and amongst the inhabitants of the earth, will not be a silent observer of such spiritual wickedness in high places, and among the rulers of the darkness of this world. For the master spirits of wickedness of all ages, and of worlds visible and invisible, will be arrayed in the rebellious ranks before the closing scene shall transpire. Now, just at this time, God will come out of His hiding place and vex the nations in his hot displeasure. By the mouth of His Prophet, He will rebuke strong nations afar off, notwithstanding their strong armies and great miracles, and cunning arts.

His servant, the Prophet, in Zion will have a marvelous boldness to rebuke them, and to lay down before them in plainness and inflexible firmness the law of the Lord. As Moses laid down the law to Pharaoh, and then continued to multiply evils and judgments until he made an utter end of Pharaoh and the Egyptians, even so will the living God prescribe the line of conduct to be pursued, and the penalties of violation, to great and mighty nations, until they rally around the ensign established upon the mountains, and go up to the house of the God of Jacob to learn His ways, or are utterly overwhelmed in keen anguish and ruin.

The ways of the God of Jacob are easily recognized in these days of general wickedness. It is true, that they are clearly revealed in the Scriptures of truth, and by a living Priesthood of inspired men, yet they have been so long and so grossly perverted by the precepts and opinions of a hireling ministry, that doubts and contentions have sprung up in every land, and the plainest and simplest truths are denied, abrogated, or accounted obsolete. God is not allowed to speak from the heavens by the mouths of Prophets as in former days. Notwithstanding there is much preaching and praying, still there is a virtual acknowledgment among all nations that God, as He was known unto the Patriarchs and Prophets of old, has forsaken the earth. And men are therefore left to discover the way to heaven by the light of nature, or the misty nebulae of a hireling Priesthood. And it is a fact, undeniable, that infidels in the school of nature have more true piety towards the living God than the hireling ministry of Christendom have.

Hence priests are doing so much, often unwittingly, to blind the eyes of the people, so that they shall not see the approaching crisis in its true character until the catastrophe is completed, and Great Babylon and all her lofty cities, great wealth, princely merchants, chief captains, and mighty sovereigns, are laid low in one general ruin. Oh ye great and strong nations! ye philosophers and religionists! ye spiritual mediums and ye revelators, sitting upon thrones over great nations! how can you fulfill the prophecies that are so clearly revealed, concerning the destructions of the last days! Ye perhaps marvel that the great men and governors over one hundred and twenty-seven provinces in ancient Babylon, with a brave monarch at their head, should have been such firm believers in the astrologers, magicians, and interpreters of dreams, in their days! But marvel not, for when the greater power of the like class of persons, under the direction of Satan, shall be brought to bear in your own day, the delusion will be so much stronger that Princes, Presidents, Governors, and chief Captains, will be constrained to bow to it. Their credulity will be taxed beyond the power of resistance. The workers of these mysterious and supernatural arts will bring to their aid both natural and supernatural causes that will challenge and defy disputation.

The senses and judgment of men cannot withstand such imperative facts as will arrest their observations. For it cannot be denied that facts and truths will constitute such a measure of the ingredients of these mysterious and wonderful arts as to give them an irresistible strength of conviction to those who are unenlightened by the Spirit of God. And so far as facts and truth are mingled, it must also be acknowledged that God, the true and living Sovereign of Heaven and Earth, will contribute to produce the delusion. He has said that "He will send them strong delusions that they might believe a lie." He gives his reason and apology for acting after this stranger manner because, knowing the truth, they do not love it unadulterated. And knowing God, they do not choose to glorify Him as God. Therefore their foolish hearts become darkened, and God suffers Satan to compound and mix up truth and error in such proportions as to be captivating and strongly delusive. As a snare, this composition will be ingeniously mixed and administered to all nations, by skillful and practiced hands.

And who shall be able to withstand? Do you think that your great sagacity and the compass of your profound, philosophical turn of mind will enable you to detect the error and delusion of these arts? Oh, man, this is a vain hope. You will not be competent to detect the delusion. God Himself will allow Satan to ply your scrutinizing eye with powers and sophistications far beyond your capacity to detect. Do you say then, I will stand aloof from investigation, I will shun all acquaintance with these mysterious workings, in order that I may not be carried away with their delusive influence. Vain hope. Oh, man, you cannot be neutral. You must choose your side and put on your armor. Those that come not up to the help of the Lord in the day of battle will be sorely cursed. The captive Hebrew Daniel stood up boldly against all the governors and whole realm of Babylon with their monarch at their head. Daniel readily acknowledged that it was not from any wisdom in him, above other men, that he could surpass the astrologers and magicians.

But holding intercourse with the God of heaven, he became endowed with supernatural comprehension that effectually shielded him against supernatural delusion. Thereby he escaped the snare that entwined around the great statesmen and governors of that immense empire of Babylon. Thereby, those who take refuge in the name of the Lord and in immediate revelation from heaven, will be safe, and no others. He that is not for God and the principle of immediate revelation will inevitably be ensnared, overcome, and destroyed because he that is not for Him must be against Him. No man in any age was ever for God that did not hold intercourse with Him personally, and receive for himself the revelations of his will. The rock of revelation, by which Peter knew Jesus Christ, is the only basis upon which any man can escape the strong delusion which God will send among the nations through Satan and his mediums and coadjutors. Reader, if you live long, you will be compelled to take a side for God or for Satan. Satan was allowed to try a compulsory process upon as good a man as Job. The whirlwind and tempestuous elements, with disease and death, were put into Satan's hand that he might compel Job to abandon his integrity. Had not Job possessed the key to revelation from God, he would have been compelled to have made peace with Satan, and forsaken the Lord. His wife urged him to do so says she, "Curse God and die"; or in other words, take the side of Satan against God.

Now, reader, if you have ships of precious merchandise, floating at sea, the time is fast coming when Satan will destroy those ships unless you bow down to his power and become a co-operator with him. And if you do bow down to him, to work wickedness and say, no eye seeth me then God will destroy those ships and you too, and peradventure He will destroy your family also, and make a clean end of you, and blot out your name under heaven. Your beautiful mansion and flourishing family still have to be consecrated to God or to Satan, whichever you may choose. The controversy is begun and the war will never end till the victory is complete and universal, and there shall not be found so much as a dog to move his tongue against the Lord, and the immediate revelations of His will. Your being a minister of some Church, will not serve as the last screen for you against the hot indignation of God, unless you have the law and the testimony of the true and living God made known to you personally.

For the time has come that God will write His law upon every man's heart, that will receive it, not with ink, but with the Spirit of the living God. And against him that hath this law, the gates of hell never have prevailed and never will prevail. Heaven and earth shall pass away before a jot of this law shall be made to succumb to wicked men or devils. The heavens have been shaken once when angels rebelled, and they are destined to another shaking even with the earth. Do you say you don't need any more revelation from God? Then the Devil will be allowed to give you some which you don't need. And by the time that he has revealed himself to you, and buffeted you, and trained you under his rigorous discipline to fight in this awful crisis against the heavens, peradventure you will not then feel so rich and increased in goods, but that you can take a little counsel from the Lord, and feel a little of your extreme poverty and destitution.

You cannot know God without present revelation. Did you ever think of this most solemn and essential truth, before? You may have been accustomed to pray, all your lifetime, and as yet you, even you, do not know God. You may have heard many thousand sermons, with a sincere desire both to remember and practice them, and yet you do not know God. But it has been decided in the court of heaven, that no man can know the Father but the Son, and he to whom the Son REVEALETH him.

Now, has Jesus Christ ever revealed God the Father to you, dear reader? Be honest with yourself, and do not err in your answer to this most important question. However much the Son may have revealed the Father to Prophets, Patriarchs, and Apostles of old, the question still remains in full force has he revealed Him to you? A revelation to another man is by no means a revelation to you. For instance, God revealed himself to Samuel and called him by name to be a Prophet. But the call to Samuel is by no means a call to you to be a Prophet. God called Abraham to kill Isaac, but that is no revelation to you to kill your son. God revealed the baptism of repentance to John the Baptist, before Christ's death, but that is not a revelation to you.

He revealed authority to Paul to preach to the Gentiles, but what was told to Paul is not told to you, nor is it required of you. Again, you need the righteousness of God to go where God is, and be happy and how will you get it except it is revealed to you personally? You cannot get it any other way. Hence the Lord says, "The righteousness of God is revealed from faith to faith." Don't say now, as some do, that revelation was anciently given in order to establish the truth, and being once established is it no longer necessary to be revealed to subsequent generations of people. Don't say this for your life, for revelation is just as necessary to establish truth now as it was then. You need the ministry of angels now, just as much as people did then. They in past ages could not know God, nor say for a certainty, from personal knowledge, that Jesus Christ was the Christ, only by the Holy Ghost and you are just as weak and dependent as they were. You most assuredly cannot call Jesus, Lord, only by the Holy Ghost. If the Holy Ghost is confirmed upon you, by the imposition of the hands of the true Priesthood, then you can know God for yourself.

Why? Because the Holy Ghost teaches all things, even the deep things of God. This generation needs present revelations from heaven, as much as any other generation ever did, because they are quite as wicked as Sodom ever was. They practice as gross sensuality and beastliness, as glaring robbery and murder, as much treachery and lying, and are as ardent for war and blood-guiltiness, as ever the ancient Canaanites were. And among the many religions that have sprung up, calculated to confuse people's minds, there is, now, as must jargon and schism, contention and strife, and persecuting zeal, as there ever was before. Now, reader, you need present revelation from God to your own dear self, in order to help you out of this nasty, confused labyrinth, and to set your feet firmly upon the solid rock of revelation. Mere flesh and blood cannot help you now. It requires an Almighty arm to effect your deliverance. Therefore, put no more trust in man, for a curse rests upon him that will be guided by the precepts of man. I do not ask you to be guided by what I say to you unless the Lord from heaven shall reveal to you that I speak the truth, even as it is in Christ. Although I know that I am declaring heaven's truth to you, in all sobriety, yet, my knowing it, does not suffice for you. You also must know it for yourself, and not for another.

This is your right and your privilege. For God has made this promise to you, and not to you, reader, only, but to all others whom He calls to repentance.

Now, go and get revelation for yourself. If you are penitently desirous with all your heart to get revelation from God to your own self, go to someone whom God has called and ordained to confer the Gift of Reader, be resolute! This is a critical and trying moment with you. And this is God's call unto you. Don't refuse when He calls you! And if you are honestly, without prejudice, meditating upon what you now read, then God's Spirit is sweetly persuading you to believe what I say. The faint dawn of the Spirit is even now upon your mind. Now, reader, cherish this little dawn of light until the daylight of more truth shines more clearly upon your mind.

Pray mightily for the Spirit of Revelation to rest upon you, that you may know the things that are freely given to you of God. And follow the Spirit of revelation, as fast as you receive its whisperings, down into the water where Jesus went, for the remission of your sins, and you will very soon become a witness to the one truth, and put your own seal upon it even as I have done. And you will not barely believe, and hope, and fear, but you will know, from present and personal revelation, that the Lord is a God at hand, revealing Himself as freely as He ever did in Patriarchal days. Will you not, then be a happy man, O reader! and you a happy woman, O reader, to come into possession of the same gift of present revelation from heaven, that holy men and holy women enjoyed in ancient times? Yes, I know you will. You will then feel deep pity and sorrow for anyone that says he doesn't need present revelation! You will then discover the pride of such an one's heart, and mourn over him as one that is blinded by the God of this world. But your peace will be great and your joy unspeakable. Although you can hardly believe me now, yet through your faithfulness, the Spirit of prophecy will in due time rest even upon you, O man! and also upon you, O woman! The spirit of prophecy has rested upon many sons and daughters in as humble walks of life as you are, and they, according to "promise", have prophesied and dreamed dreams. Now when this promise is fulfilled in your experience, you will feel very glad and very happy. And you will feel thankful that you ever read this article with a humble, prayerful heart. And when you see the promised signs following your faith, as thousands have done in this day, then you will exclaim, Surely this is not merely the form, but also the power of godliness this kind of gospel is in very deed the power of God unto salvation to every one that believeth! And then if you have money, which so many worship, you will not be afraid to give a tenth to rear up a Temple like Solomon's, in which God will place the ark of His covenant, and reveal His will, through His servants the Prophets, for the benefit of all the ends of the earth. When you yourself have the promised gift of discerning of spirits, then you will not have to ask your neighbor who is an imposter and who is not — you will know from the Fountain Head all about it just as well as the next person.

He that is spiritual judgeth all things. Many things are hard to be understood and reconciled, which the unstable and unlearned stumble at, even as formerly he that is spiritual can easily judge all things, but he that is not spiritual can judge nothing correctly, for he is blind, and he cannot see afar off.

And further, when you see also the gross and beastly sexual abominations that are practiced and are increasing among all nations, without shame or fear, you will not marvel that God is determined to raise up a righteous seed and glorious branch, by re-establishing the Patriarchal Order, as in the days of Abraham, Jacob, David, Solomon, and Elkanah . Neither will you marvel, while the Spirit of God is upon you, that man and even women should sneer at the sacred institution of marriage being an institution wholly under the control of

God, as it was in the days of Abraham. Why should you not marvel at their sneers? Because, we have been distinctly and emphatically forewarned that in the last days there shall arise scoffers, walking after their own hearts' lusts, who shall speak evil of dignities and things that they know not, have men's persons in admiration because of gain. You would have more cause to marvel and disbelieve the scriptures of truth, if sensual men and women did not speak evil of the Patriarchal Order of marriage, and of men that conform to the pure sanction and penal restrictions of that most holy Order.

Now there are several ways in which the pure and obedient get revelations. It will be your privilege in due time to become acquainted with these various ways. One way is, through the inspiration of the Spirit. The Spirit is given to every man to profit withal. All men have such a measure of the Holy Spirit as to enable them to make a profitable use of the light and opportunities that they have and to obey the law under which they are placed. All the different methods of revelation are not probably given to all men now. God dispenseth His gifts severally as He will. The inspiration of the Almighty giveth understanding. Every various method of immediate revelation, however, always accords with the inspiration of the Spirit. If an holy angel talks with a man, what the angel speaks accords with the inspiration of the Holy Spirit. If the Urim and Thummim is consulted, it accords with the teachings of the Holy Spirit. An open vision or dream, each accords with the inspiration of the Holy Ghost. Now one mark of a dream from God is, that it is distinguished for the clearness and simplicity of the impress that it makes upon the mind of him that dreams. A dream from the Lord being always true in all its legitimate bearings, will be so disembarrassed from error and uncertainty to him that has the Spirit of truth in lively exercise, that he will know it perfectly in distinction from all false hallucinations or deceptions of the mind.

Reader, take your Bible and read the Bible account of dreams. There you will see that dreams from the Lord, for any important end, are plainly distinguishable from all deceptive influences. When Jacob went toward Haran and lay upon his stone pillow, and dreamed of seeing a ladder reaching up to heaven, etc., after he awoke he knew, beyond a doubt, that the dream was from God. Hence he says, "How terrible is this place," etc. When Laban wanted to cheat Jacob out of his just wages, the Lord appeared to Jacob in a night dream and told him how to increase the number of his cattle, so that he could get the advantage of the cheating employer. Jacob understood the dream perfectly, and so managed as to have the best of the increase fall to his share. When Joseph told the simple dream of the sheaves, his brothers all understood it well. And when he told the dream of the sun, moon, and eleven stars bowing down to him, his father Jacob felt the force of the meaning, although he rebuked Joseph.

When God gives a dream to a wicked man, He makes him fully to understand it, unless He wishes to hide the meaning from him. Abimelech understood his two dreams from the Lord, concerning Sarah, Abraham's wife. The Lord gave Solomon wisdom, and riches, and dominion, in a dream, and yet Solomon knew the import of the dream, and that the Lord had appeared to him, in that dream. The Lord does not suffer wicked spirits to foul and blot and mar a dream when he wants to communicate His mind and will in a dream. Foul spirits are rebuked and commanded to depart when God wants to indict the truth upon any one's mind. The Angel of God guards the dreamer till a clear and distinct impression is made. And that impression is of an unmistakable character, it cannot be misunderstood, any more than the light of the sun can be mistaken for the darkness of midnight. An open vision is another method of revelation. David saw an Angel of the Lord with a drawn sword, even the pestilence, standing between the heavens and the earth. The Prophet having prayed that the eyes of his servant might be opened, showed him that the armies of heaven were more numerous than the host of his enemies.

Another method of revelation is through the ministry of angels. An angel forewarned Lot to leave Sodom. Angels gave the Law to Moses, upon Mount Sinai. An angel opened a great iron gate that liberated the Apostle Peter. Again, God reveals things by Urim and Thummim, and by burnt offerings, and by diverse tongues, etc.

Now, reader, I entreat you to seek the aid of present revelations from God. You need them just as much as any poor creature ever did, that has been born into the world. Without them, you never can know God, worlds without end. Don't flatter yourself that because others know God or have formerly known Him, you are any better off on that account, unless you know Him for yourself.

Are you poor and oppressed? Then you have the greatest need to receive revelations from God. There are very many poor people in these days and in these lands. Even in England, rich men oppress you, and many cheat you and defraud you, and keep back your merited wages and you, who do the greatest part of the work that is done in the land, can hardly get an honest living, while your masters roll in pomp, and fare sumptuously every day. I have seen you and your little sons and tender daughters, hurrying off early in the morning to work for them, and returning late at night, poorly fed and poorly clothed often. And all the time that you are making others rich, they are keeping you in poverty and ignorance. And your daughters are often insulted and sometimes seduced by masters, and you are threatened with workhouse if you don't grind for the oppressor, and you have but little time to see your own families, and bless them with comforts, and educate and train them up for usefulness and salvation. Now, if you knew how to take counsel from the God of heaven, as Jacob did, you would not have to submit always to such fraud and oppression.

But God would help you out of your many difficulties, and your enemies could not help themselves. God has seen your afflictions, and has sent forth his servants to all nations to preach deliverance, for the acceptable year of the Lord has now come.

And ye rich men, the voice is to you. Gather up the poor and bless them, and your riches shall not waste, but increase fourfold and great shall be your reward in heaven. But blessed are the poor who shall obtain the gifts of revelation for themselves, for they shall rejoice greatly in the Holy One of Israel. For not many rich, not many noble, will be humble enough to seek revelations from God. But beware of the counsel of any priests or ministers who are hired and paid for preaching. God never hired any man to preach, nor did He ever authorize any man to hire himself out to preach for wages. Therefore beware of all such lest they deceive you. Go not after them, neither listen to them for a moment, for they are confederate with rich men and oppressors, and they are despisers of present revelation, and consequently they neither know God themselves nor are they willing that others should know Him. And vengeance will shortly overtake all that know not God and obey not the Gospel.

(Millennial Star, 30 April 1853, Volume 15, Pages 273-276, 289-292 - The article is attributed to Pres. John Taylor, and believed it was put together by Parley P. Pratt)

Chapter Forty-One
Podcast 041 Entering into The Rest of The Lord

In the days of the Prophet Joseph Smith, they had a popular book that was read by the members of the Church. The Prophet Joseph Smith studied it himself. It was used as one of the textbooks for the early Latter-day Saints as they studied the *New Testament* and what took place in the New Testament era. It's called *Foxe's Book of Martyrs,* by John Foxe. It has historical depictions of what took place with the Christian martyrs, all the way down through time. I'd just like to read some of this to you and there's a reason I want to do this. This is what they call *"the third persecution under Trajan,"* who was the Emperor of Rome, and the date is about 108 AD. The last of the apostles of Christ that were martyred, were killed about 68 – 70 AD; Paul and Peter and some of those.

> *In the third persecution, Pliny the Second, a man learned and famous, seeing the lamentable slaughter of Christians, and moved therewith to pity, wrote to Trajan* [the Emperor], *certifying him that there were many thousands of them **daily** put to death, of which none did any thing contrary to the Roman laws worthy of persecution.*

At this particular time, Christians were busily involved both above-ground and below-ground. Above-ground, they were being butchered and slaughtered and killed. Below-ground, they had caves and caverns that we call the catacombs of Rome. Maybe some of you have been in those. I have. They lived down underneath, in the catacombs, to escape persecution. They not only lived down there, but they also held their religious meetings, and their dead were buried down there. Back to the account:

> *The whole account they gave of their crime of error amounted to this—that they were accustomed on a stated day to meet before daylight, and to repeat together a set form of prayer to Christ as a God, and to bind themselves by an obligation—not in deed to commit wickedness; but on the contrary—never to commit theft, robbery, or adultery, never to falsify their word, never to defraud any man: after which it was their custom to separate, and reassemble to partake in common of a harmless meal.*

This is what they did that they were found guilty of death under the Roman Emperors.

> *In this persecution suffered the blessed martyr, Ignatius, who is held in famous reverence among very many. This Ignatius was appointed to the bishopric of Antioch next after Peter in succession.*

This is Peter's successor:

> *Some do say, that he, being sent from Syria to Rome, because he professed Christ, was given to the wild beasts to be devoured. It is also said of him, that when he passed through Asia, being under the most strict custody of his keepers, he strengthened and confirmed the churches through all the cities as he went, both with his exhortations and preaching of the Word of God. Accordingly, having come to Smyrna, he wrote to the Church at Rome, exhorting them **not to use means for his deliverance from martyrdom, lest they should deprive him of that which he most longed and hoped for.***

Now here's a quote from St. Ignatius:

> *Now I begin to be a disciple. I care for nothing, of visible or invisible things, so that I may but win Christ. Let fire and the cross, let the companies of wild beasts, let the breaking of bones and tearing of limbs, let the grinding of the whole body, and all the malice of the devil, come upon me; be it so, only may I win Christ Jesus!"* And even when he *was sentenced to be thrown to the beasts, such as the burning desire that he had to suffer, that he spake, what time he heard the lions roaring* [he's saying he's about ready to be thrown to the lions], *saying: "I am the wheat of Christ: I am going to be ground with the teeth of wild beasts, that I may be found pure bread.*

Isn't that marvelous? And that's just one example. There are so many in this book, and you can read about these if you'll go online and look up *Foxe's Book of Martyrs*. It was studied by, as I mentioned before, the early members of the Church. They looked upon it and read these great stories, and I'm sure that what they read had an effect on the *School of the Prophets* in Kirtland, Ohio because what the Christian martyrs experienced is quoted in the *Lectures on Faith*. So, I'm sure that this was an inspiration to Joseph and the early brethren and sisters, as they read upon these things. And the question must have come up: For a person facing this kind of torture and terrible death and suffering, how is it possible for them to meet that kind of a death with such confidence, with such praise, and with such optimism in Christ? How could they do that? That's the purpose of tonight's lesson, to find out how they could do that and then to prepare **us** for anything that might come, so that we can also have that confidence and that great forward-looking optimism that they had. They knew something about a martyr's death. A person who dies a martyr's death obtains eternal life. A martyr's death reward is eternal life in the Celestial Kingdom of God. These people knew that. But, more than just knowing that doctrine, they had something more that they were involved in. Now, this is what we call in the scriptures *"entering into the rest of the Lord."* That's tonight's lesson, *entering into the rest of the Lord.*

Student 1: Are you telling us that Reformers earned celestial glory?

Mike: I'm saying that those who die a martyr's death, in the cause of Christ, in any and all ages, obtain the reward of eternal life. Let me give you one example of that. In the original Quorum of the Twelve Apostles under Joseph Smith, one of the members of the quorum was a man named David W. Patton. Brother Patton was a remarkable man of faith who performed miracles. He had the gift of performing miracles, the gift of healing. Of the Twelve, in those days, he just stood apart in his faith and what he was able to accomplish because of faith. At one time, he went to the Prophet Joseph Smith, and he said; "Brother Joseph, I have requested of the Lord that he allow me to die a martyr's death."

Joseph turned to Brother Patton and said, "Brother David, your request saddens me. For when a man of your faith requests anything from the Lord, he generally gets it." Well, at Far West, Missouri when the Saints had been driven out of Independence, out of Jackson County, out of Caldwell County, out of Davis County, and they were up in Far West, and the mobs and the persecutors were on them day and night, some LDS men were kidnapped by the mob, and David Patton led the rescue group. David Patton had a moniker that the Latter-day Saints gave him. They called him "Captain Fear-not," and he led this group to rescue these hijacked and kidnapped Latter-day Saint men. Brother Patton and his group found the mob camped on what is called Crooked River, Missouri, and the battle ensued. He was able to free the hostages. One Mormon man was killed; a mobster was shot to death, maybe two. I hadn't looked at the story before I tell it to you tonight. But, Brother Patton was shot in the bowels and wounded horribly, what we would call a "gut shot." And as they tried to make their way back to Far West he begged them to stop the litter and not move because just carrying him on a litter was so excruciating that he couldn't bear the pain. Word had gotten back to Far West and his wife, so she and some of the Latter-day Saints met the returning party with Brother Patton in tow. As she knelt next to the litter, he looked upon her and said, "Whatever you do, remain faithful and true!" And then he died on that litter. He became the first apostolic martyr in the

Latter-day Restoration. The interesting thing was that he requested that because he understood the doctrine.

Now, I'd like to go over to Matthew 11. Let's go there for just a minute and look at some scriptures. Verse 28:

> *Come unto me, all ye that labour and are heavy laden, and I will give you **rest**.*

What I'd like to propose for you tonight is that this is much more than what we think:

> *[29]Take my yoke upon you, and **learn of me**;*

Do you see that? You've got to have some knowledge in order for you to access what the Lord is going to promise in these verses. It's going to require you to have knowledge beyond what you ordinarily have:

> *for I am meek and lowly in heart: and ye shall find **rest** unto your souls.*
>
> *[30] For my yoke is easy, and my burden is light.*

Now, that's our first take-off scripture. That's a scripture that is famous throughout Christianity and is quoted hundreds and hundreds of times. To find the peace of the Lord in this life so that you can deal with, and endure patiently, persecutions and the things that take place in the mortal world. But, the *Book of Mormon* takes it further and gives us additional insight. Let's go to Alma 12. The term for *entering into the rest of the Lord* is almost exclusively *Book of Mormon* doctrine, except for one place in the *New Testament*, Hebrews 4:1-11. Alma 12 is a great one that we kick-off on, and we want to go to verse 36:

> *And now, my brethren, behold I say unto you, that if ye will harden your hearts ye shall **not** enter into the rest of the Lord;*

Look at verse 35:

> *And whosoever will harden his heart and will do iniquity, behold, I swear in my wrath, that **he shall not enter into my rest**.*

Now, back down to the middle of verse 36 again:

> *therefore your iniquity provoketh him that he sendeth down his wrath upon you as in the first provocation, yea, according to his word in the last provocation as well as the first, to the everlasting destruction of your souls; therefore,*

according to his word, unto the last death, as well as the first.

"The first provocation" you can read about is in Exodus, where the Lord wanted to take the Children of Israel up to a sacred place under Moses' direction—a temple place—up to the mountain, and He wanted to bring them into His presence. We've talked about this in the past. He told them that it would take three days to sanctify themselves. He gave a list of things they should and should not do, and to be prepared on the third day to come up to the mountain and see God face to face. That's what He wanted to do. *"The first provocation"* means they provoked Him to wrath when they refused His invitation. That's *"the first provocation."* They provoked God. When a celestial, heavenly Being visits a mortal, telestial world, and that Being comes into this world and comes in glory and power and majesty and might, the physical elements of the telestial world are going to react. There's going to be some convulsion; there's going to be some fire, some lightning, and thunder, and that's what happened on the holy mountain. It scared the Children of Israel, and they ran *"and stood afar off."* They basically told Moses, "We don't want to talk to him; He scares us. You go talk to Him and tell us what He said." Because of that, they provoked God to wrath. Now, keep your finger here in Alma 12, and we'll come back to it. Remember, the key to stopping you from entering into *the rest of the Lord* is all over the scriptures; it says that you "harden your heart." We'll come back to what that means in just a minute. Let's go to *Doctrine and Covenants* 84:23:

Now this Moses plainly taught to the children of Israel in the wilderness, and sought diligently to sanctify his people that they might behold the face of God;

That was his goal:

*[24] But they **hardened their hearts** and could not endure his presence; therefore, the Lord in his wrath, for his anger was kindled against them,*

There's your *"first provocation"* that Alma 12 is talking about: *swore that they should not enter into his rest while in the wilderness,*

That's in this world. Most people who think about this doctrine of *entering into the rest of the Lord* are pushing that into some place in the future, and it can be. But, like we've talked about so many other times, that is a default. The rest of verse 24 says:

which rest is the fulness of his glory.

Now, you want to mark that; you want to find out what *the rest of the Lord* is. That just defined it right there. *The rest of the Lord* is to enter into and obtain a fullness of His glory. We'll come back to that in just a minute. So, now let's go back to Alma 12 again. The *"first provocation"* was that they rejected the invitation for a face to face meeting with the God of Abraham, Isaac, and Jacob.

Now, what's this second provocation? The second provocation is down into our day because that invitation has been extended again. You don't want to provoke Him. The way you provoke God is you trample under your feet the Holy One. In other words, He makes an invitation for you to make a covenant with Him and you make a conscious choice to reject that invitation. That provokes Him. Being provoked means that, by law, He has to withdraw Himself from you. He will not force Himself on you. So, if He issues an invitation to you to do something like what we're talking about tonight, *to enter into His rest* and you reject that, for whatever reason, He will withdraw His Spirit. You will now inherit a legacy of darkness and confusion, instead of obtaining the promises of light and His presence and glory. In Alma 12:37 He's talking to His people in those days, but we now want to bring that up to us:

> *And now, my brethren, seeing we know these things, and they are true, let us repent, and harden not our hearts,* **that we provoke not the Lord our God...**

Do you see it? We can do it and are doing it. If we reject these kinds of doctrines, if we withdraw from the mysteries, if we harden our heart and withdraw from these mysteries, which Alma earlier in this chapter called *"the greater portion of the word,"* then He will:

> *...pull down his wrath upon us in these his second commandments which he has given unto us; but*

let us enter into the rest of God, which is prepared according to his word.

There's the invitation. Most people throughout history will reject God's invitations. Most people will reject them. Let's look at a couple of other scriptures. Let's go to Alma 13. This one follows on with what Alma was teaching in chapter 12. We want to go to Alma 13:12. Now, brothers and sisters, a point of note for you is this: the first nine verses are talking about the premortal life. You can see that verse 9 says, *"And thus it is. Amen."* That ends that discourse on the premortal life, and he's talking about obtaining promises in the premortal life. Let's go back for just a minute to verse 6. This is talking about men who are foreordained to the Holy Order of the Priesthood of God before they were born. Joseph Smith said that:

Every man who has a calling to minister to the inhabitants of the world was ordained to that very purpose in the Grand Council of heaven before this world was. I suppose that I was ordained to this very office in that Grand Council.

Now, go to verse 6. Keep in mind that this is talking about the premortal life:

[6] And thus being called by this holy calling, and ordained unto the high priesthood of the holy order of God,

This happened in the premortal life, not here:

to teach his commandments unto the children of men, that they also **might**...

"*Might*" is a key word to know we are talking about in the future:

...that they also might enter into his rest.

It's pointing toward something that is coming in mortality. Let's go on over and look at verse 12. Now, we're in the telestial world, and you have been **re**-ordained to this priesthood in the telestial world with a physical body, this priesthood that you were **fore**ordained to before you came here. Verse 12:

Now they, after being sanctified by the Holy Ghost [speaking of men in this world], *having their garments made white, being pure and spotless before God, could not look upon sin save*

> *it* were *with abhorrence; and there were many, exceedingly great many, who were* **made pure** *and entered into the rest of the Lord their God.*

So, what are some things we see there? What things are necessary for us to enter into *the rest of the Lord?*
Verse 11:

> *sanctified; their garments are washed white through the blood of the Lamb.*

Verse 12:

> *sanctified by the Holy Ghost, having their garments made white, being pure and spotless before God, could not look upon sin save it with abhorrence,*

You have a mighty change of heart. And because of that, you are made pure, white, spotless, sanctified, and:

> *...enter into the rest of the Lord their God.*

Now, that's in this life. This was the point I wanted to make to you: that's in this life. See? Look at verse 13:

> *And now, my brethren, I would that ye should* **humble yourselves** [here's another key word] *before God, and* **bring forth fruit meet for repentance**, *that ye may also enter into that rest.*

Let's skip to verse 16. See, this doctrine is heavy in the *Book of Mormon*:

> *Now these ordinances were given after this manner, that thereby the people might look forward on the Son of God, it being a type of his order, or it being his order, and this that they might look forward* [here we go, it's another prerequisite] *to him for a* **remission of their sins**, *that they might enter into the rest of the Lord.*

What's another thing required? You have to obtain something called a *remission of sins*. So, we are starting to get a pattern here. Let me ask you a question. With all of this *Book of Mormon* information that we have, here's the question: Is it possible for a person, who is not a member of the Church, to enter into, what the *Book of Mormon* calls, *the rest of The Lord* in this life, in a telestial world? I am going to say that it is not possible. Here's why; a remission of sins (in verse 16) is absolutely a prerequisite for entering into *the rest of the Lord*. I want you to go with me to 3 Nephi. Let's get the scriptures going for us; let's be scripture detectives. I've said before that forgiveness of sins is different than *remission of sins*. You don't have to be a member to receive a forgiveness of sins. There are people throughout the Christian world that have faith in Jesus Christ that can have their sins forgiven, through faith in Him. The Biblical narrative is clear on that. However, a *remission of sins* is different. A forgiveness of sins puts you in a state of *justification* and leads toward, or can lead toward, covenant relationship and ordinances. A *remission of sins* not only puts you in a position where you are not accountable for your sins before the bar of God, but it heals all of the effects of sin. You are made **whole**, and all of the spiritual scars and effects of sin and transgression are removed through the *remission of sins*. Notice what it says in 3 Nephi, chapter 12. It talks about the baptismal ordinance. We've gone over this a lot. Verse 1 is a big, long verse; go to the middle:

> *Blessed are ye if ye shall give heed unto the words*
> *of these twelve whom I have chosen from among*
> *you to minister unto you,*

It is the first *Beatitude* of the *Sermon at the Temple*, which corresponds with the *Sermon on the Mount*. But this *Beatitude* is not in Matthew. This is only found here. This is very different. The Matthew one starts down in verse 3 where it says, *"blessed are the poor in spirit,"* and in verse 4, *"blessed are all they that mourn."* You see, that's Matthew; we can get that over in Matthew. But, verses 1 and 2 are only found in 3 Nephi, and it's the first *Beatitude*. It's the missing Biblical *Beatitude*, and in the middle of verse 1 the Lord says:

> *Blessed are ye if ye shall give heed unto the words*
> *of these twelve whom I have chosen from among*
> *you to minister unto you, and to be your servants;*
> *and unto them I have given power that they may*
> *baptize you with water;*

That's the first half of the baptismal ordinance. We've talked about that. It's water baptism. Joseph said that if you don't go any further than this, you might as well baptize a bag of sand; it means nothing. But it is necessary as the first step in the ordinance, and then watch what it says:

> *and after that ye are baptized with water, behold,*
> *I* [Christ] *will baptize you with fire and with the*
> *Holy Ghost;*

That completes the baptismal ordinances. There are three phases to the baptismal ordinance. Number one is water. Number two is confirmation by the laying on of hands. And number three is the baptism of fire and the Holy Ghost, which is performed by immortals. The first half of the baptismal ordinance is performed by authorized mortal beings. They baptize you in water and using their hands. They lay their hands upon you and confirm you. But the last part, the sealing, crowning part of the baptismal ordinance is *baptism of fire and the Holy Ghost,* and Christ does that. Now, go down to verse 2:

> *And again, more blessed are they who shall*
> *believe in your words because that ye shall testify*
> *that ye have seen me, and that ye know that I am.*

This is us. We weren't there at the temple. So, this is now talking to us, reading this account:

> *Yea, blessed are they who shall believe in your*
> *words, and come down into the depths of humility*
> *and be baptized,* [with water, that's all of us, we've done that] *for* **they shall be visited with fire and with the Holy Ghost, and shall receive a remission of their sins.**

Now, if you look back in Alma 13, verse 16, you'll see that to enter into *the rest of the Lord,* you must have the completed baptismal ordinance done—the whole thing; not just by water, not just confirmed in a Sacrament meeting or after baptism, but you have to have *the baptism of fire*, which remits your sins, heals the effects of sins, and makes you whole and complete. Isn't that great stuff? Comments?

Student 4: The last line of verse 1 says, *"and be baptized, after that ye have seen me and know that I am."* And then in the middle of verse 2, He says the same thing, *"ye shall testify that ye have seen me, and that ye know that I am."*

Mike: Good insight! I have not seen that before, brother. Way to go! What we're trying to do is find out the definition of *entering into the rest of the Lord*. What have we got thus far? Baptism is necessary. You need to be baptized by authority—the complete ordinance: being made whole and complete, pure and cleansed, and sanctified by the Holy Ghost. And I'll even take it a step further: you are going to have to obtain promises from God's own mouth in order to *enter into the rest of the Lord* in this life.

Let's go to Moroni 7. Moroni chapter 7 gives us some more information. See, again I want you to understand that most people who look at this are looking at it in the future. We in this telestial world want to push the lofty things off into the next world. We've talked about this before. We want to do that with this also, but here's the point: we started out this lesson by reading an account of how early Christian martyrs could suffer what they did. I'm going to take you to the *Sixth Lecture on Faith* in just a minute. How could they have done this? Well, they could do it because they had a knowledge that surpassed the veil. They had accomplished what we call, *entering into the rest of the Lord*, and when you do that, what happens to you in this life and the physical body doesn't matter anymore. Moroni 7:3:

> *Wherefore, I would speak unto you that are of the church, that are the peaceable followers of Christ,*

Now, that right there tells you that we are in a very select group of people. These are people who have been baptized members of the Church. Next:

> *and that have obtained a sufficient hope*

Now, we've talked about *hope* before, and that's not the worldly hope of, "Lord willing and the creek don't rise, I hope I make it and everything will work out right." That's a hope that puts you out of control, and it's based on wishing. The *hope* that Moroni is talking about here is a *sure* knowledge that can only come to you from revelation, and I'm going to say **higher** revelation. So, those who *"have obtained a sufficient hope:"*

> *by which ye can enter into the rest of the Lord, from this time henceforth* [from this time means in mortality forward] *until ye shall rest with him in heaven.*

Obtaining *the rest of the Lord* in the telestial world **guarantees** that you will have that *rest* in the world to come. It's a guarantee. You cannot obtain it here and not have it there. So, now we are coming into areas where we talk about *calling and election made* *sure*; all the doctrines we have talked about. *Entering into the Rest of the Lord* in this life means you know something above and beyond the veiled existence of the telestial world. You've obtained something.

Now, in conclusion here, to show you what we are talking about, I'd like to take you to the *Sixth Lecture on Faith*. It kind of ties this all together. In the *Sixth Lecture on Faith*, we have what is called the *Law of Sacrifice*. Now, if we were going to interpret and describe and define *entering into the rest of the Lord*, I think we would say that you've had your *calling and election made sure*, you've obtained something called *the more sure word of prophecy*, which in the temple is referred to as *conversing with the Lord through the veil*. That's making your *calling and election sure* through a process called *the more sure word of prophecy*. This is where the brother of Jared obtained a sure promise from God's own mouth, which gives him (here's a key word) the **confidence** necessary to rip that veil, and with that **confidence**, demand that the Lord show Himself to him. And that's exactly what he did. In Ether 3:9, when he sees His finger, the Lord said:

> *Sawest thou more than this?*
> *[10] And he answered, Nay; Lord, show thyself unto me.*

That's the difference there. And he obtains that **confidence** because of promises he had gotten earlier by conversing with the Lord through the veil. Let me just read to you a couple of things from the *Sixth Lecture on Faith*. This is marvelous and is one of my favorite lectures of all of them, Six and Seven. Five I like, but Six is a great one. It starts out by saying:

> *Having treated in the preceding lectures of the ideas of the character, perfections, and attributes of God, we next proceed to treat of the **knowledge which persons must have** that the course of life which they pursue is according to the will of God, in order that they may be enabled to exercise faith in him unto life and salvation.*

What this lecture is saying is that each one of us must obtain for ourselves a knowledge from God that the course you're pursuing is according to His will. That's not a supposition or a, "Gosh, I hope I'm doing the right thing. I hope he's pleased with me." You have to **know** He is. When you start to get into this area of obtaining this knowledge, you are now knocking on the door of *entering into the rest of the Lord*. In paragraph 2, he goes on and says:

> *This knowledge supplies an important place in revealed religion; for it was by reason of it* [this knowledge]

Now, think about how we started out the lesson tonight with the Christian martyrs. It was by reason of this knowledge:

> *that the ancients were enabled to endure as seeing him who is invisible.*

You see, they hadn't obtained the *Second Comforter* yet. They had not seen and touched something, but they had **heard** something. They had heard the voice of God call them by their familiar name and had obtained promises by His own voice, from His own mouth, with an oath from Him that these promises are secured and will be realized in their lives:

> *An actual knowledge to any person that the course of life which he pursues is according to the will of God, is essentially necessary to enable him to have that confidence in God, without which no person can obtain eternal life. It was this that enabled the ancient saints to endure all their afflictions and persecutions, and to take joyfully the spoiling of their goods, knowing (not believing merely) that they had a more "enduring substance."*

Paragraph 3:

> *Having the assurance...*

Think of that word assurance and the word right in the middle of assurance is *sure*:

> *that they were pursuing a course that was agreeable to the will of God... knowing (not merely believing) that when this earthly house of their early tabernacle was dissolved, they had a building of God, a house "not made with hands, eternal in the heavens."*

One of those Christian martyr stories that is so touching, took place under Nero. It's a whole family that was brought into the Coliseum arena. Now, get a picture of this, will you? These are baptized members of the Church, of the *New Testament* Church. They are in the Coliseum; there are 60,000 people screaming around them and here's a mother and a father with their little children standing huddled with each other, with their arms around each other, standing in the middle of the arena. They open the arena doors and they let loose lions and tigers and bears that have been starved on purpose. These animals are starved, and they are ferocious with starvation. And do you know what that father and that mother did? I can hardly talk about it. They sing a hymn as these animals come in and kill the whole family in front of 60,000 screaming Romans. Now, that father and that mother: where did they get that from? They got it from what we are talking about here tonight! The *New Testament* saints obtained, brothers and sisters, the *Church of the First Born*. They had communion with the *General Assembly in the Church of Enoch*. They were familiar with the *spirits of just men made perfect* and translated beings, who came down from the city of Enoch and ministered to them. They had that! They had *entered into the rest of the Lord*. So, as it says here in paragraph 3:

> *knowing (not merely believing) that when this earthly house of their tabernacle was dissolved, they had a building of God, a house "not made with hands, eternal in the heavens. (1 Corinthians verse 1)*

Let me read to you something else the Prophet Joseph Smith said. It's all about views, how you view yourself in this world and your relationship with other people. Listen to what the Prophet Joseph Smith said. This is what happens when you come into this level of discipleship:

> *We consider that God has created man with a mind capable of instruction, and a faculty which may be enlarged in proportion to the heed and diligence given to the light communicated from heaven to the intellect; and that the nearer man [or woman] approaches perfection, **the clearer are his views**, and the greater his enjoyments, till*

> *he has overcome the evils of his life and lost every desire for sin;*

Now think about these ancient saints as Joseph goes on:
> *and like the ancients, arrives at that point of faith where he is wrapped in the power and glory of his Maker, and is caught up to dwell with Him.*

That's what we're talking about here. One last thing as we end tonight's lesson. From *Lecture Six*, part 4:
> *Such was, and always will be, the situation of the saints of God, that **unless they have an actual knowledge** that the course that they are pursuing is according to the will of God, **they will grow weary in their minds and faint**;*

This is what's happening to the tens of thousands of Latter-day Saints who are leaving church activity. I had a man this week ask me a question about why I thought there were so many people that choose to leave the Church. In my mind, there are lots of different reasons, and I outlined five or six of them. But number one in my mind is that they have not obtained the *baptism of fire and the Holy Ghost*. And the reason they haven't obtained it is because too many of them think they got it when they were confirmed a member and somebody put their hands on their heads and said, "Receive the Holy Ghost." Why should you seek for something if you feel you have already obtained it? This is like what we talked about last week, the Lord said in Isaiah 5:13:
> *Therefore **my people** are gone into captivity, because **they have no knowledge**.*

Going back to part 4:
> *they will grow weary in their minds and faint; for such has been, and always will be, the opposition in the hearts of unbelievers and those that know not God, against the pure and unadulterated religion of heaven (the only thing which **ensures** eternal life),*

See, what we are talking about here tonight, brothers and sisters is *"the pure and unadulterated religion of heaven."* But, you have to get into the scriptures to know this. You can't be scripturally illiterate and not putting forth an effort to search

God's word and expect to obtain these holy promises. You can't do it. Going on it says:

> *that they will persecute to the uttermost all that worship God according to his revelations, receive the truth in the love of it, and submit themselves to be guided and directed by his will, and drive them to such extremities that* **nothing short of an actual knowledge of their being the favorites of heaven,**

I love that statement! That ties in with another *Book of Mormon* doctrine that says you are *"highly favored of the Lord."* See, all of this is talking about higher things here. None of this is *"the lesser portion of the word."* This is *"the greater portion."* These are the *mysteries of God* that you can have if you will ask, seek, and knock:

> *nothing short of an actual knowledge of their being the favorites of heaven, and of their having embraced* **that order of things**

See, that's a higher order of things. It's a higher order of knowledge, a higher order of blessings, a higher order of covenants, a higher order of priesthood, and a higher order of promises:

> *which God has established for the redemption of man, will enable them to exercise that confidence in him necessary for them to overcome the world, and obtain that crown of glory which is laid up for them that fear God* [fear/reverence].

Then the rest of the lecture talks about how you obtain this is through sacrifice. The whole *Sixth Lecture* is on sacrifice. If you want to *enter into the rest of the Lord*, it is going to require sacrifice. If you want to have the blessings of Abraham, Isaac, and Jacob, you're going to be required to sacrifice to the same extent they did, to obtain the place that they have.

On the back of the dust-cover of Neal A. Maxwell's book, *A Disciple's Life* is one sentence I want to share. The book is about 560 pages, but on the back is this one sentence taken out of it:

> *If we are serious about our discipleship, Jesus will eventually request each of us to do those very things which are the most difficult for us to do.*

That's the summary statement of that whole book on Neal Maxwell; sacrifice. Remember one thing, the Lord will not require of you that which you are not prepared to offer and fulfill. He won't do it. One of the things you may want to consider to ask in your prayers is, *"What is required of me Father, at this point to obtain these blessings of which I am learning?"*

Tonight's lesson is *the rest of the Lord*. It's a summary of about five or six other podcasts on holy promises that God gives to those who will pay the price. There is a sacrifice called the *Abrahamic Sacrifice*. Each person who wants an inheritance with Abraham, Isaac, and Jacob and all the Holy Fathers who go no more out, will have to come up to the knowledge and pay the price through the sacrifice required to enter in. I want you to know that when the Lord requires it from you, you are fully prepared to do it or He won't require it. He is not in the business of condemning and destroying His children. But if you want to be where He is, there is only one pathway to it, and sacrifice is emblazoned along the way. Do any of you have any comments?

Student 4: Basically then, when the Lord appeared to these people (2,500 at first, in the *Book of Mormon)*, they really were taught all the principles of the gospel, now they had seen, now they had heard, now they had felt, and now they had *entered into the rest of the Lord*, and this was why they were able to preserve themselves over two hundred years. Is that what you're saying?

Mike: That's well said. What I'm saying is that with this, we can meet any of the tests that are coming that are required for us, and we knew about them before we were born. There is nothing happening to you in this life that you did not know about and agree to before you came here. This is your path. You knew about it; you researched it with heavenly beings, probably beings who had been on that path before you, and who could counsel you in wisdom because they had already traversed it. They were counselors to you as you entered into the one room school house. Maybe some of them said, "That might be a little bit more for you at this time and this experience than you want to take on." There must have been wisdom and prudence involved in those preschool counseling sessions because again, the purpose is to succeed, not fail; succeed! This is where knowledge comes in.

You have the knowledge of this, and this is the beauty of it, none of this was new to any of us. We've just been caused to forget it, and now we're experiencing something similar in this life to what we did in the premortal life, only with a body. Don't think for a minute that you didn't have your trials and sacrifices, your anointings, your endowments, your blessings and ordinations before you came here. Everything that's taking place in this life is a pattern of the way things were before and the way things will be in the world to come. That's how you discern the *mysteries of God*, by learning to seek for and understand patterns. So yeah, they were able to do this.

What do you think it was that David W. Patton knew as a result of his time in the *School of the Prophets*? It was personal revelation, piercing the veil, having the ministration of angels and the *spirits of just men*, communing with the *Assembly of the Church of the First Born*. What do you think he learned through it all that would enable him to go to Joseph and say, "Joseph, I have asked the Lord to allow me to die a martyr's death." Certainly, we don't think that that was just an off the cuff, random statement. That statement comes because Brother Patton had deep revealed knowledge of the *mysteries of God*. He understood something, or he would have never made that request. So yes, all of these things, step by step.

I love Brother John Pontius' writings! I was listening to "The UnBlog Reunion." This is where a bunch of the people gathered before Brother Pontius died. And as I was listening to this blog the other day, he said again, "God will never ask you or require you to do anything, but that he doesn't prepare you for the task. And if you feel called to a certain direction, know this, that you would not feel the call unless the preparation to fulfill that assignment accompanied it." Basically, that's 1 Nephi 3:7:

> *...the Lord giveth no commandments unto the children of men, save he shall prepare a way for them that they may accomplish the thing which he commandeth them.*

So, as you listen to any of these podcasts or anything that has to do with the Restoration, if you feel impressed, if the Holy Ghost inspires you, enlightens your mind, and you have a new idea or you feel that's your future, or this is something I've heard before, that is part of preparing you to fulfill the very thing that's been revealed to you.

Well, thank you so much. It has been fun to be with you tonight. So, bless your hearts and God bless you, keep you safe and increase your faith until it becomes unshakeable.

References:
Foxes' Book of Martyrs, by John Foxe
Alma 13:12 *"...[enter] into the rest of the Lord..."*
Matthew 11:28-30
Hebrews 4:1-11, *New Testament* reference to entering the rest of the Lord.
Alma 12:35-36
D&C 84:23
Exodus 20:18 "...and stood afar off."
Alma 12:37
Alma 12:10 "...the greater portion of the word..."
Alma 13:1-9 (referring to premortal life)
Joseph Smith, *History of the Church*, 6:364
Alma 13:6, 11-13, 16
3 Nephi 12:1-2
Joseph Smith: "You might as well baptize a bag of sand as a man, if not done in view of the remission of sins and getting of the Holy Ghost." *History of the Church,* 5:499
Moroni 7:3
Ether 3:9-10
Lectures on Faith 6:1-4
Joseph Smith, *History of the Church,* 2:8
Isaiah 5:13
1 Nephi 1:1; Alma 48:20; Ether 1:34 "highly favored of the Lord"
Alma 12:10 "...lesser portion of the word..."
A Disciple's Life: The Biography of Neal A. Maxwell, by Bruce C. Hafen
John Pontius 2012 UnBlog Family Reunion recordings:
https://unblogmysoul.wordpress.com/books-downloads-more/unblog-family-reunion/
1 Nephi 3:7

Chapter Forty-Two
Podcast 042 Peace and Safety

This week as I was reading the scriptures I had a strong impression that I needed to talk about something with you tonight, and it may be very time-appropriate with everything that's been going on in the world. I'd like to share with you a few things about me for just a moment. The reason I'm doing that is to set a precedent, kind of a foundation about what I want to talk about during the class.

I came from a background of inactivity. My mom and dad were both members but were not active in the Church. So, as a young man, I grew up never going to Primary or Aaronic Priesthood functions. I grew up in a home where I had good parents, but as far as religion and church were concerned, I didn't have much influence there. But, I did fall in love with a girl who was a very active Latter-day Saint young woman. We dated for a couple of years, but after I took her out on our first date, she let it be known to me that she would never marry or consider marrying anyone but a returned missionary, and it had to be in the temple. That had been her goal from day one, and I was about as far away from those kind of things as you could be. I grew up in the streets of Salt Lake City and belonged to a gang there called the "Panthers." My dad was a police officer, and my mom and dad had no idea what their boy was involved in behind the scenes. They didn't find out until later on when I was an adult and had repented sorely for some of my activities there. I wanted to marry this gal when I was 19 years old. She was three years younger than me, but she just let it be known that that was not in the ballpark. I tried to persuade her with every bit of convincing dialogue that I had that we should get married, that we loved each other, etc. About this time, things went south on me. I had a hot rod Chevrolet, a '56 Chevy with a Corvette motor in it. It got me into all kinds of trouble. I had my driver's license taken away for exhibition of acceleration, lost my job, and about this time my bishop, that I only saw because I went to church with my girlfriend, called me into his office and asked if I wanted to consider going on a mission. After I had a good laugh and looked at him and saw that he was dead serious, I declined and went away. At that point, things seemed to go further south for me. Everything seemed to go badly. After a period of time, this same bishop called me in and said, "Are you sure you wouldn't like to consider going on a mission?"

At that point, my thought was, "Well, why not." My girlfriend needs to get a few more years under her belt; she needs to graduate from high school. My interesting thought about serving a mission was that maybe I could learn a foreign language. I thought this in the back of my pea-head brain that maybe a foreign language would be a benefit to me as I searched out a career and decided what I wanted to do with my life. So, I said "Yes," and I don't believe there was anybody as unprepared to go on a mission as I was at that time. I don't believe I had ever said a prayer and had never read the scriptures. If there were any prayers ever spoken, it was when dad and I went to go duck hunting or pheasant hunting, and mom had a little prayer with us to make sure that we came back safely. That was about the extent of our prayers.

And so, it wasn't too long until the bishop asked me, "By the way, where would you like to go?"

I said, "Anywhere but Germany!" The reason I had such a bad feeling for Germany was that I didn't graduate from high school on time because I failed an English course. So, half of that year they let me take a foreign language, instead of English. Well, I took German, and it was because of the German language I studied that I didn't graduate from high school. I had to go back to night school and make up my degree. So, I had kind of a bad taste in my mouth about Germans. I thought they were all Nazi's at that point.

So the mission call comes, and my mom and dad are so excited for me. We opened it up, and it said, "You have been called to serve a mission in Bavaria." I remember thinking, "Bavaria? Isn't that a communist country? Where is Bavaria?" We looked it up and, low and behold it's southern Germany! You talk about poetic justice. So, I got called for 2 ½ years to go on a mission to Germany. The reason we went 2 ½ years in those days was because there was no Language Training Mission; there was no MTC. You just went up to a mission home, which was where the Deseret Gym used to be, across the street from the Church Office Buildings. You went in there for a week, you received your temple endowments, and they set you apart. Boyd K. Packer set me apart to serve that mission. So, we went for 2 ½ years, and that extra six months served as your Language Training Mission. They put you out on the streets, and you had six months to learn the language and two years to preach the gospel.

There were no native German companions in those days, so all of them were English speaking Americans. They gave you a missionary companion that spoke excellent German and that man was told by the mission president, "Do not speak any English at all with your companion." So, it was literally "root hog or die" in learning the German language. You learned it just because that was all you could do. There was no other way to do it within six months. So, it worked, and I was speaking, reading, and writing German fluently. But an interesting thing happened. I was so unprepared. I was in the mission field for one reason. I loved this girl, and she would not marry me unless I served a mission and could take her to the temple. It wasn't six weeks into the mission when I found out this was a horrible mistake! I was with a great missionary companion, a man that just wanted to be on a mission and he taught at BYU, and his name was Elder Calvin Bartholomew. Brother Bartholomew was just the kind of missionary that you wanted to be, and I was everything opposite of what you should be. One thing led to another, and he and I had an altercation, and I left him asleep one night, hopped a train and went to Munich, and I was going home. I'd made up my mind that this was a big mistake and even though I didn't really want to go home, I felt that there was just no way I could look at 2 ½ years doing this. How can I teach the gospel to the German people and be an ambassador for Christ? I don't even know that it's true. I don't know anything about it. So, that next morning, I found myself at the mission home on the front door of the President's office. He came in early in the morning and asked, "What are you doing here? And where's your companion?"

I said, "I left him asleep down in Southern Bavaria, and I'm here because I'm going home. This was a big mistake."

He said to come on in for a minute, and so I went in and stood there. He said, "Why don't you sit down?"

I said, "I'm not going to sit down; I'm not going to be here that long. I'm just here for one reason. I want to find out if you're going to help me get home or do I have to hitchhike across Europe and stow away on a ship? One way or another, I'm going home."

He said, "Sit down."

I said, "All right, but we're not going to take very long at this." Then I told him what had happened and I told him what a big mistake it was. On the train that night I had thought about all the reasons he was going to give me about why I should not go home and how he would try to get me to stay. I thought I had what he was going to say all figured out. I told him what was happening and what I wanted to do, and he looked at me, and when it was all said and done, he just stopped.

Now, this is President Owen Spencer Jacobs who was a potato farmer from Idaho. He looked at me and said, "Do you know what your problem is Elder Stroud?"

I said, "No, why don't you tell me what my problem is."

He said, "Well, you're nothing but a fat, rotten, spoiled brat!" And that was exactly the thing that I had **not** rehearsed him saying to me.

I stood up, leaned across the desk, and I put my fist in the middle of the desk, and said, "Why, for two cents I'd pick you up and throw you through that window."

He came up out of his chair and put his fist in the middle of the desk, and it was nose to nose and eyeball to eyeball. I outweighed him by probably eighty pounds and was a foot taller than he was, and he looked at me, and he said, "Son, you're not man enough. Sit down!" He just took all the wind out of my sail, and I didn't know what to do. He just took away everything I had by what he said.

Then we sat down for a while, and we talked and determined that I really didn't want to go. I didn't want to disappoint my girlfriend, and I didn't want to disappoint my mom and dad. Everybody was so thrilled that I was in the mission field; everybody but me! And so, we sat down and talked about what the problem was and came up with a solution. The solution was this: "I'll make you a deal," President Jacobs said. "I'm going to transfer you up close to the mission home here in Munich. I don't want you to work in the field. I want you to do an experiment. I want you to read the *Book of Mormon* through from cover to cover. I want you to pray about it every day. I want you to start at the very first page, and I want you to go to the last page. And when you get to the last page, if you still want to go home, then I will see to it that you go home. I want you to call me and report in every day and tell me about your progress." Well, I thought that was fair enough, because really, again brothers and sisters, I didn't want to go home. I just couldn't see myself staying there for 2 ½ years and feeling what I was feeling at that point: frustrated, scared, and angry. All of the human emotions were just boiling around me. But I decided to take him up on that. He gave me a companion who was a surfer from Redondo Beach, California, and he was more like me. He had come from a little bit of a rebel background but had gotten his life squared away before he came. His name was Elder Erwin. Then I had another one called Elder Scott, and those were the only missionaries I remember because they played such an important role in my life.

Before we left the mission president's office, he asked me to come over and kneel down and pray with him, and he asked me to say the prayer. I'd never said a prayer, and I told him that. I said, "I don't know how to pray!" Isn't that a sad situation? Think about what missionaries are required to do now and how the bar was raised a few years back. Well, they wouldn't take a missionary like me now, but I'm so grateful they did then.

I told him I didn't know how to pray and we knelt down, and he said, "I'll help you." So, he taught me like a primary teacher helping a little primary kid to say a prayer. You know: bow your head, close your eyes, and fold your arms. "Heavenly Father, we thank thee," that kind of a thing. And then he prayed for me. I can't remember the words, but I remember what I felt. I felt something I hadn't felt before. I felt like this man was actually talking to somebody in that room! When we got up, he embraced me, and like I said, I was probably a foot taller than he was and outweighed him by eighty pounds. But he just put his arms around my chest, and I remember looking down on his little bald head, and he said, "Elder Stroud, I love you." And that started our experiment. You know, he treated me like a non-member. He treated me for what I was. At that point in 1963, I knew nothing, and I mean nothing!

We started our experiment reading the *Book of Mormon*. I started reading 1 Nephi. I read it every day, and I prayed about it the best I could and tried to apply it and do what he taught me to do. My companion was very, very patient with me. We didn't work. He was to babysit me while I was involved with this experiment. Every day I'd check in, and he'd say, "Are you praying about it?"

"Yes."

"What's happening?"

"Nothing." I got into Alma, and when I reported in, I said, "Boy, this is sure boring. What's all this war and all this kind of stuff in there? I'm just so bored."

And he said, "Remember our deal? You've got to go all the way to the end of the book."

And so, one night we were in our apartment in Munich. It was an attic apartment and had one of these skylights you could open up. My companion was asleep over in his bed, and I was sitting at the table reading in 3 Nephi. I came to verse 8, where that huge storm hit the Nephite people, and the tremendous destruction occurred. Something happened then. Now, I don't know what it was, but as I was looking at the pages in the book, I seemed to almost be able to view the terrible destruction and calamity that was going on. It was so real that I thought I could almost hear the screams and yells of the people. It was so real to me that it wouldn't take much to smell the smoke of the burning buildings. I went through that whole thing. As I read those words, it was more like viewing what happened than it was reading the words on the book. It went through the three days of darkness, and I got a feel for what that was like. Then I had a feeling when Christ appeared in the eleventh chapter. And when He came down and appeared at the temple in the city Bountiful and said to the people, *"Behold, I am Jesus Christ, whom the prophets testified shall come into the world,"* I received a witness by the Holy Ghost that that actually happened. I've never forgotten that and it has provided an anchor for me.

In the ensuing years, there have been times when I struggled with activity. There have been times when I struggled with addictive behavior, but that anchor has always been there; a place where I could return to. When I was in turmoil, and when the trials and adversity were the greatest, and with everything else that has happened to me in my life—various priesthood assignments, and almost thirty years in the Church Education System—with all of that, it was the *Book of Mormon* and personal revelation that provided an anchor for me. It was just burned into my soul, and even though I might doubt some things, I could never, and have never doubted the truthfulness of the *Book of Mormon*. I received that abiding testimony. And I just wanted to share that experience.

I'd like to share with you a thought that I had this week. We're living now, at a time in our day, where the events that took place and that I saw and viewed in 3 Nephi, are taking place again. President Benson said that these chapters at the end of Helaman on up to 3 Nephi, portray our day and are a pattern of what will happen in our day. Those of you who are Isaiah students and have studied Avraham Gileadi's writings, isn't it interesting to see that history repeats itself and that when the prophets, especially Isaiah, speak, they speak of things that are happening in their day and things that have happened in their past, and that they portray those things as the exact pattern of things that will happen in the future? It's just remarkable.

So, I've got a lot of thoughts on my mind that I'd like to share with you. Let's go over to 3 Nephi, chapter 6 for just a minute. We can see some things that are taking place. If you'll go to the chapter heading, it says:

> *The Nephites prosper—Pride, wealth, and class distinctions arise—*

I don't think it takes a rocket scientist to see those very things in our day. The class distinctions are part of the removal of the middle class and the allocation of wealth so that those on the top end have it all, and there's no middle class by design, and the rest of the population reside in poverty. Now, Margie and I have been on missions in places in the world where we have seen societies where the middle class was eradicated. We've seen where corruption at the top and in the government was so rampant, filled with political intrigue, political assassinations, and huge wealth redistribution. I was telling a granddaughter of mine this week, "I have seen poverty you can't imagine. I've been in the Philippines and seen a mother with a newborn sitting in a gutter, selling her baby for $20 so she could have something to eat." I've seen those things, and I've seen the great distinctions that are in the various countries in the world. The United States right now is torn by division like it's never been in my lifetime. Not even during the civil rights days of the 60's did we have the division that we have right now because of the leadership of our country, not only over the last 8 years, but over the last 16 plus years we're seeing the fruits of that right now. Look at this:

> *Many prophets cry repentance and are slain—*
> *Their murderers conspire to take over the government.*

Let's look at verse 11:

> *For there were many merchants in the land, and also many **lawyers**, and many officers.*

Now, that's an indicator there that we've got some problems. Go on down to verse 21:

> *Now there were many of the people who were exceedingly angry because of those who testified of these things; and those who were angry were chiefly the chief judges, and they who had been high priests and **lawyers**; yea, all those who were*

***lawyers** were angry with those who testified of these things.*

I think that when we talk about "draining the swamp" in Washington D.C., that one of the pollutants there are too many lawyers. If you go on down to verse 28:

And they did enter into a covenant one with another, yea, even into that covenant which was given by them of old, which covenant was given and administered by the devil, to combine against all righteousness.

Look at the previous verse:

*[27] Now it came to pass that those judges had many friends and kindreds; and the remainder, yea, even almost all the **lawyers** and the high priests, did gather themselves together, and unite with the kindreds of those **judges** who were to be tried according to the law.*

So, you see these lawyers, and you see a lot of judges. Let's go over to chapter 7 and look at the chapter heading, right at the beginning;

The chief judge is murdered,

Now, we just had one of the chief judges of the United States, Scalia, die at a ranch in Texas. I think that history will show that it was a political assassination and that he was murdered. I think the reason he was murdered was to shift a balance of power to a more liberal edge, which is what Mr. Obama tried to do. Thank goodness the government stood up and stopped him and said that the new chief judge would be appointed by the incoming president-elect. Otherwise, you'd have an imbalance in the court there that could have completely destroyed what's left of the Constitution. So, I think we have already had a chief judge murdered. And I think that history, in time, will point that out. Notice the next statement in the chapter heading:

the government is overthrown,

Go down to verse 2:

And the people were divided one against another; and they did separate one from another into tribes, every man according to his family and his

> *kindred and friends; and thus they did destroy the government of the land.*

So, look at your dates here. This is 30–33 AD, and the Savior comes in 34 AD. So, 2-3 years before the appearance of Christ and especially before the storm (the storm starts in 2-3 years from now), you have the government that fails, the chief judge is murdered, and if you go to verse 5:

> *Now all this was done, and there were no wars as yet among them; and all this iniquity had come upon the people because they did yield themselves unto the power of Satan.*
>
> *[6] And the regulations of the government were destroyed,*

Now, I was thinking about everything that has happened here recently, and I've been thinking about Donald Trump. I had some interesting feelings about him. Now, I don't mean for this to be a political thing at all; I'm not doing that on purpose, just sharing with you some ideas. Isaiah, 140 years before the Persian Empire steps in and destroys the Babylonian Empire, Isaiah prophesied in the Bible and if you want to go there with me for just a minute, go on over to Isaiah chapter 45. I thought this was really interesting. You have the children of Israel, and they have been in Babylonian captivity for about 70 years. Actually, let's go to chapter 44 first. This was spoken 144 years before Solomon's Temple is destroyed. Here is this prophecy of Isaiah and he talks about a man named Cyrus, who hasn't been born yet. This is 140 years before the birth of Cyrus. The Lord says of Cyrus in verse 28:

> *He is my shepherd, and shall perform all my pleasure: even saying to Jerusalem, Thou shalt be built; and to the temple, Thy foundation shall be laid.*

Now, keep in mind that the children of Israel were in Babylonian captivity, and they are there for 70 years before this man, Cyrus, comes on the scene and destroys the Babylonian captivity. The new kid is on the block, and it's the Persian Empire, which succeeded the Babylonian Empire.

Look at chapter 45, verse 1:

> *Thus saith the Lord **to his anointed**, to Cyrus,*

Now, Cyrus is not a member of the House of Israel. He is what we call a pagan, an idolater, a heathen, a Gentile, and he is outside the covenant line. He is an **outsider**. I want you to remember that. Cyrus is an outsider:

whose right hand I have holden,

Notice that the Lord has picked an outsider to come in and notice in the chapter heading for 45:

Cyrus will free the captives of Israel from Babylon—

He chose an outsider that he anoints and takes by the right hand. Back to verse 1:

to subdue nations before him; and I will loose the loins of kings, to open before him the two leaved gates [the gates of Babylon]; *and the gates shall not be shut;*

This is the Lord speaking to Cyrus:

[2] I will go before thee, and make the crooked places straight: I will break in pieces the gates of brass,

Again talking about the leaved gates of Babylon that represent that huge world empire:

and cut in sunder the bars of iron.

[3] And I will give thee [Cyrus] *the treasures of darkness* [the wealth of Babylon/the world], *and hidden riches of secret places, that thou mayest know that I, the Lord, which call thee by thy name, am the God of Israel.*

[4] For Jacob my servant's sake [who is in bondage right now], *and Israel mine elect, I have even called thee* [Cyrus, an outsider] *by thy name: I have surnamed thee, though thou hast not known me.*

Then in verse 5 again, look down at the bottom:

I girded thee, though thou hast not known me:

Go over to verse 13. Again, the Lord speaking through Isaiah about Cyrus, 140 years before he's even born. He says:

I have raised him up in righteousness, and I will direct all his ways: he shall build my city [Jerusalem], *and he shall let go my captives, not for price nor reward, saith the Lord of hosts.*

I thought about that, about how the Lord chose an outsider. There was a big controversy about Donald Trump being an outsider. I want you to notice also, that the chapter that talks about Cyrus, the ancient outsider who freed the captives of Israel, is chapter 45. I wonder—knowing the Lord loves numbers and has perfect knowledge of all things past, present, and future—isn't it interesting that Donald Trump is going to be the 45th President of the United States? Could he be an outsider who has stepped in to free His people and to set them loose from spiritual captivity and bondage? Is this the modern day Cyrus the Great? Is this the one?

Then, I thought about something else. I thought about all the prophecies. You see, everybody is so excited right now. The stock market has hit an all-time high and seems to be just going up and up and up. They call it the "Trump bump." It's because of confidence in people, among other things. Sure, it's manipulated, but there's a new confidence in people. Things are looking brighter; things are looking better. The job market is looking to be improved, the Carrier Factory episode that took place over in Indiana, and all of these different things are seemingly better. And so, we've got tremendous excitement and confidence and anticipation like we haven't had for a long time in this country. There's a huge surge of patriotism. I love where I watch the rallies that start out with prayer, and we have various pastors and ministers that offer heartfelt prayers. I love it when they pledge allegiance when they sing the national anthem. It's just like a rebirth of patriotism that's taking place in our country. It feels so good, and everybody's excited. I'm excited about what's happening! And yet, I know the prophecies. I know what's written in section 29 about the events that precede the Second Coming. I know what's written in section 45. I know what's in section 88 and 101. I know what's in Matthew JST 24. I know these things, and I understand them. I know what the prophets have written.

When I came home from my mission in 1966, I had received a witness of the prophets and apostles. I remember that I started storing wheat in 1966. I put away our first wheat because we were told to put away a year's supply. Since 1967, I have always had a year's supply of food—always! I followed President

Kimball's advice to plant trees, berry bushes, grape vines, and have a garden. I've been gardening for 40 years. I'm in Eagar for a reason. I came to Eagar because I had an opportunity to transfer with the Church Education System, and I could choose anywhere in the world to go. And I came here because I did my homework on what it would be like to be here in the case of a societal collapse and if the power ever went out and we went backward 200 years. I hand-picked this place. I studied all of the prevailing winds based on what could happen if there were atomic fallout and believe me, I've done my homework since 1966. I live in a place here in Eagar that is totally self-sufficient. We're off the grid. We can stay in this house for years and take care of up to 40 people and never have to shop. So, I know all of the prophecies. I've read all of the books. I've read all of the books by Roger Young. I've read all of the books on dreams and visions that came from Another Voice of Warning. I've studied all of this. I don't believe there's a seminary teacher anywhere in the Church that could teach the end-times scenario and the signs of the times more effectively than I can. I know the scriptures. I've been a student of them all of my life and particularly, signs of the last times.

Many of you have asked me, and not a week goes by without questions on what my feelings are on a "call-out." I'll say it again: "call-out" is a true principle. It's scripturally based; it's everywhere. If people don't know that the Lord calls out his covenant people from dangerous areas to supplant them in places of safety, they're not students of the scriptures. You can't read the scriptures and not know that the "call-out," as its so-called today, is a scriptural principle. So, yes, I believe in that. I believe that I am living in a place that will be a place of safety. This place where I am was established by Mormon pioneers as a part of the Little Colorado Mission. Brigham Young sent Mormons from Utah down into this area. They followed the Little Colorado River up to its headwaters where I am. I'm at the foot of the White Mountains, and it was a terrible life in the beginning. This area was filled with outlaws and thieves, and the Mormons settled in here at the peril of their lives. The two communities I live in, to this day, are still separated by a hundred-plus-year-old animosity that goes all the way back to outlaws and sheepherders and cattlemen. The Mormons came in here and settled this area at great cost. I believe that when asked about a "call-out," I was ready to go out to Cabela's and spend some significant money on materials for bug-out bags, tents, and everything else because I believe in the "call-out" principle. And yet when it came time to push the button and order the materials, we couldn't do it. We just didn't feel like it and eventually, what happened was that the Spirit settled on us and said, "You live in a place where people will come to escape for their lives." And I believe that this place was sanctified by the turmoil, the sorrow, the travail, and the adversity of the early pioneers who settled here and that their children will reap the benefits of a safe place because of the sacrifice of their pioneer fathers. I believe that there are places like that all throughout the country that have been made hallowed and sanctified.

Will the Church issue a "call-out?" I don't know. I believe there is a "call-out" going on right now. I believe the Spirit of the Lord is hovering over men and women, moms and dads, and their families, and inspiring them to do certain things to prepare for the events that are sure to come. Some of those things that they're being inspired to do is to move and to sell what they have and to move to places. I know people, personally, and others as a result of podcasts that have shared their stories with me, that said, "We've up and moved without knowing where we were going." Like Nephi in 1 Nephi 4:6, when he goes up over the walls of Jerusalem:

> *And I was led by the Spirit, not knowing beforehand the things which I should do.*

That's happening now. So, whether there will be a membership-wide "call-out" as a result of instructions given by the president of the Church, I don't know, and frankly, it doesn't matter to me. What matters to me more, brothers and sisters, is that we sanctify ourselves and live so close to the Spirit of the Lord, that that Spirit will instruct us in every detail as to what we should do, where we should go, and we don't have to worry because it won't be *"the philosophies of men mingled with scripture."* It won't be what one person thinks might happen or how they interpret the scriptures. Your move will be guided by the Spirit through personal revelation, and that is always pure, and it is always right. It is never wrong.

So, it kind of leads me to what this is all about. I wanted to share one other thing. I was reading the story of Jonah this week, and I thought about how Jonah was called to go to Nineveh. Now, Nineveh, at the time of Jonah's call in the 7th century was the biggest and the most sophisticated city on the face of the earth. It was established by the great hunter of men, Nimrod. So, it is closely associated with where the Tower of Babel was and all of that area which would be today's modern day Iraq. Well, Jonah who was of the tribe of Zebulon, lived down by the Sea of Galilee area. He was called by the Lord to go and prophesy the destruction of Nineveh. Now, it's interesting that Jewish tradition says that Jonah was the son of the widow Zarephath, and was raised from the dead by Elijah the Prophet. Isn't that an interesting thing? That's a Jewish tradition. If this is true, this is the man who is now called on a prophetic mission to go to Nineveh, the largest pagan city, capital of wickedness in the world and try to get them to repent. You all know the story. He went up there and fulfilled his mission, and they repented. And as a result, Jonah's mission forestalled the destruction of God's people by 100 years. It bought them 100 years. I'm wondering, have we had some time purchased for us with the election of Donald Trump? Have the American people sufficiently repented that God will give them some extra time? I don't know, just some things to think about. But, Jonah's mission to the Assyrians bought Israel and the covenant people of the Lord, 100 years. Roughly 100 years before they slipped into wickedness and the Assyrians came down and destroyed them and carried them away into captivity. Just some musings I'm having on this.

So, this week, as I was studying the scriptures, I came to this scripture that I want to talk to you about tonight. Let's go to 1 Thessalonians chapter 5 in your *Bible*. We'll just tie some things together. I've been following a lot of preparedness sites. I've belonged to "Another Voice of Warning" for about 11 years. I'm one of the old timers there. I'm a lurker. I don't participate much, but I have picked up material from that site that has blessed my life. So, I've watched these sites, and various others I have perused over the years, and there's a lot of anxiety in them right now; a lot of concern and a lot of people talking about the dreams and visions that people have had. As I said, I have all three of those books. I've read all of Roger Young's books. I've read so many books. I've got a library here on all of these kinds of things, and I want to take you into a little different direction tonight. I'd like us to be anxious, but not frenzied. I get a feeling of frenzy as I read the preparedness sites from the Latter-day Saints. The reason that there's this feeling of frenzy is that too many of us have not received the truth and taken the Holy Spirit for our guide, so we are relying on everything that is in print, and that's a lot in the information age and the day of the internet. We are relying on what's happening to others, what others are seeing in their dreams, what others are experiencing in their visions, and what others are interpreting from the scriptures to mean, etc., etc. I think we just kind of need to back away a little bit and take a deep breath. I'm not saying relax because I think we are in a period of jeopardy and seriousness like we've never been, ever, in the history of the world. But let's back off and take a different look at things. Let's go to 1 Thessalonians 5:1:

> *[1] But of the **times and the seasons**, brethren, ye have no need that I write unto you.*

Paul is talking now about the signs and times, and seasons of times, leading up to the Second Coming.

> *[2] For yourselves know perfectly that the day of the Lord so cometh as a **thief in the night**.*

Now, this was written roughly between 65 AD and 70 AD. This was written before the apocalypse of the Roman Army destroying the Jewish nation in 70 AD, with follow up destruction seven years later. So, Paul is talking about the Second Coming, our day, and the times and the seasons that lead up to that. Notice verse 2. This is where Roger Young gets the title of his book from, *A Thief in the Night*. Now, there's a difference between a thief and a robber. It's an interesting little thing you want to look at. A robber always confronts you face to face, takes what you've got, usually with bodily harm. You are usually injured, if not killed, by a robber. A thief comes when you're asleep, and you remain asleep, and he just takes everything you've got. It's interesting, *"as a thief in the night."* I might tell you, based on the other parables, that He is going to come at a particular time, we think He's probably going to come at midnight—and that could be—when it's the darkest when we are in our deepest sleep. Look at verse 3:

> *For when they* [that's those people living at this time] *shall say,* ***Peace*** *and* ***safety****;*

Now, that's what I want you to look at and you ought to circle those two key words. When the thief comes in the night, it will come at a time when most people are saying, "Finally, we have peace," and, "Finally, we are safe!" A lot of the dreams, visions, a lot of the things point toward a couple of things that I find interesting, and the Spirit has whispered to me that these are two areas to look to. My own personal feelings are that when it talks about peace, we can also add prosperity. Even though it's not mentioned, prosperity comes at a time of peace and safety. One of the fruits of peace and safety is prosperity. You look at the stock market, and you'll see it is at an all-time high, and just seems to be going up. They call it the "Trump bump." People are singing, "Happy days are here again." A lot of the dreams and visions have pointed out that an economic collapse would take place at a time when the markets were high. We've never seen them higher than they are now.

Another indicator of times when things will start to fold up is a severe winter. Now, these have all been laid out. I find it interesting that here in Round Valley, where I live at about 7,200 feet, we are having the coldest November and December that we've had in years. It gets cold up here, but it's never been like this in November and December. So, are we looking at that winter? Is the stock market an indicator of these kinds of things? These are kinds of things to watch for. But again, not frenzied, just a quiet, quiet movement forward; preparing quietly and orderly. Then notice what it says:

> *when they shall say, Peace and safety; then sudden destruction cometh upon them,*

It comes, and he draws a parallel about what it would be like when the water breaks on a pregnant woman. She's in the last stages of her labor, and the child's coming:

> *as travail upon a woman with child; and they shall not escape.*

Now, we break it into two groups of people. Here we go, the foolish and the wise virgins again:

> *[4] But ye, brethren, are not in darkness, that that day should overtake you as a thief.*

We live in the information age, and there has never been more written and more available about signs of the times and biblical and Latter-day Saint interpretations than there is now. But I'm saying that you are in the darkness. Even in the midst of all that information, you remain in the darkness if you rely on others to interpret the events that are going on around you. That's the point of my lesson today. Notice what he says:

> *But ye, brethren, are not in darkness, but that day shall overtake you as a thief.*
>
> *[5] Ye are all the children of **light** and the children of the **day**:*

Those two words you ought to circle, *day* and *light*. Those are words the Lord has referred to as *"the day star."* He is the Lord of Light. His voice is Light:

> *we are not of the night, nor of darkness.*
>
> *[6] Therefore let us not sleep, as do others;*

I'm gonna say that one of the ways you're asleep is if you are accepting the philosophies of men, mingled with scripture. If you're following the uninspired dictates of others, instead of seeking for personal revelation for yourself and for your family and teaching your family to do the same thing. Each one of us has to stop standing on borrowed light. We have to obtain revelation for ourselves. I don't think that there has ever been a more critical time for that than now.

> *but let us watch and be sober.*

Notice now that he pulls in an allegory of being drunken and sober:

> *[7] For they that sleep in the night; and they that be drunken are drunken in the night.*
>
> *[8] But let us, who are of the day, be sober, putting on the breastplate of faith and love; and for an helmet, the hope of salvation.*
>
> *[9] For God hath not appointed us to wrath,*

Did you catch that? If you're awake, and you're quietly preparing and receiving revelations, and not in a frenzied state or worried about this, that, and the other because you have received the truth and taken the Holy Spirit for your guide, you're not appointed to wrath. You'll get through the day that's coming. The Lord will take you, like Cyrus, by the right hand and lead you in every step of the way that you need to go:

> *but to obtain salvation by our Lord Jesus Christ,*

Skip to 11:

> *Wherefore comfort yourselves together, and edify one another, even as also ye do.*

Now, look at verse 14:

> *Now we exhort you, brethren, warn them that are unruly, comfort the feebleminded, support the weak, be patient toward all men.*

Verse 17:

> *Pray without ceasing.*

These are all the things that you do to qualify for personal revelation so that you can see what's coming with clarity and have that comfort and peace that comes from those who abide in the Spirit:

> *[19] Quench not the Spirit.*
> *[20] Despise not prophesyings.*

Those are just some thoughts there.

Let's go to *Doctrine and Covenants* 63 and let me show you a couple of other things here. I'm kind of rambling a little bit. I hope you'll forgive me and pick up what I am trying to say. Section 63 is a section we don't look at as often as we should, but I'd like to go to verse 5. He's talking about signs that are going to come. Look at what it says:

> *Behold, I, the Lord, utter my voice, and it shall be obeyed.*
> *[6] Wherefore, verily I say, let the wicked take heed, and let the rebellious fear and tremble; and let the unbelieving hold their lips, for the day of wrath shall come upon them as a whirlwind,*

That's what we're looking at. That's what's coming in our day. Is it going to be an economic collapse that causes that? <u>I personally believe</u> that with a 20 trillion-dollar debt the answer isn't in politics; there has to be a reset. Notice what else it says:

> *and all flesh shall know that I am God.*

> *[7] And he that seeketh signs shall see signs, but not unto salvation.*

See, that's again relying on the arm of flesh. That's not faith; it's "I'll believe it when I see it!" We need to move in a different direction, Latter-day Saints, especially those of us who are preppers. You need to move in a different direction and not rely upon the arms of flesh and the interpretation of others. You need to seek for and obtain revelation for yourself. Verse 9:

> *But, behold, faith cometh not by signs, but signs follow those that believe.*

Then it talks about these signs. Let's go over to verse 29. We have a charge ahead of us that no other people on the face of the earth have ever had, and that is to establish a society of Zion that will be in place when the Lord comes. The Lord of Lords and King of Kings has to come to a people who are Lords and Kings. You have to come to a society of Priesthood Kings and Queens. You can't be the King of Kings if there aren't any Kings for you to be King over, and that has to be done with a Zion society:

> *[29] Wherefore, the land of Zion shall not be obtained but by purchase or by blood,*

This was in the days when the Lord was telling members of the Church to purchase up lands for their inheritance, which they did. Notice the bottom of verse 29:

> *otherwise, there is none inheritance for you.*

So, Zion is going to be obtained by one way or another way; by either purchase or by blood. Now, they purchased it, and the interesting thing is that the deeds to the original purchases of land, many of those deeds of trust, which are legal documents, still remain in the hands of family descendants of the original purchasers. There are people in this Church that hold deeds of land to areas in and around Kansas City and Independence, Missouri. They have legal deeds. It will be interesting to see what they are going to do with those things:

> *[30] And if by purchase, behold you are blessed;*

This is what they tried to do. They purchased the land and then they were driven out of it at the point of a bayonet and took their deeds of purchase with them, which are still held by the families.

> *[31] And if by blood,*

And that's the way it's going to be in our day. I believe that the purchase of the lands of inheritance will be reassigned, will come back into their possession, not by purchase again, but by blood:

> *as you are forbidden to shed blood, lo, your enemies are upon you, and ye shall be scourged from city to city, and from synagogue to synagogue, and but **few shall stand to receive an inheritance**.*

Now, that is a double prophecy. That has a prophetic fulfillment in the early days in the history of the Church when they were driven out of Jackson County, Missouri. It's interesting that at the time this was given was when they were in Kirtland, Ohio, and you have two Church headquarters. You had the headquarters of the Church in Kirtland, where Joseph resides at that time, and you have a second headquarters of the Church in Jackson County. Well, they were not successful. They were driven out of the state by an extermination order. You know the history. And they were "**called-out**" of Missouri and moved up into Illinois, and were "**called-out**" of Illinois and moved into Mexico. Now, this double prophecy, where it talked about early days, there were *"but few that shall stand to receive an inheritance,"* and there were because they were driven right out of the country. But I'll tell you also, that in a future day, because of the *"whirlwind"* in verse 29 that we talked about earlier, few will be able to stand and receive an inheritance. But there will be a few; that's your key. I want you to circle that word *"few"* because that's the word the Lord uses to describe the *remnant* that He is going to use to start the process of a society-wide Zion people:

> *[32] I, the Lord, am angry with the wicked; I am holding my Spirit from the inhabitants of the earth.*

You know what happens when He does that when He withdraws His Spirit? You saw what happened when He withdrew His Spirit from the Nephites. The Lord said, *"my Spirit will not always strive with man;"* and *"[will] not always suffer them to take happiness in sin."* Are we coming into that point? It appears like we've been able to buy a little time. Have we been able to buy a little time? Or will we see an assassination of the chief

High Priest, chief judge, i.e., President of the United States? I fear and worry about that. Don't think for a minute that the Gadiantons have gone away. They are behind closed doors and secret chambers, plotting how they can turn around this defeat that they've suffered—a historical, world-wide, political defeat—how they can turn it around and regain their power. We're not out of this at all, by any means. Yet, I hope that we've bought a little bit of time. Then it goes on and says:

> *[33] I have sworn in my wrath, and decreed wars upon the face of the earth, and the wicked shall slay the wicked, and fear shall come upon every man;*
>
> *[34]* **And the saints also shall hardly escape***; nevertheless, I, the Lord, am with them, and will come down in heaven from the presence of my Father and consume the wicked with unquenchable fire.*

Well, these are just some thoughts, brothers and sisters. You know, if you want to have an interesting experience go on YouTube and look up Ted Koppel's video called *Lights Out*. Watch that and read what it is. It has to do with what would happen if there was a cyber attack on the grid or what if there was an electromagnetic pulse. A cyber attack is more likely than the electromagnetic pulse, in my mind. Ted Koppel did a year or so of work on this. He wrote a book called *Lights Out*, and you can see a little video of some news conferences that he held on what would happen if the lights went out in the United States. If we had a prolonged grid failure nationwide for thirty days, it's estimated that thirty million people would be dead. A million people a day.

My mom and dad lived through the Depression, and as I was working on being prepared, I'd go to them and say; "What happened here and what were the circumstances here?" My mom came from Goshen, Utah and my dad was from Salt Lake. So, one was on a farm in rural Utah, and the other one was up in the city. Up in the city, they felt the pains of the Great Depression. Down in the rural areas they hardly knew it was even going on, other than the fact that hobos and transients were moving from coast to coast looking for work and looking for something to eat.

So, I talked to my mom and dad a lot about this. My dad brought up the same thing that Ted Koppel points out in *Lights Out*. He said, "Think about if we were ever to lose the electricity. Just look at how interconnected we are!" According to Homeland Security, or whoever is in charge of national defense, the number one thing that could jeopardize our country is not an attack from foreign invaders. It's not even a nuclear attack. It's a hack on the grid where we lose the power. If that were to be prolonged, it would literally put us back in time 200 years. So, based on what my mom and dad said about growing up in the Depression, I decided to build an outhouse. I went online and got the plans from the WPA, which was a Roosevelt work project during the Depression, and they built outhouses. So, I got plans for an outhouse, and I built one. I now have an outhouse on my property, and I have it on skids so that it can be moved from one hole to another. Open up the door, and inside is a nice oak seat. I asked my mom about this because I'd never built an outhouse and never hardly used one. She said, "Well, what you want to do is measure it. If you're sitting on the throne, and your knees don't hit the door, and you can put your feet out, and dangle your feet and move them back and forth then you've got the right distance from the door to where the seat is." Now, that's valuable information from people who went through the Depression.

I have a bucket in there filled full of corn cobs, and it's kind of a joke to show the distance between this generation my generation. I'd open that up, and my grandkids would say, "What's in there grandpa?"

"Come over here and let me show you."

I'd open it up, and they can recognize it, "Why, that's a toilet, isn't it? But what's that white bucket over there with all those corn cobs in it?"

And then I tell them, "That is what those were used for before you had a Montgomery Ward or a Sears catalog. And if you were too poor to have those two books in there for toilet paper, you used those corn cobs, and that's where the saying *'rougher than a cob'* comes from." Anyway, I had some fun with that. I've taken and used every available square inch of my property. I've got turkeys and rabbits and chickens, and have horses available. I used to own horses, but I haven't got any horses now, since I've been home from missions, but I've got availability to horses, and we're just set to go. If the lights go out, we're okay. I've got a well that will provide water, and if the whole house went off the grid, I have a solar system. So, I'm a believer in these kinds of things. But rather than follow the promptings of others (which I have done in the past), when I now pray I lean more towards asking my Father in Heaven in a special way with upraised hands, "Father, what's coming that I need to know so that I can be prepared for me, my family, and for those that will seek refuge and safety in a time when things become very difficult?" I believe we are on the cusp of this.

Anyway, back to Zion. We've talked about this in the past. It appears that Zion-people are not going to voluntarily humble themselves very much. It appears that instead of voluntary humility, we're going to experience compelled humility, which reverses pride. Think about voluntary humility while there is still time. Those of us who still have jobs, still have a nice home, have food, clothing, and shelter, who could still sense the urgency and the need to be about preparing. The most important preparation you can make is to sanctify yourselves. I remember in a seminary and institute in-service, we were discussing what the most important thing is that we can do for our students. One of the institute teachers said, "The most important thing you can do for yourselves, for your students, and for anybody you come in contact with is to sanctify yourself." Now, in reality, you can't sanctify yourself. All you can do is put yourself in a position where you receive light and knowledge and truth, and **that** sanctifies you.

Well, brothers and sisters, as we wrap it up here, let's go to *Doctrine and Covenants* 103:12, and it's talking about Zion:

> *For after much tribulation, as I have said unto you in a former commandment, cometh the blessing.*

That former commandment says:

> *[13] Behold, this is the blessing which I have promised after your tribulations, and the tribulations of your brethren—your redemption, and the redemption of your brethren, even their*

> *restoration to the land of Zion, to be established,*
> ***no more to be thrown down****.*

Now, that was never done in Joseph's day! That's our day! So, this whole thing in section 103 is talking about us:

> *[14] Nevertheless, if they pollute their inheritances they shall be thrown down; for I will not spare them if they pollute their inheritances.*

They did, and that's why they were driven out of their inheritances:

> *[15] Behold, I say unto you, the redemption of Zion must needs come by power;*

That's the only way it's going to happen. It's going to happen by one man and one woman at a time, who have power in their priesthood, who have the ministry of angels, who have the visitation of *just men made perfect*, who have beings from the city of Enoch who are sent to prepare them, who have free and open intercourse with the *general assembly of the Church of the Firstborn*, and have met the Lord face to face; *Jesus the Mediator of the New Covenant*. That's the power it's going to take to redeem Zion:

> *[16] Therefore, I will raise up unto my people **a man**, who shall lead them like as Moses led the children of Israel.*

Go down to verse 21:

> *Verily, verily I say unto you, that my servant Joseph Smith, Jun., **is the man** to whom I likened the servant*

That seems to indicate, and this ties into *Visions of Glory*, that the prophet Joseph Smith is going to make his appearance again at a future day. Now, we're going to have the leadership of Joseph once again. Back to verse 17:

> *For ye are the children of Israel, and of the seed of Abraham, and ye* [this is us, now] *must needs be led out of bondage by power, and with a stretched-out arm.*

Look at your footnote on 17c, and you'll see that it says, *"Bondage, Physical."* Here's the pattern: as the children of Israel were in Egyptian bondage, so we can look to be in a captivity/bondage in the future for a period of time. That's why in the Book of Alma it talks about two groups: Limhi and his group and Alma and his group, both under Lamanite captivity. It shows what one group tried to escape by their own means, using their own intellect, with the strength of their own arm, and they lost most of the population of their men. You had Alma and his people, who thoroughly trusted in the Lord and were delivered by miraculous means and didn't lose one person. We're going to have a chance to practice that in a future day. We are going to lose our freedoms for a period of time. There will be invaders on American soil. We will go into captivity for a short period. The Assyrian from the north will come down:

> *[18] And as your fathers were led at the first,*
> *even so shall the redemption of Zion be.*

With all this captivity, there will also be mighty miracles; miracles that will eclipse anything that has happened in the past:

> *[19] Therefore, let not your hearts faint,*

Isn't that interesting? We're going to go into captivity and bondage, but the Lord says, "Don't let your hearts faint."

> *for I say not unto you as I said unto your fathers:*
> *Mine angel shall go up before you, but not my presence.*

That's what happened in ancient times. The Lord withdrew Himself because they rejected Him at Sinai and He sent down the angel of the Lord to guide them in the wilderness. It was an Aaronic Priesthood guidance. But look in verse 20, in our day:

> *But I say unto you: Mine angels shall go up before you,* ***and also my presence****, and in time ye shall possess the goodly land.*

Look at verse 26:

> *And my presence shall be with you even in avenging me of mine enemies, unto the third and fourth generation of them that hate me.*

So, we are moving into a marvelous day. Will you be a part of that? As long as we are in a frenzy and seeking to interpret what others interpret, instead of seeking for our own guidance through the Holy Spirit to us individually, we'll be susceptible to anxiety, a lack of peace, and there will be a frenzied-ness about us in our preparations. I pray that we'll prepare under the direction of the Holy Spirit and be like Nephi of old, as he leaves his brothers outside the gates to go over the walls into the ancient city of David and find the brass plates. He said:

And I was led by the Spirit, not knowing beforehand the things which I should do.

That's our example. God bless us to seek for and obtain a greater outpouring of the Spirit of the Lord, to have a greater companionship of the Holy Ghost to sanctify us and to testify to us, teaching us of the things we need to know in this world, preparatory to our encounter with the Lord Jesus Christ as the *Second Comforter*. God bless you all! Thank you.

Resources:
3 Nephi 11:10 "Behold, I am Jesus Christ, whom the prophets testified shall come into the world."
3 Nephi 6 chapter heading
3 Nephi 6:11, 21, 27-28
3 Nephi 7 chapter heading
3 Nephi 7:2, 5-6
Isaiah 44:28
Isaiah 45 chapter heading
Isaiah 45:1-5, 13
1 Nephi 4:6
1 Kings 17:17-24 Elijah raised widow's son
1 Thessalonians 5:1-9, 11, 14, 17, 19-20
2 Peter 1:19 "...the day star..."
D&C 63: 5-7, 9, 29-34
Lights Out by Ted Koppel
Ether 2:15 "...my Spirit will not always strive with man;"
Mormon 2:14 "...would not always suffer them to take happiness in sin."
D&C 103:12-22, 26
1 Nephi 4:6 "And I was led by the Spirit, not knowing beforehand the things which I should do."

Chapter Forty-Three
Podcast 043 Will Ye Also Go Away

Good evening, brothers and sisters. It's good to be with you again tonight. Let's go over to John chapter 6, in the *New Testament* for just a moment. I want to take a look at a scripture here. In this chapter, we have something called *the bread of life sermon*. I'm sure you've read that, and we won't take time to go into it, but I just want to pay attention to a couple of places in this sermon. It begins in verse 16 and goes all the way to the end of the chapter, to verse 71. You may want to take a look at that sermon again. At the end of that sermon, the disciples are upset because some of the things that Jesus has said and done are really contrary to their traditions. It simply says this, if you'll look at verse 60:

Many therefore of his disciples, when they had heard this,

You can read the prior verses and see what he said:

said, This is an hard saying; who can hear it?

I want to point out now, that these are baptized members of the Church, men and women who have listened to some doctrine that flies in the face of their Jewish traditions. Another thing in content and context is, this sermon follows Jesus' feeding 5,000 men. There were probably many more people there because it only numbers the 5,000 men. It doesn't mention women and children. But again, when we get down to verse 60, and the disciples said, *"This is an hard saying; who can hear it?"* Look at what Jesus says:

> *[61] When Jesus knew in himself that his disciples murmured at it, he said unto them, Doth this offend you?*

Then He says a couple of other things that have to do with His pronouncement of Him being the Son of God. Look at verse 66:

> *From that time many of his disciples went back and walked no more with him.*

Again, I'm going to emphasize; these are baptized members of the Church. They have witnessed this miracle of feeding the 5,000 people and probably many other miraculous things up to that point. And yet, because of what He says here, what they observed and what He does and says, they walk away. Verse 67:

> *Then said Jesus unto the twelve,*

You can see Him standing there watching this multitude walk away. "We're not going to have anything to do with this. We want our membership removed from the records of the Church." And Jesus said to the twelve:

> *Will ye also go away?*

What a poignant statement that is to the members of the twelve:

> *[68] Then Simon Peter answered him, Lord, to whom shall we go? Thou hast the words of eternal life.*

That's a question I'd like to ask us tonight.

The purpose of this lesson is to address this "going away" that's taking place in the Church membership. Where will you go if you leave the membership of the Church? Everything you know about the Restoration, about the Prophet Joseph Smith, about modern-day scripture, about priesthood, about temple ordinances, about the doctrines of the kingdom, come as a result of your membership in the Church of Jesus Christ of Latter-day Saints. All of the things that you know, you could not have known outside of membership in the Church. You would have been like all of the rest of the Christian world who have the *Bible* and limited scripture resources. They can only go so far in their knowledge, and they bump up against a wall. You who are walking away have access to all of this information, and yet you are making a decision. Your friends and family talk to me during the week about you being in the middle of a crisis of faith. Well, congratulations, that's exactly what you're supposed to be doing here on the earth. Every one of us, at some time or another, are going to come up face to face and experience some kind of a challenge that will challenge our faith. That's one of the main purposes of the telestial world. Why would you walk away from the very thing that's given you all the knowledge that you have up to this point? If you've experienced any joy and you have had any spiritual experiences if you've participated in any miracles if you've had priesthood active in your life, why would you walk away from that at this point? I ask you the same question that Jesus asked them, "Will you also go away?" And I would say, "Where will you go?" You have access through your membership to all of the answers to life's questions and *mysteries of Godliness* that have been hid from the foundation of the world that are made available to you now. You can only access and have access through your membership in the Church of Jesus Christ of Latter-day Saints.

So, what are the reasons that people leave? When we were in the mission field, Margie and I got this from Brother Pontius, and we practiced this while we were in the mission field in the Philippines and had continued to practice it up until just the last couple of weeks. We tell every new investigator, every new member, and anybody and everybody who is new in the faith, and therefore weak in the faith, that they're going to have three things that are going to happen to them either before they are baptized or, for sure, after they are baptized. I promise you that somewhere in your sojourn, in your journey as a member of this Church, these three things **will** happen to you. There is an old saying, "Being forewarned is forearmed." So this gives you power through knowledge so that when this happens to you, it won't take you away. We've traveled throughout the world on missions and worked with people and have been involved heavily with the rescue, and without exception, the number one reason why people leave the Church throughout the world is because they were offended by another member of the Church.

So, as they are getting ready to come to church for the first time, one of the three things that we tell them in their investigation process is, "You know you need to come to church for a certain number of times, as determined by the mission president, before you can be baptized." We tell them right up front, "Either before you join the Church or after you join the Church, you're going to be offended. Just plan on it! Another member is going to say something that will hurt your feelings. The words will be planted in your mind by a devil or an unclean spirit, and you're going to say, 'Well, I'll never go back to that Church again if that's the way they are!' Or, 'Who do they think they are treating me like this?' Now, those statements that you have placed in your mind come from hell." I tell them upfront.

Here's the other thing you need to understand when an offense comes from another member of the Church. More often than not, 95 to 97 % of the time, it's not intended. It's just that in the Church we have stupid people that do stupid things. They don't think! They put their foot in their mouth and say things that they don't give a thought to. So, we warn people upfront, "This is going to happen. Know this, that it's not intended. It's just that in the Church you have all kinds of people who are at different levels and different stages of their progression. You're going to come into contact with those people, and somewhere in that contact period, you're going to have your feelings hurt and be offended. Know this, that it has happened to all of us. Not only have we been offended, but some of us have been the offenders. We just needed to grow up in the gospel, repent, and have that weakness in us transformed into a strength. Just give it some time, don't worry about that."

That's one of the three things that we tell people. And it is, without a doubt, the number one reason why people leave the church. Well, we've had several people come back within a week, sometimes that very next Sunday, and say, "Elder Stroud, remember that you told us about three things that would take place?"

"Yes, and which one took place?"

"Sunday, I had a person who said this to me."

I said, "Wow! That was offensive!"

They looked at me and said, "Yeah, but you know what? We remembered what you said, and it's no big deal!" And they went right over it. It's wonderful!

The second thing that's going to happen is that you're going to be tempted not to attend church. What's the big deal? So, we tell them, "Why is the devil plying these three tactics against you, as a new member or an investigator? We have to ask what the reason is behind this. Well, the reason he's going to tempt you to not go to church is to keep you from partaking of the sacrament. That's the primary reason. There are other reasons that have to do with fellowship and service, etc., but the primary reason is to keep you from partaking of the sacrament. In that sacrament, what you do is, you agree, for the next seven days, to take upon you the name of Jesus Christ, always remember Him and to keep His commandments which He has given you. You agree to do that when you partake of those emblems, those tokens of His atoning sacrifice, the bread, and the water. If you righteously and with full intent, accept that agreement, He, in turn, promises that for the next seven days He will give you the Holy Spirit to be your guide. You do that every seven days because frankly, we live in a world where if you don't do it every seven days, you're going to find yourself in a snare, in a trap, and captivated by the power of the evil one. So, that's an insurance to help you continue to grow and receive revelation and guidance because you agreed to take upon yourself, for the next seven days, the name of Christ, always remember Him, and keep His commandments. And he's going to provide you with a compass. He is going to give you a lantern, a lamp unto your feet, and a light unto your path. You're going to get your own little personal Liahona for the next seven days, where you can be warned and guided, receive instruction from time to time, and be blessed because you are trying to do what you should."

When we explain why they're tempted not to go to church, they can easily see that. This is where knowledge becomes power. We tell them upfront, "This is what's going to happen to you. Here's what's going to happen if you give in to that temptation, and here's what's going to happen if you're obedient to the Lord's counsel to attend church and partake of the sacrament."

The third thing is, you're going to come across anti-Mormon material. In our day, the information age, the internet has made just about everything that was ever written about the Church of

Jesus Christ of Latter-day Saints [Mormonism] available at the click of a mouse. It used to be that this material was only put into print by apostates or anti-Mormons who hated the Church and wanted to destroy your faith. So, they would take portions of the history of the Church out of context or take parts of it out of history and put it in such a way that it would cause your faith to be attacked. Now, you don't have to go to the Gerald and Sandra Tanner press in Salt Lake City or any of the other anti-Mormon press. You can get all that you want that will challenge your faith on the internet from our own history. Now that's the point I want to emphasize. This is kind of bringing me into what I want to talk about tonight. Why are people leaving? Why are they going?

It appears, brothers and sisters, that somewhere along the line, a decision was made decades ago that any parts of our history, the history of the Church of Jesus Christ of Latter-day Saints, that was not faith promoting, should not be made public. That was a decision that was made. I don't know who made it. I don't know when it was made, but it appears that somewhere, either that decision was made or we've slipped into that somehow because not everything in our history is savory. That's a fact! I think that President Hinckley will go down in history as having the hallmark of his ministry be the *Joseph Smith Papers Project*. Some people have said that the hallmark of his ministry would be the great temple builder. I'm not taking anything away from that because he was the great temple builder. But, when it comes to the salvation of the members of the Church (and certainly temples are a part of that), I believe this is one of the great revelations to come to President Hinckley, and I believe this came from the Lord through His prophet. President Hinckley decided that we should gather all of the information that we can find, that's existent and available on the Prophet Joseph Smith, compile it, make it into volumes, and make it available to all of the public, the members of the Church, and anybody else that wants it. That is the birth idea of the *Joseph Smith Papers Project*.

Margie and I were involved in that a little bit and had a chance to travel with these esteemed BYU scholars, Church history scholars, experts on the Prophet Joseph Smith, and Marlin K. Jensen, who was the Church Historian. We had the chance to go on that tour, so I have an inside look into what was happening there. When the idea was first presented by President Hinckley to this group of scholars, one of them who was a spokesman for the group, I can't remember the name, but he came out, and he said, "Everything, President Hinckley? Everything?"

Now, these men knew and had access to the material that had been archived and kept in First Presidency vaults and in archives in the Harold B. Lee Library at BYU. They also had access to any other place that was restricted to anyone that did not have clearance as a Church historian, a scholar, or someone else that had clearance to view these records. It was restricted, not available to the general membership of the Church. They knew that in those records there were things that were not savory. There were also things that would butt heads against some of what has been taught as truth in the Church, and if they pulled these first-hand records out and made them public they were going to have a lot of people saying, "Wait a minute, that isn't what I've been taught!"

And be it to President Hinckley's everlasting glory, he said, "That's all right. We want it all. And the Prophet Joseph Smith's history will stand on its own." Well, that's been a two-edged sword. So, with two things, with the advent of internet access and the information age, and the *Joseph Smith Papers*, we're now involved in an interesting thing that's taking place in the Church. Members of the Church are being forced to face their own history, and it is shaking them up! As a result of that, I just want to say that the Church has printed us some essays, and you can find this on lds.org under *general topic essays*. Here are some of the names of the essay titles that the Church has put out over the last two or three years, as a result of the confusion and turmoil that has taken place, as members of the Church have faced first-hand accounts on their own history. Some of these essays are: *Becoming Like God, The Book of Mormon and DNA Studies, Book of Mormon Translation, First Vision Accounts, Joseph Smith's Teachings about Priesthood, Temple, and Women, Mother in Heaven, Peace and Violence Among 19th Century Latter-day Saints*, (and that one, in particular, is going to talk about the Mountain Meadows Massacre), *Plural Marriage in the Church of Jesus Christ of Latter-day Saints, Race and the Priesthood,* and *Translation and Historicity of the Book of Abraham.* These are all things that we've had answers to. As a Church Education Systems teacher, I've taught for years about blacks and the priesthood and this, that, and the other. I'm not going to go into that tonight. I'm just going to say that what we have taught and what we've believed and what we now read in first-hand accounts that are coming forth from our church about our church history and the *Joseph Smith Papers Project* appear to be in conflict. And I put, "appear" to be in conflict.

You see, it goes back to the story in John again. The Savior taught some things, He did some things, and the members of the Church looked at that and said, "Whoa, wait a minute, wait a minute! This isn't the way we understand things here. This is different than we think things should be." And even then, in the Savior's own ministry, and throughout time, this has always happened, people turned and walked away. When in reality, some knowledge, some information, some discussion, and more important than all that, a witness from the Holy Ghost through the Holy Spirit, so that you can once again feel that Spirit, would resolve a lot of these issues. But, we are right now in the middle of this conundrum, if you will, in the Church. Let me just say a couple of other things in order to help you understand this. I like that more and more I hear the Brethren say things like this, "Take what you hear in general conference and go home and ask Heavenly Father, in the name of Jesus Christ, to confer this information that you've heard by the Holy Spirit, by the Holy Ghost. Receive a witness for yourself that it's true."

Somewhere along the line, we have slipped into this feeling that prophets and apostles in the restoration don't ever make any mistakes. Somewhere we've come into that. I don't know how we got into that. How we could ever assume or adopt such a philosophy, knowing the history of the Church and the coming forth of the *Book of Mormon* is beyond me! We go right on up to Joseph Smith and the 116-page manuscript, where he went against what the Lord told him to do, acted on his own counsel, and as a result, we all know the story of what took place there. All the way through the prophet's life, throughout his whole life, he's chastised by the Lord for doing things that he shouldn't be doing. Let me give you one example. Joseph Smith received a remission of his sins many times. You can read about it in the scriptures. I just want to show you one example. Go to section 93 in the *Doctrine and Covenants*. This was given in May of 1833 in Kirtland, Ohio. This was at a time when knowledge was being poured out upon this great prophet, seer, and revelator that was just outstanding. Section 93 is what I call the "Holy of Holies" of the *Doctrine and Covenants*. It's got such deep, significant, and profound doctrine in it that from verse 1, where it gives you a five-step formula on how to receive the *Second Comforter*, on through to talking about *intelligence, glory, spirit,* and *truth.* It's just unbelievable what's in here. And yet, go to verse 47. Some of the deepest doctrines of the Restoration are found in the first 40 verses of section 93, given through this great prophet Joseph Smith. You read this stuff, and there is no way that you can say he made it up. This is so far beyond the Prophet Joseph in 1833.

Look at verse 47. The Lord pours all this knowledge out upon Joseph, and then He speaks to Joseph and says this:

> *And now, verily I say unto Joseph Smith, Jun.—*
> *You have not kept the commandments, and must*
> *needs stand rebuked before the Lord;*

I just love that! All the way through it, into Nauvoo, the Prophet Joseph was not the greatest judge of human character. In the Nauvoo period and the Kirtland period he took into his bosom some nefarious characters and entrusted them with things that were closest to his own bosom. He made mistakes, brothers, and sisters, and had to repent sorely for it. He was rebuked and chastised and called to repentance by the Lord numerous times. This is the prophet of the Restoration. This is the man that stands in the presence of God the Father and His Son, Jesus Christ, who has all of these things that he's famous for, and yet he made mistakes all the way through his life. And here's the important part, watch this: **God allowed him to**. Joseph said this in the *Teachings of the Prophet Joseph Smith* page 268:

> *I told them I was but a man, and they must not expect me to be perfect; if they expected perfection from me, I should expect it from them; but if they would bear with my infirmities and the*

> *infirmities of the brethren, I would likewise bear with their infirmities.*

The History of the Church page 278, the Prophet Joseph Smith said:

> *I told them that a prophet was a prophet only when he was acting as such.*

I like this statement by David O. McKay. This is a conference report given in General Conference April 1962. Speaking about this, on what we'll call "the humanity of the prophet." That's a good term to use here. President McKay said:

> *Someone has said that when God makes the prophet, he does not unmake the man. I believe that.*

Isn't that a great quote? *"When God makes the prophet, he does not unmake the man."* Lorenzo Snow was quoted by Neil A. Maxwell in General Conference in 1984:

> *I can fellowship with the President of the Church if he does not know everything I know...I saw the...imperfection in [Joseph Smith]...I thanked God that He would put upon a man who had those imperfections the power and authority He placed on him...for I knew that I myself had weakness, and thought there was a chance for me.*

Gordon B. Hinckley said this, in the 1992 April Conference:

> *I have worked with seven Presidents of this Church. I have recognized that all have been human. But I have never been concerned over this.*

Somewhere we have come up with this feeling of the infallibility of the Mormon prophets and apostles. We're no better than the Catholic Church and the infallibility of the Pope. Yet, none of this was ever taught by the founders of the Restoration. And I don't believe that it is taught by the leaders today, at least not intended the way it's taken by the Latter-day Saints. I believe that it's the members of the Church that have built up this tradition in here, that prophets and apostles never make any mistakes. And what's more, God allows them to make mistakes, and we'll talk about that in just a minute. President Hinckley continued, saying:

> *They may have had some weaknesses. But this has never troubled me. I know that the God of heaven has used mortal men throughout history to accomplish His divine purposes.*

Isn't that a great quote?

Here's one by Boyd K. Packer that was given in a CES symposium in August of 1981. Elder Packer said:

> *The Brethren then and now are men, very ordinary men, who have come for the most part from very humble beginnings.*
>
> *Do you know how inadequate we really are compared to the callings we have received? Can you feel in a measure the weight, the overwhelming weight, of responsibility that is ours? If you look for inadequacy and imperfections, you can find them quite easily. But you may not feel as we feel the enormous weight of responsibility associated with the callings that have come to us. We are not free to do some of the things that scholars think would be so reasonable, for the Lord will not permit us to do them, and it is His church. He presides over it.*

I thought that was a great comment.

Here's a couple more that are really good. Brother Bruce R. McConkie said this in *Mormon Doctrine*:

> *With all their inspiration and greatness, prophets are yet mortal men with imperfections common to mankind in general. They have their opinions and prejudices and are left to work out their problems without inspiration in many instances.*

Bruce R. McConkie again, in an address given at the Institute of Religion at the University of Utah, in October of 1966 said this:

> *Thus the opinions and views, even of a prophet, may contain error, unless those opinions and views were inspired by the Spirit.*

And one last quote by Elder McConkie. This was used in a Teaching Seminary Preservice in 2004. It is from an open letter by Bruce R. McConkie, about 1980:

> *But every word that a man who is a prophet speaks is not a prophetic utterance. Joseph Smith taught that a prophet is not always a prophet, only when he is acting as such. Men who wear the prophetic mantle are still men; they have their own views; and their understanding of gospel truths is dependent upon the study and inspiration that is theirs. Some prophets—I say it respectfully—know more and greater inspiration than others.*

In essence, prophets and apostles are first and foremost, aside from their holy calling and the anointing they receive for that, are men in a fallen world working out their own salvation with the fear and trembling like everyone else. They have a holy assignment and a mission. Here's another thing: God allows them to make mistakes because they learn from their own experiences like you and me. Now, in our day of the Church, we have councils, and we have quorums where they meet together and discuss, and input, and that, accompanied with the Holy Spirit, ensures that few mistakes are made. History has shown that in every ministry of a president of the Church, there have been decisions made that may not have been inspired, and the Lord allows that. How are we going to learn from our mistakes? Joseph learned from the 116-page manuscript. He said this:

> *Whatever God requires is right, no matter what it is, although we may not see the reason thereof till long after the events transpire.*

And if he learned that good lesson, it was worth everything that took place there. I think in the Garden of Eden, even when Adam was told by the Lord that if he yields to temptation, They will provide a Savior for him. The whole purpose of having a Savior is because we make mistakes. We learn from those mistakes, repent, and hopefully we won't make those same mistakes very often. Individually, that's the way we learn, and the Lord allows that to take place.

Think of Oliver Cowdery for example, and let's go into 1839 in Far West when Oliver is in a stage of apostasy, as well as the majority of the members of the Quorum of the Twelve and two counselors in the First Presidency. They were in open opposition to Joseph Smith. How would you have felt if you had been a member of the Church, just a common, ordinary member at that time, witnessing this dissension in the Church? What would you have done? Oliver Cowdery was a man who'd seen God, heard His voice, obtained promises, had the ministration of angels, and yet, in 1839 he's saying things to Joseph Smith like, "If I left the Church, the whole Church would fall apart." He was warned early in the *Doctrine and Covenants* to beware of pride. Can you imagine a person who has had all of these experiences saying, "If I left the Church, the Church would fall apart without me."

Joseph looked at him and said, "Oliver, you just try it." Well, he did, and he walked away for nine years. He was gone for nine years and then came back humbly, at Winter Quarters in 1846 and asked to be re-baptized so he could come across the plains with the Saints. But, for nine years he was out of the Church! Why would you walk away? You're going to walk away because we have a tradition that needs to be corrected here, that God allows his leaders to make mistakes? What's the big deal? It's always been that way. Yet, it doesn't change a thing as far as the overall performance and mission of the Church and the gospel. It doesn't change a thing.

You ought to pull out a talk that was given by Ronald L. Halstrom, and it centers on the difference between The Church of Jesus Christ of Latter-day Saints and the Gospel of Jesus Christ. There is a difference between the two. Brothers and sisters, the Church can't save you. The President of the Church can't save you, nor can the First Presidency, nor any member of the Twelve, nor any other general authority. They cannot save you! They are to guide us with inspired counsel. I looked on lds.org to see if I could find anywhere in the scriptures where a prophet said, "Follow me." I couldn't find anything. Everywhere I found prophets, what they were doing was pointing those that they had stewardship over toward the place where Christ was. In essence, they were saying, "I'm not Him. He's over there. Let me show you the way. I have a little more experience. I have some inspiration you may not have at this point. Let me point the way. He's over there." They are pointing you towards Him. It is Christ who says, "Follow me." I don't find anywhere in the scriptures where a prophet says, "Follow me," but I find all kinds of places where it says to follow Christ. Our prophets and apostles are guides. They are directors. They have received the holy convocation from the Lord and an anointing. For many different reasons, the Lord has chosen them to help us come to the Savior. They act as a conduit for revelation to be poured down upon the general membership of the Church. What the prophets want us to do is to become so experienced in revelation and prophecy within our own sphere of influence, which is generally our family, that we become prophets and prophetesses for our own family. They are setting the example for how that works by being called apostles and prophets to the general membership of the Church. They're pointing this out, this whole thing of leadership by general authorities, apostles, and prophets, is a template of what the Lord wants to see done in every individual family. Why find fault with this? When all is said and done, it doesn't matter to me whether the Church spends money on malls or game preserves. It doesn't matter to me. I am not concerned about what the salaries of the general authorities are. You know why I'm not concerned? Because my membership in the Church of Jesus Christ has brought me to a point where I am independent of relying upon those men and women for what the Lord wants Mike Stroud to accomplish. It has fulfilled its purpose. I am so grateful for my membership because everything that I enjoy now—the peace and happiness, the direction, the guidance—everything I have comes as a result of my membership in The Church of Jesus Christ of Latter-day Saints. I would have none of this. I would enjoy none of this. There would be no doors open. There would be no channels of light without my membership in the Church. I would be like a biblical Christian banging my head up against a wall because I've gone as far as I could. You want to leave that because you think President Monson was uninspired in building a mall? That's the reason you're going to go? I will admit also that there are some things that are just not answerable at this point. There are some things that people find a cause to find fault and consider moving away. You're just going to have to sit it on the shelf and have faith that at some time you'll be able to receive an answer for that. But, don't leave because everything is not available to you right now. By the way, it's probably not available because you're not paying the price to access it. There's a price for this stuff.

I've found out that everything that I want from God is attached to a law and a formula, accompanied by a covenant. If I find out what that law is, and I align myself with that law, through repentance and obedience, I can have the heavens opened and receive anything I want. No restrictions. So, we get our feelings hurt, and we're going to walk away from this and let this take us away from the one thing that opens the windows of heaven and allows you to call down the powers of such?

Well, brothers and sisters, let me read a couple of other things to you by the Prophet Joseph Smith. This is marvelous. I go back to what Alma the Younger said in Alma chapter 30. He's talking to Korihor, and Korihor is a lot like those of us who are having difficulties and finding fault with the Church and finding fault with the leadership. It's nothing new. This has been going on since Adam. You can see in Alma chapter 30, the microcosm or pattern of what's going on in the Church today. People are being led away because they say things like Korihor. He is accusing leadership of the Church:

> *[31] ...and [he] did revile against the priests and teachers, accusing them of leading away the people after the silly traditions of their fathers,*

See? Now, skip over to verse 35 and Alma has a comment he makes after he listens to Korihor rail on and on. By the way, Korihor is a member of the Church, probably a priesthood bearer, so this is not an outsider. If you read closely the whole 30th chapter, you'll get a feel for that. Alma says:

> *[35] Then why sayest thou that we preach unto this people to get gain, when thou, of thyself, knowest that we receive no gain? And now, believest thou that we deceive this people,* ***that causes such joy in their hearts****?*

There's an indicator. Those of you who have walked away from the Church or those of you who are contemplating walking away, take a deep breath and take a different view. Nothing in the telestial world is stable. Nothing in this world is stable. This is not the real world, and you in the telestial body, the natural man, is not the real you. You are a spiritual being who has been called to get your glory and power and knowledge, so that you can be sent into a classroom behind the veil, forget everything, and pass through sorrow, that you might learn the good from the evil. "It is better for us to do this." Notice that the "passing through" indicates it's temporary at best. You're in a school room, and you're taking a test. Don't let one or two items cause you to throw the whole thing out the door. It's the proverbial "throwing the baby out with the bathwater." It doesn't make sense. And yet, that's what you're doing. Take a different view. Take the view that Church leaders always have, do, and always will, make mistakes. Take a different view and know that God allows it. If God were to correct and protect every decision that comes down on how to direct the Church and guide the members, what is the need for the gift of the Holy Ghost and why the purpose for the agency of man? If you have to be directed in everything, then what's the purpose of the Holy Ghost?

Let me read you a statement made by Brigham Young in 1853:

> *Now those men, or those women, who know no more about the power of God, and the influences of the Holy Spirit, than to be led entirely by another person, suspending their own understanding, and pinning their faith upon another's sleeve, will never be capable of entering into the celestial glory, to be crowned as they anticipate; they will never be capable of becoming Gods. They cannot rule themselves, to say nothing of ruling others, but they must be dictated to in every trifle, like a child. They cannot control themselves in the least, but James, Peter, or somebody else must control them. They never can become Gods, nor be crowned as rulers with glory, immortality, and eternal lives. They never can hold scepters of glory, majesty, and power in the celestial kingdom. Who will? Those who are valiant and inspired with the true independence of heaven,*

Did you catch phrase that right there? That's what you want to grab. That's what you're being lied about to, and you're forsaking, if you walk away from the organization that's providing you the opportunity to be independent:

> *who will go forth boldly in the service of their God, leaving others to do as they please, determined to do right, though all mankind besides should take the opposite course. Will this apply to any of you? Your own hearts can answer.*

You see, brothers and sisters, if you have to be told what to do in everything if you don't make a move until you're instructed by your leadership, you forfeit exaltation. The leadership is there to provide for you until you become experienced and perfected in receiving revelation for yourself, and you become, within your own circle of influence, a prophet, like your leaders are, in the circle of the Church membership.

Margie likes to call everything that we do in the Church "training wheels." When you take the training wheels off, you don't throw away the bike. The training wheels are there to help you to come up and obtain something higher. In the meantime, you stay in balance. And if you come up against something that upsets you or you don't understand, don't make a drastic decision at that point. Put it aside. Let it work on you. Joseph said:

> *The things of God are of deep import; and time, and experience, and careful and ponderous and solemn thoughts can only find them out.*

Notice the first thing necessary in the formula to find out the deep things of God is time; give it time. Brother Packer used to say that if you have time, take time! Don't be in a rush to make decisions that could affect your eternal destiny. The war in heaven was fought over this principle. There was a mighty general there that said, "You can't think for yourself. Let me take care of you. If you think for yourself, there's too big a chance, too big of a risk that you'll never make it back and you'll fail and lose the whole thing. I will take care of you." It's the same message big government gives to its populations. "You're not talented enough. You're not intelligent enough to take care of yourself. If we leave it up to you, you'll mess up and not only mess up your life, but everybody else. So, let us take care of you. Just do what we say and don't give it a thought." Sound familiar?

I hope that I'm not misunderstood here. A couple of things that I just tried to explain are causing way too many people to be offended and to *"go away."* All we need to do is adjust our thinking and come back to what was revealed and what is doctrine that was taught by the early foundation brethren and sisters of the Church that somehow we'd gotten away from a little bit. I'm not finding fault; it's not my place to correct the Church or correct the course if it needs to be. I think that the Church has been exactly what it's supposed to be. It's taking the gospel to the convert level membership of the Church. Those of you who want more are going to have to step outside of that comfortable little box of the *"traditions of the fathers," "the precepts of men,"* and *"the philosophies of men mingled with scripture."* You're going to have to pay a price to seek for and obtain personal revelation. You're going to have to align yourself with the laws and covenants that will put you in a position where you can obtain that revelation; then there is nothing that can or will be withheld. I pray with all the fervor of my heart that you understand correctly what I am saying here and that you take a different view of things; look at things differently.

I had a lady that visited me, and I asked her if I could share this, and she gave me permission. She came up to the house, and we had a marvelous visit. She shared with us a vision that she'd had. And I asked her if I can share it on my podcast. She said, "Please do." So, without mentioning her name, she told me that in this vision she'd seen an arm, from the mid-shoulder, upper-arm down to the hand. In the hand was a handle, and the handle was connected to a stem that led to a little red wagon. You can kind of get a picture of this. She's had this vision given to her of this arm and hand holding onto the handle of a little red wagon. In the little red wagon were all kinds of wonderful gifts. They were just luminescent. They were vibrating with light and life. It was just filled to the brim with these wonderful gifts. Then she said this, "The little red wagon was rusted, it was patched, the hard rubber wheels had big pieces and chunks of rubber out of the wheels. The little red wagon had seen better days. But, it was filled with all kinds of gifts, and that arm and that hand had hold of that handle. I immediately got the message of the vision.

I said, "The little red wagon is pretty beat up, but it's **His** little red wagon."

She looked at me with a smile and said, "That's exactly right, Mike. It is **His** little red wagon, and it's filled with gifts. But, you have to look past the dilapidated, beat up, rusted, chunked-out tires of the little wagon and remember whose hand is at the helm and the gifts that are available."

God bless us to not let the devil deceive us and captivate us by his cunning lies. Take a different view, take a deep breath. If you're experiencing a crisis of faith or you have, take another look at it and look at things differently. Prophets and apostles are men. They're working out their salvation with fear and trembling. This is how we justify what Nephi says:

> *I will not put my trust in the arm of flesh; for I know that cursed is he that putteth his trust in the arm of flesh. Yea, cursed is he that putteth his trust in man or maketh flesh his arm.*

Follow Christ and while you're in your beginning, elementary, rudimentary stages of learning how to receive revelation, let those prophets and apostles point the way. Let them guide you. Pray for them that they'll be inspired by the Lord. Imagine what it would do for the Brethren as they guide the Church, if they knew that the vast membership of the Church (while exercising their right to the gift of the Holy Ghost and acting independently, not being acted upon), prayed for the First Presidency, the Twelve, and other Church leaders, regularly, to receive inspiration. Do you think the membership, operating in that kind of power would have an effect upon the leadership of the Church? Would it bless their lives? And contrary to that, what does constant accusation, name-calling, lawsuits, and other satanic approaches and pursuits do to hinder the growth of the Church and to make it difficult for the Brethren? I pray that the Lord will bless us in this. God bless us all. I hope that you understand this. In the name of Jesus Christ, amen.

Resources:
John 6:16-71
John 6:65-66
lds.org, General Topic Essays
D&C 93:47
Teachings of the Prophet Joseph Smith page 268 and 278
David O. McKay, *"The Divine Church,"* Conference Report, April 1962, pp. 5-9
Neal A. Maxwell, quoting Lorenzo Snow in *Conference Report*, October 1984, p. 10
Gordon B Hinckley *Conference Report*, April 1992, p. 77
Boyd K. Packer at a CES symposium in August of 1981
Bruce R. McConkie Ordinary Men, Extraordinary Callings, New Era Sept. 2007
Bruce R. McConkie Institute of Religion at the University of Utah, October 1966
Bruce R. McConkie *Teaching Seminary Preservice Readings Religion 370, 471, and 475,* (2004), 42–46 Joseph Smith, *Teachings of the Prophet Joseph Smith,* 255–56
Alma 30:31,35
President Brigham Young, Discourse at SLC Tabernacle, Feb. 20, 1853
Joseph Smith, History of the Church, 3:29
2 Nephi 4:34

Come, Join with Us
By President Dieter F. Uchtdorf
Second Counselor in the First Presidency
October 2013

To Those Who Leave

The search for truth has led millions of people to The Church of Jesus Christ of Latter-day Saints. However, there are some who leave the Church they once loved.

One might ask, "If the gospel is so wonderful, why would anyone leave?" Sometimes we assume it is because they have been offended or lazy or sinful. Actually, it is not that simple. In fact, there is not just one reason that applies to the variety of situations.

Some of our dear members struggle for years with the question whether they should separate themselves from the Church.

In this Church that honors personal agency so strongly, that was restored by a young man who asked questions and sought answers, we respect those who honestly search for truth. It may break our hearts when their journey takes them away from the Church we love and the truth we have found, but we honor their right to worship Almighty God according to the dictates of their own conscience, just as we claim that privilege for ourselves.5

Unanswered Questions

Some struggle with unanswered questions about things that have been done or said in the past. We openly acknowledge that in nearly 200 years of Church history—along with an uninterrupted line of inspired, honorable, and divine events—there have been some things said and done that could cause people to question.

Sometimes questions arise because we simply don't have all the information and we just need a bit more patience. When the entire truth is eventually known, things that didn't make sense to us before will be resolved to our satisfaction.

Sometimes there is a difference of opinion as to what the "facts" really mean. A question that creates doubt in some can, after careful investigation, build faith in others.

Mistakes of Imperfect People

And, to be perfectly frank, there have been times when members or leaders in the Church have simply made mistakes. There may have been things said or done that were not in harmony with our values, principles, or doctrine. I suppose the Church would be perfect only if it were run by perfect beings. God is perfect, and His doctrine is pure. But He works through us—His imperfect children—and imperfect people make mistakes.

In the title page of the Book of Mormon we read, "And now, if there are faults they are the mistakes of men; wherefore, condemn not the things of God, that ye may be found spotless at the judgment-seat of Christ."6

This is the way it has always been and will be until the perfect day when Christ Himself reigns personally upon the earth.

It is unfortunate that some have stumbled because of mistakes made by men. But in spite of this, the eternal truth of the restored gospel found in The Church of Jesus Christ of Latter-day Saints is not tarnished, diminished, or destroyed.

As an Apostle of the Lord Jesus Christ and as one who has seen firsthand the councils and workings of this Church, I bear solemn witness that no decision of significance affecting this Church or its members is ever made without earnestly seeking the inspiration, guidance, and approbation of our Eternal Father. This is the Church of Jesus Christ. ***God will not allow His Church to drift from its appointed course or fail to fulfill its divine destiny.***

There Is Room for You

To those who have separated themselves from the Church, I say, my dear friends, there is yet a place for you here.

Come and add your talents, gifts, and energies to ours. We will all become better as a result.

Chapter Forty-Four
Podcast 044 From Eternity to Eternity

Brothers and sisters, it's good to be here with you again tonight on this Sabbath evening. Twice today, I've had discussions with people who are frustrated because they seem to go one step forward and five steps backward in their progression. I pointed out that everything in this world is unstable, that we are actually in hell. We're in a place where devils and demons dwell. That, by definition, is a hell. It's a beautiful place, but it's designed, on purpose, to be a place where you come into it disadvantaged and fallible. Everything in this world is flawed. It's a probationary state. You are surrounded by individuals who seek your misery, and it's flawed by its very nature. Everything and everybody in this world is flawed. Christ is the only unflawed person who has ever set foot on this earth, from the time that Adam left the garden until the present time. Understand that everything else is flawed for a purpose. It's designed for us to pass through sorrow that we may learn the good from the evil. I remember that when Adam finally partook of the fruit, he said, *"I see that this must be. I will partake that man may be,"* to Eve, his little sweetheart.

And in the background, you hear a voice say, *"That is right."* They turn around, and there is Lucifer with a big grin on his face thinking he has thwarted all the purposes of God. In reality, he is simply fulfilling the plan that was foreordained before this earth was created, as the *Pearl of Great Price* says, *"For he knew not the mind of God."* Because he sinned against light, he doesn't remain where he was. He goes backward, continually losing light and identity and stature, until, as the early Brethren taught, he'll go back to native intelligence and lose his very identity, which is always represented in this world by beheading. So, every time you see a person who is beheaded, whether it's Laban or Goliath, (because ancient societies always did that) it represents the loss of an identity. Remember, everything from the neck up controls everything from the neck down. If you take the head off, the whole system is shot. They understood that principle, if not scientifically, they at least understood it enough that it severely handicaps a person in the next world. You see that all through native and ancient societies. But, here is the very purpose for us being here. After Satan says, *"That is right,"* they turn and look at him, and Eve reaches up and turns Adam's face toward her. I love this! Brethren, this is why we have wives. This is women! Without them, **we don't stand a chance in this world**. She takes and turns his head, looks into his eyes, puts her hand on his cheek, and says, *"It is better that we pass through sorrow that we may know the good from the evil."* I want you to pay attention to the words *pass through*. This very life is referred to in the scriptures as a *temporal* life. Another word for *mortality* is *temporal. Temporal* comes from what word? *Temporary.* So, we are here to come against things that are illusionary. The real person is what's inside you. It's not who you see looking back at you when you look into an earthly mirror. Everything is illusionary here. The real life is not here. The real identity is not here. This is the perfect schoolhouse, the perfect learning laboratory for the Mothers and Fathers in heaven to send their children off to be tutored. *"It is **better** to pass through..."* You see, it's never meant to be permanent; *temporal, temporary,* ***pass through***. You're on a journey here. This is not your abode; this is not home. You've been sent away to go to school so you can learn lessons here that cannot be learned in any other way, nor in any other place. It's wonderful what we are seeing here! But, it's important to remember that everything and everyone in this world are flawed. You need to grab hold of that. So, the only thing we can do to help us get through this is through our experiences. Hopefully, we are learning wisdom and prudence.

Prudence means to be cautious. It's wise to be cautious. *Prudence* and *wisdom* are two words the Lord uses side by side when He speaks. It's wise for us to use those two words in our sojourn here. One of the wisdom principles is that everything and everyone around you are flawed, so you need to look for a source that is not flawed. If you want to be like Christ and be with Christ, then you're not going to get there by obtaining adulterated, twisted truth. You have to seek for a source of truth that you can absolutely, unerringly rely on. That will not be found among any mortals in this world. So, what we need to do is to take the Holy Spirit for our guide. There's a hierarchy, and you can see that in the temple. In the temple, you see the person who plays the Father, gives instruction to the person who plays the Son, and the Son gives instruction to messengers who come down. Actually, the hierarchy in the telestial world is Father, to Son, to Holy Ghost, to angels, to man.

Go with me to 2 Nephi 32 and let me show you something. You've all read this scripture before. What we're looking for is a hierarchy, a power structure, to tap into unadulterated truth. John Taylor said that a lot of the problems we have in our last days, a lot of the delusion that will come (that, in part, God allows to come) is because his people love truth **adulterated**. Isn't that a sad comment? We'd rather go down into the pasture and dip water out of the pasture where the cows have walked through it, rather than to go upstream and find the source. Notice that the source is always upstream. It's never downstream. You've always got to go up to find a pure source. Well, the telestial world is the pasture. The water that's in the pasture, many, many times, too often has been polluted, diluted, and prostituted. 2 Nephi 32:3:

> *Angels speak by the power of the Holy Ghost; wherefore, they speak the words of Christ.*

Do you see a hierarchy there?

> *Wherefore, I said unto you, feast upon the words of Christ; for behold, the words of Christ will tell you all things what ye should do.*

Skip to verse 5:

For behold, again I say unto you that if ye will enter in by the way, and receive the Holy Ghost, it will show unto you all things what ye should do.

So, there's a hierarchy. Angels minister to men in the telestial world. Their boss is the Holy Ghost, so to speak. The God of the telestial world is the Holy Ghost. And He has His helpers. He has many different kinds of helpers. He has angels in the form of resurrected beings. He has translated beings. He has *spirits of just men made perfect*, and other righteous spirits who are commissioned to bless and help those of us who are in the flesh. But, angels work under the direction of the Holy Ghost. The Holy Ghost works under the direction of the Son of God, and the Son of God works under the direction of the Holy Father. There is your power pole. That's your structure. So, what we want to do now, in this world where we're down wandering through the pasture with the water diluted is to go upstream and find the source. We want to tap into that source. When you tap into information in that source, it is never wrong; it is always right. Always! It is the only true, sure source in this world to receive unadulterated truths.

I've said this before. Since Adam left the garden and entered into the lone and dreary world, there have been many restorations. All of them are followed by an apostasy, which was then followed by another restoration, followed by an apostasy, and so forth. Throughout the existence of mortal man in the telestial, fallen world, that's the pattern. I've looked at that and pondered that and here's what happens. The minute God reveals truth through His restoration prophet at that time, and that prophet speaks that pure unadulterated word of God, the moment the word leaves the prophet's mouth, all hell combines to adulterate, prostitute, and destroy that revealed word. This is where the term *secret combination* come from. So, all hell **combines** to destroy that because all hell knows that that's the power source, that when tapped into, spells the destruction of the dark side.

Let's go to Ether chapter 12 and let me show you an interesting little scripture. I've had a couple of calls from brothers and sisters this last week who have just said, "Oh, I'm so upset!" And usually, there has been an abuse: a verbal abuse by a family member, or something. Something has been said to break the heart of the person I'm talking with. They are so discouraged and feel so hopeless as to what they can do about the situation. When you feel like you're beat up, you need to take a different view on it. I'm all about viewing things differently. Put your finger here and let me take you to another place. We'll come back to Ether 12. But, I just had this thought come into my mind, and we just have to go with it.

Let's go to Mosiah chapter 5. This chapter is the great discourse on that *"Mighty change of heart"* that took place with a whole congregation of people:

> *[1] And now, it came to pass that when king Benjamin had thus spoken to his people,*

That's the last three chapters: 2, 3, and 4. I think that if we didn't have anything else in the *Book of Mormon*, other than Mosiah chapters 2-4, there's enough information there to get you back home successfully. That's the power of the *Book of Mormon*. There's enough information in these chapters to get you back to Christ, to usher you into his presence in this life, and be redeemed from the Fall:

> *he sent among them, desiring to know of his people if they believed the words which he had spoken unto them.*
>
> *[2] And they all cried with one voice, saying: Yea, we believe all the words which thou hast spoken unto us; and also, we know of their surety and truth, because of the Spirit of the Lord Omnipotent, which has wrought a mighty change in us, or in our hearts, that we have no more disposition to do evil, but to do good continually.*

We've talked about that in other podcasts. So, because of what has just happened here, because of what we just read in verse 2:

> *[3] And we, ourselves, also, through the infinite goodness of God, and the manifestations of his Spirit, have **great views** of that which is to come; and were it expedient, we could prophesy of all things.*

The reason they can prophesy of all things is because their *views* have changed. Listen to this statement by the prophet Joseph Smith and think about these views:

> *We consider that God has created man with a mind capable of instruction, and a faculty which may be enlarged in proportion to the heed and diligence given to the light communicated from heaven to the intellect;*

What a great statement. That's a ponderable statement. I was thinking about this this week. I was working with some animals out here—I've got some chickens, turkeys, rabbits, some cats, a horse and this, that, and the other—and I'm looking at them and seeing that none of these creatures, these creations of God, have the power of imagination. Power to imagine is only found in God's children. Notice what he said, *"...God has created man with a mind capable of instruction, and a faculty which may be enlarged in proportion to the heed and diligence given to the light communicated from heaven to the intellect."* In other words, you listen to the voice of Christ. You partook of the sacrament today, and you committed to doing three things: take upon yourself the name of Christ, always remember Christ, and keep Christ's commandments. If you do that, then you have the promise. If you commit to doing that on Sunday morning or sometime Sunday, he's going to give you His Spirit, the Light of Christ, which teaches right and wrong, a director, a compass, your own personal compass for the next seven days. If you'll listen to that, it will enlarge your intellect. The rest of the quote says:

> *and that the nearer man approaches perfection,* **the clearer are his views**, *and the greater his enjoyments, till he has overcome the evils of his life*

See! We can do that!

The question comes up, "Can we ever get to a point where evil has no effect upon us while we're still in mortality?" And the answer is yes! You see that alluded to in the temple when the Father says to Christ, *"Instruct Peter, James, and John to go down to Adam and his posterity in the telestial world and cast Satan out of their midst,"* and that's while they are still in the

telestial world. You can come to a point where evil has no more effect on you. Look at the rest of it:
> *till he has overcome the evils of his life and lost every desire for sin;*

This is all happening as a result of your heed and diligence given to light that's communicated to your intellect. It's all based upon that. I want you to remember, the more you learn, the greater your views are. It changes everything. You see things differently:
> *and like the ancients, arrives at that point of faith where he is wrapped in the power and glory of his maker,*

Visualize that for a minute. That's talking about on this earth. None of this quote has anything to do with hereafter:
> *and is caught up to dwell with Him.*

Caught up from where? The telestial world.

Now, let's go back to Ether 12. So, what you want to do is, when things seem to be ganging up on you, when hell seems to be combined against you, you need to look at it differently. If that's truly happening, I say congratulations to you. I say rejoice because that dark mud would not be stirred up unless they were concerned about something. See, they work on prioritizing things on the dark side on the other side of the veil, like we should be doing here. If they've already got people who are doing their bidding and doing it well, then it's not going to be such a concern to the powers that be, in the dark armies, as they are on a person who begins to awaken. Now, when you start to awaken, and you're awakened by doing what? You give *"heed and diligence...to the light communicated from heaven to the intellect."* You have a faculty that can do that. Only God's children have that power. Your faculty for that kind of thing is capable of being eternally enlarged. So, you determine whether that's going to move forward to a fullness, whether you're going to remain stationed where you are, or go backward and lose what you've got. So, I say congratulations to you because obviously, you're doing something that is stirring up these dark-side spirits and causing concern over there. It's like Joseph Smith said:
> *It seems as though the adversary was aware, at a very early period of my life, that I was destined*

> *to prove a disturber and an annoyer of his kingdom;*

Well congratulations, that's what's happening to you. So, if you find that as you are listening to any of these podcasts and they are blessing you, it's coming because knowledge is giving you power. And that's not because of me, but because of the spirit that we try to teach with, and the spirit by which you listen. Now, when you have that power, it's going to result in actions that are going to cause hell to awaken and become concerned. They don't want to lose their converts. So, again, I just say good for you! It's like we said before, the "bells of hell" are ringing, and your name just moved to the top of the agenda sheet discussed in dark places and in combined forces. So, I think that's a wonderful thing.

If you find that you just don't seem to be getting ahead and you say to yourself, like Nephi, *"O wretched man that I am!"* You recognize in yourself that there are deficiencies, and it makes you sad. You want to do better, but it doesn't appear that you're making any progress. I want you to know that you're making great progress or you wouldn't even recognize and be distressed that there's something wrong. The ones I'm concerned with are those doing these kinds of behaviors and don't see anything wrong with it. That's room for concern. But, if you're now looking at your life and seeing behavior that disgusts you and distresses you, I say good for you! Something's happening. You're in the midst of a formula that's working. Now, let's look at that formula.

Now, let's go to Ether 12:27. I remember when I first saw this, it was so exciting for me and this scripture has changed the way I view so much. I've been able to use this scripture to help so many people to view things differently. It starts out, and there's a list here, and we can number them. Number one:

> *And if men [/women] come unto me*

That's your first step. Notice this whole process is a formula for transformation. When you start the process and go all the way through, you come out on the other side transformed in a glorious manner. Step number two:

> *I will show unto them their weakness.*

"Weakness," not weaknesses. He will help you identify the natural fallen man or woman that you are in this world; that's the *weakness*. He'll show it to you. You'll start to see some things about yourself. I learned that if you want to be upset and really have an interesting experience, ask the Lord to show you your weakness and those areas that are keeping you from moving forward. I promise you He'll do that. It's a real eye-opener because most of what He considers barriers to your progress, you consider no big deal. Number three:

I give unto men weakness

Look at that! The very thing that troubles you and distresses you and grieves you and causes you to mourn over who you are are your gifts. Notice that he says, *"I give."* That's a gift. When He gives something to you, you have received a gift. Your weaknesses are gifts! How's that for taking a different view? What's the purpose of that? Here's number four:

that they may be humble;

So, what's the purpose of God showing you your weakness after you come to Him? It's so that you can be humbled because humility is the launch pad for transformation. Humility is the absolute foundational launch pad, base-level, for the transformation of man into anything Godly. It all starts with humility. Number five:

and my grace is sufficient

Whatever that *grace* is, God says there's enough of it. There's enough for everybody. You'll never run out. There's always enough. *Grace* is power and strength. If you want another term for *grace*, put in "the Lord's strength and God's power." He's got enough. There is enough and to spare:

for all men [/women] *that humble themselves before me;*

Did you catch that last one, step number 5? You can't access that *grace*, which is strength and power unless you humble yourself. If you can't voluntarily humble yourself by seeking for it and asking for it and praying for that gift, well, *"God will have a humble people,"* according to President Benson. Either you can **choose** humility, or you can be **compelled**. We have a great day of compulsion coming, folks. There **is** a great day of compulsion coming! That reminds me of a scripture. Go over to Helaman

12:1. You want to see what our day is bringing and what we can to look forward to? This is a scripture that President Eyring has memorized and uses in a lot of his talks:

> *[1] And thus we can behold how false, and also the unsteadiness of the hearts of the children of men;*

Of course, we are unsteady; we're in an unsteady place. We're not going to be steady in an unsteady place:

> *yea, we can see that the Lord in his great infinite goodness doth bless and prosper those who put their trust in him.*
>
> *[2] Yea, and we may see at the very time when he doth prosper his people, yea, in the increase of their fields, their flocks and their herds, and in gold, and in silver,*

Just change the words with those things that fit 2016:

> *and in all manner of precious things of every kind and art; sparing their lives, and delivering them out of the hands of their enemies;* **softening the hearts of their enemies that they should not declare wars against them;**

I have that one triple underlined:

> *yea, and in fine, doing all things for the welfare and happiness of his people; yea,*

In other words, when God does all of that:

> *then is the time that they do harden their hearts, and do forget the Lord their God, and do trample under their feet the Holy One—yea, and this because of their ease, and their exceedingly great prosperity.*

Now, in this next verse, think about what we've been talking about in Ether 12: voluntary humility or compelled humility:

> *[3] And thus we see that except the Lord doth chasten **his** people with many afflictions, yea, except he doth visit them with death and with terror,*

Who is he visiting here? **His** people! Not all people on the earth are **His** people. **His** people are people who have made covenants:

> *and with famine and with all manner of pestilence, they will not remember him.*

Go back over to Ether 12:27 again. If we humble ourselves, not only will we see our weakness, but He will endow us with sufficient *grace* to do what's next. Look at what happens:

> *...for if they humble themselves before me, and have faith in me,* **then** *will I make weak things become strong unto them.*

If you lose your temper, that's a definite weakness in this world. Understandably, there are a lot of things to set you off and pull the trigger. What's the opposite of that? We want to see what the gift is that's waiting for you. The opposite is patience and long-suffering, understanding. You can take that fierce anger that you have, and if you apply this formula, that beast that's always just raging under the surface, ready to come out at any time, will be overcome and turned into a strength. If you try to overcome that and control any of these inconsistencies in this flawed world by your own effort, at best you will have limited success. It will be one step forward and five back; I promise you because you're trying to do it with the strength of your own arm. That's why you've got to apply this formula, and the first step is, "Come unto Me." The opposite of that weakness with anger is patience and longsuffering. And so, your greatest weakness now becomes your most Godly strength.

What a great formula that is. So, if you find that you are looking at yourself and saying, "I'm so weak. I despise myself," I say good for you because you're in the middle of the formula. You would have never seen that in yourself to despise it if you weren't in the process of coming to the Savior. So, the formula is in effect, and you are moving forward. God bless you! Good for you! Let's all rejoice! That's wonderful! Congratulations! You're winning in the telestial battlefield because everything in the gospel is about coming up and being transformed. I thought I would just share that with you because I have had some thoughts and feelings on it.

I want to chat with you for the remainder of the time about something that I've been having on my mind lately. You can look these up in the scriptures. Just go into your search engine on lds.org and type in the phrase, *"from eternity to eternity,"* and you'll see that it's listed several times in the *Book of Mormon* and the *Doctrine and Covenants*. I think it's in the *Pearl of Great Price* also. It seems to be a restored doctrinal term. I don't know if it's in the *Bible* or not, but it's definitely in the other works. And another one is, *"from everlasting to everlasting."* What I'd like to propose to you is that even though it seems to be an oxymoron, eternity has a beginning and an end. In our thinking, we use the word *eternal* and especially *eternity*, as something that has no beginning and has no end. Yet, the very fact that you go *from eternity to eternity* seems to indicate a beginning, an ending, and another beginning. Hold that in mind for just a minute. In the temple sealing, we have the words: *kingdoms, thrones, principalities, powers, dominions,* and *exaltations.* All those words are used in the plural. Yet, we teach and seem to understand that once you've "obtained exaltation" that you have arrived. I would like to change the wording and say, instead of "obtaining exaltation," that we say, "obtain **an** exaltation." I think that by the time you reach the Celestial Kingdom and have the gift of eternal life, if you choose, you've just begun your progress. You've arrived at one level, eternal life in the celestial world where you have **an** inheritance in the same kingdom as the Father and the Son. But, there seems to be much, much more, if you choose to go beyond that.

I wonder about the words in the temple ceremony that say:
> *If you proceed and receive your full endowment, you'll be required to take upon you sacred obligations, the violation of which will bring upon you the judgment of God, for God will not be mocked.*

Now, this next sentence:
> *If any of you desire to **withdraw**, rather than accept these obligations of your own free will and choice, you may now make it known by raising your hand.*

Now, if we look at that within the hour and a half endowment ceremony, none of us receive our full endowment. You've had the initiatory, which initiated you into the endowment, but you only have the first half of the endowment when you leave the temple that day after you have received your temple blessings.

It's incomplete! I think that we in the Church believe that what we've received there is all there is. Again, it's just the beginning. The full endowment does not come back until you receive **second** anointings. You've already received the first one. And they say, *"If you...receive your full endowment..."* The endowment that's spoken of is not complete until you're sealed up to eternal life, obtain the fullness of the Melchizedek Priesthood, and are ordained a king and a queen, a priest and a priestess. So, you see, we haven't received a full one. We've talked about that in the past. You can either receive it through a church ordinance from church authority, or you can receive it, or the equivalent of it, with all its rights and blessings, from under the hand of heavenly messenger beings or from God Himself. The point is, you've only got a portion of it here. All of us who have been through and received our temple endowments, that have not received the *Second Anointing* blessings, have not received the full endowment.

Notice also it says, *"If you desire to withdraw."* In the temple, when it asks if you desire to withdraw it means, "I've received my initiatory, but I don't want to go any further." So, you raise your hand and you are ushered out of the endowment room, for whatever reason you didn't want it. What if those statements that we hear, that we think pertain to the hour and a half to two hours in the temple endowment allegory, are eternal principles that apply in eternity? What if you go forward and receive **an exaltation** in the Celestial Kingdom. There are no exaltations in the terrestrial world. Exaltation is a term referred to and reserved for the celestial world. So, let's say you have inherited an exaltation in the form of eternal life. You and your wife now are a couple, sealed, and now have an inheritance in the celestial world. What if you get there and somebody says to you at that point, "Do you desire to proceed, or do you desire to withdraw?" What if you are given an option once you are there? You are qualified. You wouldn't have been given an option unless you had obtained that promise. What if, when you get there, and you have that promise, there's more? The principle of the agency of man always being in effect is an eternal principle. There is no place in the universe where agency isn't applicable. It isn't something that just belongs to the telestial world and to a fallen man. It exists always, everywhere! So, what if at that point, you have these words or the equivalent of these words spoken to you? "If you want to proceed and receive something fuller, you need to make a choice, or you can decide to stay here," and you exercise agency as to whether you go on from there or you stay. I don't think there's any movement anywhere in eternity—from the premortal life, all the way through the state of probation—where you are not given an opportunity to proceed, stay, or withdraw, unless you are a son of perdition. They are totally acted upon, and when you are acted upon, the principle of agency is negated. You have chosen to negate your ability to choose. So, just some thoughts on that.

Here's something else on this *"from eternity to eternity."* Let's say that at each one of these beginnings, we have a new Mother and Father who've attained exaltation in the celestial world, and they are a husband and wife, mother and father, king and queen, priest and priestess, but they have no posterity. We talked about what Brigham Young said in a previous lesson, that the first authorization for them is that they are authorized by those Grandfathers and Grandmothers that they descend from in higher living spheres of exaltation, to beget spiritual progeny. That's the first authorization. Then you begin to have your family in eternity. What if that **begins an eternity**? What if every time a Mother and a Father are authorized by the Elohim to begin the process that makes **them** part of the Elohim, what if that begins an eternity? What if that eternity goes from there, all the way through to where the Savior of those children and those worlds, under the direction of that new Mom and Dad, completes the mission given to Him where everybody is saved except those who are sons of perdition, and everybody has obtained an exaltation. The Savior of that system presents that to the Father. At that point, the work is finished. That ends an eternity, and it moves *from eternity to eternity, from everlasting to everlasting.*

When Joseph Smith received the Michael Chandler papyri, and the Church purchased them in Kirtland, there were amazing things that were on those papyri with those mummies. Michael Chandler bought them from his uncle Antonio Lebolo, who got them out of the tombs of the Valley of the Kings. I've been over to the Valley of the Kings, and I've seen that pit where the

Abraham mummies and papyri came out. It's interesting to sit there and put your feet on top of the ground where those things came out and read the book of Abraham. Try that if you want an interesting experience! When Joseph was working on those, they were also working on something called the *Abrahamic Alphabet*. It was an alphabet from Egyptian papyri. Joseph was killed before he could complete that. There was so much on those papyri, but he was continually distracted. He was kept on the run, mobbed with false lawsuits and harassed on purpose because the combined powers of hell did not want him to complete and make public the information that was on the Abraham papyri. Here's something we do have: William W. Phelps was working with Joseph on it, and one of the things that they came across was an interesting statement that said:

> *And that eternity, agreeably to the records found in the catacombs of Egypt, has been going on in this* **system** *(not this world) almost two thousand five hundred and fifty-five millions of years.* [2.5 billion years].

There's the word you want to underline, **system**. Think about what we just talked about: **an eternity**. What if another word for *system* is ***an*** *eternity*, beginning with the birth of spiritual progeny of our Father and our Mother, of which Christ was an ordained child to be the Savior of that system and to come to this earth and perform an atonement? What fantastic information that is. You see, every one of the men who sit enthroned with the Holy Fathers and Mothers, who *"go no more out,"* have all gone through a stair-step process of progression. The King Follett Discourse gives us some information. Here are some things that we can deduce. Let me read a couple of things to you that go back to this. What does it mean to contemplate being an heir to God and a joint heir with Christ? Joseph answers this:

> *What is it? To inherit the same power, the same glory and the same exaltation, until you arrive at the station of a god, and ascend the throne of eternal power, the same as those who have gone before.*
> *What did Jesus do?* [Joseph asked]

> *"Why, I do the things I saw my Father do when worlds came rolling into existence. My Father worked out His kingdom with fear and trembling, and I must do the same; and when I get my kingdom* [this is Jesus speaking]*, I shall present it to My Father, so that He may obtain kingdom upon kingdom, and it will exalt Him in glory.* **He will then take a higher exaltation, and I will take His place**, *and thereby become exalted myself."*
> *So that Jesus treads in the tracks of His Father, and inherits what God did before; and God is thus glorified and exalted in the salvation and exaltation of all His children.*

What do we deduce from that? Well, Joseph gave us this masterful pattern; that before God the Father was who He is now, He was an Eternal Son, and intimates that when He says:

> *I do the things I saw my father do.*

What did He see His Father do?

> *To lay down my life as my Father did, and take it up again* [for the sins of the world].

Intimating that before our Father was who He is, that He was the Savior on an older planet in another **system** and that His son Jesus is following in His footsteps, the same as all others have done before. What a marvelous principle that is. To talk about that just speaks volumes to me of hope and glory and to know that I have within me the DNA heritage of all those Fathers and Mothers, an endless line of Holy Mothers and Holy Fathers from which I am descended. What is it They want for me? What is Their work? To bring to pass my immortality and eternal life. That's Their whole purpose! So, what do They do to do that? They sacrifice. The way They exalt Their children in these school rooms and bring them up to be who They are and where They are is through sacrifice. What a wonderful plan we're involved in here. What a beautiful plan!

Over in *Doctrine and Covenants* 121, we start to see now, you and I are talking about things older societies have known. I'm not going to say that individual people haven't known, but for sure we have this knowledge available to us as a society of the Latter-day Saints, and especially in our day when we have the great light, and dark Urim and Thummim called the internet. We have access to information like never before in the history of the world. Verse 26:

> *God shall give unto you knowledge by his Holy Spirit, yea, by the unspeakable gift of the Holy Ghost, that has not been revealed since the world was until now;*

The bottom of verse 27 says that this knowledge was held in reserve. Verse 28:

> *A time to come in the which nothing shall be withheld,*

Nothing! This is our day! The bottom of verse 31 says:

> [It] *shall be revealed in the days of the dispensation of the fulness of times—*

Now, brothers and sisters, *the dispensation of the fullness of times* is broken up into two general categories. We are in the first section of *the dispensation of the fullness of times*. The first part of it can be referred to as part A, *the dispensation of the Gentile* or the time of the Gentile. The scriptures talk about when the time of the Gentile ends or when the fullness of the Gentile comes in. That's the ending of part A of the *dispensation of the fullness of times*. You and I are on the cusp of that. We're on that part where the majority of the Gentiles will not make the leap into part B of this dispensation. They won't make it! The reason they won't make it is that they *"trample under their feet the Holy One"* and *"they set him at naught."* They will not listen to His voice; therefore they are not considered the elect of God because they harden their hearts against his voice. They won't make the transition. There are few Gentiles who will repent and be numbered among those of part B, and part B is *the dispensation of Israel*. So, there are two parts, and we are about to see the end of one and the ushering in of the second one. It's those of us who are considered Gentiles, and I am a Gentile. I have the blood of Israel flowing in my veins, but for all the reasons we talked about in the Gentile lesson, I am a Gentile. I'm among that group that, if I repent, I can be numbered among the House of Israel, when the Melchizedek Priesthood **really** begins to shine forth.

I want to give you something to think about. Ponder this for just a minute. In the temple ceremony, the only priesthood that is used in the telestial world, that you officiate in is Aaronic. Think about that. In the telestial world, the only priesthood that is operative, as far as the temple allegory goes is Aaronic. Just prior to moving from the telestial endowment room and entering the terrestrial room, you have the robes of authority placed on you in preparation for officiating in the Melchizedek Priesthood. You don't officiate in the Melchizedek Priesthood until you enter the terrestrial, millennial, third estate world. Something to think about.

That's not to say that we don't see miracles in this world and in the *day of the Gentile*; we certainly do. No matter where a group of people, an institution of people, or a society finds itself, there are always people within those groups who can rise up and do something more, and they do. But in the coming day, before we are ushered into the Millennium, we have a period of time called the *day of Israel*, in which a few repentant Gentiles will be invited to participate. <u>I believe</u> that in that little period of time, which wraps up *the dispensation of the fullness of times*, you're going to see miracles that will eclipse anything that has taken place in the scriptural record, from Adam down to the present. But I don't believe it's going to happen in the *day of the Gentile* because it's going to require a society that has tremendous faith.

I was speaking with one Navajo woman who wrote me, and we were talking back and forth about the Native Americans and what their future is. Right now, they are pretty much in a state of apostasy and darkness. But, Wilford Woodruff said:

> *It will be a day of God's power among them, and a nation will be born in a day. Their chiefs will be filled with the power of God and receive the Gospel, and they will go forth and build the new Jerusalem, and we shall help them.*

For example, a huge percentage of the Navajo Nation are already baptized members of the Church and yet, the majority of them are not in their covenants and don't have the light and knowledge they need in order to come forth and shine forth. That's going to change. When the day of the Gentile ends, this remnant of Native Americans (along with others), will go and compel humility and make it so that as many as possible, who won't harden their hearts and will become better instead of bitter, can be numbered among the house of Israel in the second half of *the dispensation of the fullness of times*. That period of time, which is sometime between now and the Second Coming, you're going to see Melchizedek Priesthood operative. They'll be performing powerful miracles, raising the dead, controlling the elements, moving mountains, parting the sea, and bringing translated beings down from the city of Enoch where *"we will fall upon their necks, and they shall fall upon our necks."* I think we are going to see that. My belief is that the ordinance of translation, which is not in effect now, will be introduced one more time at the end of the *day of the Gentile* and the opening of the *day of Israel*, prior to the Second Coming. You're going to need translated beings on the earth doing things in order to prepare for the Second Coming of the Lord Jesus Christ. I want to be one of them! How about you?

God Bless you all. I hope this has been interesting and informative for you. Have a great week, and we'll see you next week.

References:
Moses 4:6 "...for he knew not the mind of God..."
2 Nephi 32:3, 5
Joseph Smith, History of the Church, 2:8
Joseph Smith, History of the Church, 1:4
Ether 12:27
"God will have a humble people." *Beware of Pride,* by Ezra Taft Benson, April 1989
Helaman 12:1-3
W. W. Phelps, *Times and Seasons*, vol. 5, pg. 758, 1 Jan. 1844
King Follett Sermon
D&C 121:26, 28, 31
Helaman 12:2 "...trample under their feet the Holy One..."
1 Nephi 19:7 "...they set him at naught..."
Moses 7:63 "...we will fall upon their necks, and they shall fall upon our necks..."
Wilford Woodruff, Journal of Discourses page 282
"the dispensation of the fulness of times" (Ephesians 1:10; D&C 128:20).
Book of Moses 7:63 *"fall on their necks."*
2.5 Billion years, *Times and Seasons* 5 no. 24 (1 January 1844). The Times and Seasons was a church newspaper published monthly, and sometimes biweekly in Nauvoo, Illinois

Added here is the Joseph Smith King Follett Sermon:
Chapter XIV CONFERENCE OF THE CHURCH, APRIL, 1844 (CONTINUED)—THE KING FOLLETT SERMON— THE CHARACTER OF GOD—RELIGIOUS FREEDOM—GOD AN EXALTED MAN—ETERNAL LIFE TO KNOW GOD AND JESUS CHRIST—EVERLASTING BURNINGS—MEANING OF THE HEBREW SCRIPTURES—A COUNCIL OF THE GODS—MEANING OF THE WORD CREATE—THE IMMORTAL INTELLIGENCE—THE RELATION OF MAN TO GOD—OUR GREATEST RESPONSIBILITY—THE UNPARDONABLE SIN—THE FORGIVENESS OF SIN—THE SECOND DEATH.

Sunday, April 7, 1844.—[Conference Report Continued.]

At quarter past three, p.m., the President having arrived, the choir sang a hymn, Elder Amasa Lyman offered prayer.   President Joseph Smith delivered the following discourse before about twenty thousand Saints, being the funeral sermon of Elder King Follett. Reported by Willard Richards, Wilford Woodruff, Thomas Bullock and William Clayton.

Beloved Saints: I will call [for] the attention of this congregation while I address you on the subject of the dead. The decease of our beloved brother, Elder King Follett, who was crushed in a well by the falling of a tub of rock, has more immediately led me to this subject. I have been requested to speak by his friends and relatives, but inasmuch as there are a great many in this congregation who live in this city as well as elsewhere, who have lost friends, I feel disposed to speak on the subject in general, and offer you my ideas, so far as I have ability, and so far as I shall be inspired by the Holy Spirit to dwell on this subject.

I want your prayers and faith that I may have the instruction of Almighty God and the gift of the Holy Ghost, so that I may set forth things that are true and which can be easily comprehended by you, and that the testimony may carry conviction to your hearts and minds of the truth of what I shall say. Pray that the Lord may strengthen my lungs, stay the winds, and let the prayers of the Saints to heaven appear, that they may enter into the ears of the Lord of Sabaoth, for the effectual prayers of the righteous avail much. There is strength here, and I verily believe that your prayers will be heard.

Before I enter fully into the investigation of the subject which is lying before me, I wish to pave the way and bring up the subject from the beginning, that you may understand it. I will make a few preliminaries, in order that you may understand the subject when I come to it. I do not calculate or intend to please your ears with superfluity of words or oratory, or with much learning; but I calculate [intend] to edify you with the simple truths from heaven.

The Character of God

In the first place, I wish to go back to the beginning—to the morn of creation. There is the starting point for us to look to, in order to understand and be fully acquainted with the mind, purposes and decrees of the Great Eloheim, who sits in yonder heavens as he did at the creation of the world. It is necessary for us to have an understanding of God himself in the beginning. If we start right, it is easy to go right all the time; but if we start wrong we may go wrong, and it will be a hard matter to get right.

There are but a very few beings in the world who understand rightly the character of God. The great majority of mankind do not comprehend anything, either that which is past, or that which is to come, as it respects their relationship to God. They do not know, neither do they understand the nature of that relationship; and consequently they know but little above the brute beast, or more than to eat, drink and sleep. This is all man knows about God or His existence, unless it is given by the inspiration of the Almighty.

If a man learns nothing more than to eat, drink and sleep, and does not comprehend any of the designs of God, the beast comprehends the same things. It eats, drinks, sleeps, and knows nothing more about God; yet it knows as much as we, unless we are able to comprehend by the inspiration of Almighty God. If men do not comprehend the character of God, they do not comprehend themselves. I want to go back to the beginning, and so lift your minds into more lofty spheres and a more exalted understanding than what the human mind generally aspires to. I want to ask this congregation, every man, woman and child, to answer the question in their own hearts, what kind of a being God is? Ask yourselves; turn your thoughts into your hearts, and say if any of you have seen, heard, or communed with Him? This is a question that may occupy your attention for a long time. I again repeat the question—What kind of a being is God? Does any man or woman know? Have any of you seen Him, heard Him, or communed with Him? Here is the question that will, peradventure, from this time henceforth occupy your attention. The scriptures inform us that "This is life eternal that they might know thee, the only true God, and Jesus Christ whom thou hast sent."

If any man does not know God, and inquires what kind of a being He is—if he will search diligently his own heart—if the declaration of Jesus and the apostles be true, he will realize that he has not eternal life; for there can be eternal life on no other principle.

My first object is to find out the character of the only wise and true, God, and what kind of a being He is; and if I am so fortunate as to be the man to comprehend God, and explain or convey the principles to your hearts, so that the Spirit seals them upon you, then let every man and woman henceforth sit in silence, put their hands on their mouths, and never lift their hands or voices, or say anything against the man of God or the servants of God again. But if I fail to do it, it becomes my duty to renounce all further pretensions to revelations and inspirations, or to be a prophet; and I should be like the rest of the world—a false teacher, be hailed as a friend, and no man would seek my life. But if all religious teachers were honest enough to renounce their pretensions to godliness when their ignorance of the knowledge of God is made manifest, they will all be as badly off as I am, at any rate; and you might just as well take the lives of other false teachers as that of mine. If any man is authorized to take away my life because he thinks and says I am a false teacher, then, upon the same principle, we should be justified in taking away the life of every false teacher, and where would be the end of blood? And who would not be the sufferer?

The Privilege of Religious Freedom
But meddle not with any man for his religion: all governments ought to permit every man to enjoy his religion unmolested. No man is authorized to take away life in consequence of difference of religion, which all laws and governments ought to tolerate and protect, right or wrong. Every man has a natural, and, in our country, a constitutional right to be a false prophet, as well as a true prophet. If I show, verily, that I have the truth of God, and show that ninety-nine out of every hundred professing religious ministers are false teachers, having no authority, while they pretend to hold the keys of God's kingdom on earth, and was to kill them because they are false teachers, it would deluge the whole world with blood.

I will prove that the world is wrong, by showing what God is. I am going to inquire after God; for I want you all to know Him, and to be familiar with Him; and if I am bringing you to a knowledge of Him, all persecutions against me ought to cease. You will then know that I am His servant; for I speak as one having authority.

God An Exalted Man
I will go back to the beginning before the world was, to show what kind of a being God is. What sort of a being was God in the beginning? Open your ears and hear, all ye ends of the earth, for I am going to prove it to you by the Bible, and to tell you the designs of God in relation to the human race, and why He interferes with the affairs of man.

God himself was once as we are now, and is an exalted man, and sits enthroned in yonder heavens! That is the great secret. If the veil were rent today, and the great God who holds this world in its orbit, and who upholds all worlds and all things by His power, was to make himself visible,—I say, if you were to see him today, you would see him like a man in form like yourselves in all the person, image, and very form as a man; for Adam was created in the very fashion, image and likeness of God, and received instruction from, and walked, talked and conversed with Him, as one man talks and communes with another.

In order to understand the subject of the dead, for consolation of those who mourn for the loss of their friends, it is necessary we should understand the character and being of God and how He came to be so; for I am going to tell you how God came to be God. We have imagined and supposed that God was God from all eternity. I will refute that idea, and take away the veil, so that you may see.

These are incomprehensible ideas to some, but they are simple. It is the first principle of the gospel to know for a certainty the character of God, and to know that we may converse with Him as one man converses with another, and that He was once a man like us; yea, that God himself, the Father of us all, dwelt on an earth, the same as Jesus Christ Himself did; and I will show it from the Bible.

Eternal Life to Know God and Jesus Christ
I wish I was in a suitable place to tell it, and that I had the trump of an archangel, so that I could tell the story in such a manner that persecution would cease forever. What did Jesus say? (Mark it, Elder Rigdon!) **The scriptures inform us that Jesus said, as the Father hath power in himself, even so hath the Son power— to do what? Why, what the Father did. The answer is obvious—in a manner to lay down his body and take it up again. Jesus, what are you going to do? To lay down my life as my Father did, and take it up again.** Do you believe it? If you do not believe it you do not believe the Bible. The scriptures say it, and I defy all the learning and wisdom and all the combined powers of earth and hell together to refute it. Here, then, is eternal life—to know the only wise and true God; and you have got to learn how to be gods yourselves, and to be kings and priests to God, the same as all gods have done before you, namely, by going from one small degree to another, and from a small capacity to a great one; from grace to grace, from exaltation to exaltation, until you attain to the resurrection of the dead, and are able to dwell in everlasting burnings, and to sit in glory, as do those who sit enthroned in everlasting power. And I want you to know that God, in the last days, while certain individuals are proclaiming His name, is not trifling with you or me.

The Righteous to Dwell in Everlasting Burnings
These are the first principles of consolation. How consoling to the mourners when they are called to part with a husband, wife, father, mother, child, or dear relative, to know that, although the earthly tabernacle is laid down and dissolved, they shall rise again to dwell in everlasting burnings in immortal glory, not to sorrow, suffer, or die any more, **but they shall be heirs of God and joint heirs with Jesus Christ. What is it? To inherit the same power, the same glory and the same exaltation, until you arrive at the station of a god, and ascend the throne of eternal power, the same as those who have gone before. What did Jesus do? Why, I do the things I saw my Father do when worlds came rolling into existence. My Father worked out His kingdom with fear and trembling, and I must do the same; and when I get my kingdom, I shall present it to My Father, so that He may obtain kingdom upon kingdom, and it will exalt Him in glory. He will then take a higher exaltation, and I will take His place, and thereby become exalted myself.** So that Jesus treads in the tracks of His Father, and inherits what God did before; and God is thus glorified and exalted in the salvation and exaltation of all His children. It is plain beyond disputation, and you thus learn some of the first principles of the gospel, about which so much hath been said.

When you climb up a ladder, you must begin at the bottom, and ascend step by step, until you arrive at the top; and so it is with the principles of the gospel— you must begin with the first, and go on until you learn all the principles of exaltation. But it will be a great while after you have passed through the veil before you will have learned them. It is not all to be comprehended in this world; it will be a great work to learn our salvation and exaltation even beyond the grave. I suppose I am not allowed to go into an investigation of anything that is not contained in the Bible. If I do, I think there are so many over-wise men here that they would cry "treason" and put me to death. So I will go to the old Bible and turn commentator today.

I shall comment on the very first Hebrew word in the Bible; I will make a comment on the very first sentence of the history of creation in the Bible— Berosheit. I want to analyze the word. Baith—in, by, through, and everything else. Roch—the head, Sheit— grammatical termination. When the inspired man wrote it, he did not put the baith there. An old Jew without any authority added the word; he thought it too bad to begin to talk about the head! It read first, "The head one of the Gods brought forth the Gods." That is the true meaning of the words. Baurau signifies to bring forth. If you do not believe it, you do not believe the learned man of God. Learned men can teach you no more than what I have told you. Thus the head God brought forth the Gods in the grand council.

I will transpose and simplify it in the English language. Oh, ye lawyers, ye doctors, and ye priests, who have persecuted me, I want to let you know that the Holy Ghost knows something as well as you do. The head God called together the Gods and sat in grand council to bring forth the world. The grand councilors sat at the head in yonder heavens and contemplated the creation of the worlds which were created at the time. When I say doctors and lawyers, I mean the doctors and lawyers of the scriptures. I have done so hitherto without explanation, to let the lawyers flutter and everybody laugh at them. Some learned doctors might take a notion to say the scriptures say thus and so; and we must believe the scriptures; they are not to be altered. But I am going to show you an error in them. I have an old edition of the New Testament in the Latin, Hebrew, German and Greek languages. I have been reading the German, and find it to be the most [nearly] correct translation, and to correspond nearest to the revelations which God has given to me for the last fourteen years. It tells about Jacobus, the son of Zebedee. It means Jacob. In the English New Testament it is translated James. Now, if Jacob had the keys, you might talk about James through all eternity and never get the keys. In the 21st. of the fourth chapter of Matthew, my old German edition gives the word Jacob instead of James.   The doctors (I mean doctors of law, not physic) say, "If you preach anything not according to the Bible, we will cry treason." How can we escape the damnation of hell, except God be with us and reveal to us? Men bind us with chains. The Latin says Jacobus, which means Jacob; the Hebrew says Jacob, the Greek says Jacob and the German says Jacob, here we have the testimony of four against one. I thank God that I have got this old book; but I thank him more for the gift of the Holy Ghost. I have got the oldest book in the world; but I have got the oldest book in my heart, even the gift of the Holy Ghost. I have all the four Testaments. Come here, ye learned men, and read, if you can. I should not have introduced this testimony, were it not to back up the word rosh—the head, the Father of the Gods. I should not have brought it up, only to show that I am right.

A Council of the Gods
In the beginning, the head of the Gods called a council of the Gods; and they came together and concocted [prepared] a plan to create the world and people it. When we begin to learn this way, we begin to learn the only true God, and what kind of a being we have got to worship. Having a knowledge of God, we begin to know how to approach Him, and how to ask so as to receive an answer. When we understand the character of God, and know how to come to Him, he begins to unfold the heavens to us, and to tell us all about it. When we are ready to come to him, he is ready to come to us.

Now, I ask all who hear me, why the learned men who are preaching salvation, say that God created the heavens and the earth out of nothing? The reason is, that they are unlearned in the things of God, and have not the gift of the Holy Ghost; they account it blasphemy in any one to contradict their idea. If you tell them that God made the world out of something, they will call you a fool. But I am learned, and know more than all the world put together. The Holy Ghost does, anyhow, and he is within me, and comprehends more than all the world; and I will associate myself with him.

Meaning of the Word Create
You ask the learned doctors why they say the world was made out of nothing, and they will answer, "Doesn't the Bible say He created the world?" And they infer, from the word create, that it must have been made out of nothing. Now, the word create came from the word baurau, which does not mean to create out of nothing; it means to organize; the same as a man would organize materials and build a ship. Hence we infer that God had materials to organize the world out of chaos—chaotic matter, which is element, and in which dwells all the glory. Element had an existence from the time He had. The pure principles of element are principles which can never be destroyed; they may be organized and re-organized, but not destroyed. They had no beginning and can have no end.

The Immortal Intelligence
I have another subject to dwell upon, which is calculated to exalt man; but it is impossible for me to say much on this subject, I shall therefore just touch upon it, for time will not permit me to say all. It is associated with the subject of the resurrection of the dead,—namely, the soul—the mind of man—the immortal spirit. Where did it come from? All learned men and doctors of divinity say that God created it in the beginning; but it is not so: the very idea lessens man in my estimation. I do not believe the doctrine; I know better. Hear it, all ye ends of the world; for God has told me so; and if you don't believe me, it will not make the truth without effect. I will make a man appear

a fool before I get through; if he does not believe it. I am going to tell of things more noble.

We say that God Himself is a self-existing being. Who told you so? It is correct enough; but how did it get into your heads? Who told you that man did not exist in like manner upon the same principles? Man does exist upon the same principles. God made a tabernacle and put a spirit into it, and it became a living soul. (Refers to the Bible.) How does it read in the Hebrew? It does not say in the Hebrew that God created the spirit of man. It says,

"God made man out of the earth and put into him Adam's spirit, and so became a living body."

The mind or the intelligence which man possesses is co-equal [co-eternal] with God himself. I know that my testimony is true; hence, when I talk to these mourners, what have they lost? Their relatives and friends are only separated from their bodies for a short season: their spirits which existed with God have left the tabernacle of clay only for a little moment, as it were; and they now exist in a place where they converse together the same as we do on the earth, I am dwelling on the immortality of the spirit of man. Is it logical to say that the intelligence of spirits is immortal, and yet that it has a beginning? The intelligence of spirits had no beginning, neither will it have an end. That is good logic. That which has a beginning may have an end. There never was a time when there were not spirits; for they are co-equal [co-eternal] with our Father in heaven. I want to reason more on the spirit of man; for I am dwelling on the body and spirit of man—on the subject of the dead. I take my ring from my finger and liken it unto the mind of man—the immortal part, because it had no beginning. Suppose you cut it in two; then it has a beginning and an end; but join it again, and it continues one eternal round. So with the spirit of man. As the Lord liveth, if it had a beginning, it will have an end. All the fools and learned and wise men from the beginning of creation, who say that the spirit of man had a beginning, prove that it must have an end; and if that doctrine is true, then the doctrine of annihilation would be true. But if I am right, I might with boldness proclaim from the house-tops that God never had the power to create the spirit of man at all. God himself could not create himself.

Intelligence is eternal and exists upon a self-existent principle. It is a spirit from age to age and there is no creation about it. All the minds and spirits that God ever sent into the world are susceptible of enlargement.

The first principles of man are self-existent with God. God himself, finding he was in the midst of spirits and glory, because he was more intelligent, saw proper to institute laws whereby the rest could have a privilege to advance like himself. The relationship we have with God places us in a situation to advance in knowledge. He has power to institute laws to instruct the weaker intelligences, that they may be exalted with Himself, so that they might have one glory upon another, and all that knowledge, power, glory, and intelligence, which is requisite in order to save them in the world of spirits.

This is good doctrine. It tastes good. I can taste the principles of eternal life, and so can you. They are given to me by the revelations of Jesus Christ; and I know that when I tell you these words of eternal life as they are given to me, you taste them, and I know that you believe them. You say honey is sweet, and so do I. I can also taste the spirit of eternal life. I know that it is good; and when I tell you of these things which were given me by inspiration of the Holy Spirit, you are bound to receive them as sweet, and rejoice more and more.

The Relation of Man to God
I want to talk more of the relation of man to God. I will open your eyes in relation to the dead. All things whatsoever God in his infinite wisdom has seen fit and proper to reveal to us, while we are dwelling in mortality, in regard to our mortal bodies, are revealed to us in the abstract, and independent of affinity of this mortal tabernacle, but are revealed to our spirits precisely as though we had no bodies at all; and those revelations which will save our spirits will save our bodies. God reveals them to us in view of no eternal dissolution of the body, or tabernacle. Hence the responsibility, the awful responsibility, that rests upon us in relation to our dead; for all the spirits who have not obeyed the Gospel in the flesh must either obey it in the spirit or be damned. Solemn thought!—dreadful thought! Is there nothing to be done?—no preparation—no salvation for our fathers and friends who have died without having had the opportunity to obey the decrees of the Son of Man? Would to God that I had forty days and nights in which to tell you all! I would let you know that I am not a "fallen prophet."

Our Greatest Responsibility
What promises are made in relation to the subject of the salvation of the dead? and what kind of characters are those who can be saved, although their bodies are mouldering and decaying in the grave? When His commandments teach us, it is in view of eternity; for we are looked upon by God as though we were in eternity; God dwells in eternity, and does not view things as we do. The greatest responsibility in this world that God has laid upon us is to seek after our dead. The apostle says, "They without us cannot be made perfect"; for it is necessary that the sealing power should be in our hands to seal our children and our dead for the fulness of the dispensation of times—a dispensation to meet the promises made by Jesus Christ before the foundation of the world for the salvation of man.
Now, I will speak of them. I will meet Paul half way. I say to you, Paul, you cannot be perfect without us. It is necessary that those who are going before and those who come after us should have salvation in common with us; and thus hath God made it obligatory upon man. Hence, God said, "I will send you Elijah the prophet before the coming of the great and dreadful day of the Lord: he shall turn the heart of the fathers to the children, and the heart of the children to their fathers, lest I come and smite the earth with a curse."

The Unpardonable Sin
I have a declaration to make as to the provisions which God hath made to suit the conditions of man—made from before the foundation of the world. What has Jesus said? All sins, and all blasphemies, and every transgression, except one, that man can be guilty of, may be forgiven; and there is a salvation for all men, either in this world or the world to come, who have not committed the unpardonable sin, there being a provision either in this world or the world of spirits. Hence God hath made a provision that every spirit in the eternal world can be ferreted out and saved unless he has committed that unpardonable sin which cannot be remitted to him either in this world or the world of spirits. God has wrought out a salvation for all men, unless they have committed a certain sin; and every man who has a friend in the eternal world can save him, unless he has committed the unpardonable sin. And so you can see how far you can be a savior. A man cannot commit the unpardonable sin after the dissolution of the body, and there is a way possible for escape. Knowledge saves a man; and in the world of spirits no man can be exalted but by knowledge. So long as a man will not give heed to the commandments, he must abide without salvation. If a man has knowledge, he can be saved; although, if he has been guilty of great sins, he will be punished for them. But when he consents to obey the gospel, whether here or in the world of spirits, he is saved.
A man is his own tormentor and his own condemner. Hence the saying, They shall go into the lake that burns with fire and brimstone. The torment of disappointment in the mind of man is as exquisite as a lake burning with fire and brimstone. I say, so is the torment of man.
I know the scriptures and understand them. I said, no man can commit the unpardonable sin after the dissolution of the body, nor in this life, until he receives the Holy Ghost; but they must do it in this world. Hence the salvation of Jesus Christ was wrought out for all men, in order to triumph over the devil; for if it did not catch him in one place, it would in another; for he stood up as a Savior. All will suffer until they obey Christ himself.
The contention in heaven was—Jesus said there would be certain souls that would not be saved; and the devil said he would save them all, and laid his plans before the grand council, who gave their vote in favor of Jesus Christ. So the devil rose up in rebellion against God, and was cast down, with all who put up their heads for him. (Book of Moses—Pearl of Great Price, Ch. 4:1-4; Book of Abraham, Ch. 3:23-28.)

The Forgiveness of Sins
All sins shall be forgiven, except the sin against the Holy Ghost; for Jesus will save all except the sons of perdition. What must a man do to commit the unpardonable sin? He must receive the Holy Ghost, have the heavens opened unto him, and know God, and then sin against him. After a man has sinned against the Holy Ghost, there is no repentance for him. He has got to say that the sun does not shine while he sees it; he has got to deny Jesus Christ when the heavens have been opened unto him, and to deny the plan of salvation

with his eyes open to the truth of it; and from that time he begins to be an enemy. This is the case with many apostates of the Church of Jesus Christ of Latter-day Saints.

When a man begins to be an enemy to this work, he hunts me, he seeks to kill me, and never ceases to thirst for my blood. He gets the spirit of the devil—the same spirit that they had who crucified the Lord of Life—the same spirit that sins against the Holy Ghost. You cannot save such persons; you cannot bring them to repentance; they make open war, like the devil, and awful is the consequence.

I advise all of you to be careful what you do, or you may by-and-by find out that you have been deceived. Stay yourselves; do not give way; don't make any hasty moves, you may be saved. If a spirit of bitterness is in you, don't be in haste. You may say, that man is a sinner. Well, if he repents, he shall be forgiven. Be cautious: await. When you find a spirit that wants bloodshed,—murder, the same is not of God, but is of the devil. Out of the abundance of the heart of man the mouth speaketh.

The best men bring forth the best works. The man who tells you words of life is the man who can save you. I warn you against all evil characters who sin against the Holy Ghost; for there is no redemption for them in this world nor in the world to come.

I could go back and trace every object of interest concerning the relationship of man to God, if I had time. I can enter into the mysteries; I can enter largely into the eternal worlds; for Jesus said, "In my Father's house are many mansions; if it were not so, I would have told you. I go to prepare a place for you." (John 14:2). Paul says, "There is one glory of the sun, and another glory of the moon, and another glory of the stars; for one star differeth from another star in glory. So also is the resurrection of the dead." (1 Cor. 15:41). What have we to console us in relation to the dead? We have reason to have the greatest hope and consolation for our dead of any people on the earth; for we have seen them walk worthily in our midst, and seen them sink asleep in the arms of Jesus; and those who have died in the faith are now in the celestial kingdom of God. And hence is the glory of the sun.

You mourners have occasion to rejoice, speaking of the death of Elder King Follett; for your husband and father is gone to wait until the resurrection of the dead—until the perfection of the remainder; for at the resurrection your friend will rise in perfect felicity and go to celestial glory, while many must wait myriads of years before they can receive the like blessings; and your expectations and hopes are far above what man can conceive; for why has God revealed it to us? I am authorized to say, by the authority of the Holy Ghost, that you have no occasion to fear; for he is gone to the home of the just. Don't mourn, don't weep. I know it by the testimony of the Holy Ghost that is within me; and you may wait for your friends to come forth to meet you in the morn of the celestial world.

Rejoice, O Israel! Your friends who have been murdered for the truth's sake in the persecutions shall triumph gloriously in the celestial world, while their murderers shall welter for ages in torment, even until they shall have paid the uttermost farthing. I say this for the benefit of strangers.

I have a father, brothers, children, and friends who have gone to a world of spirits. They are only absent for a moment. They are in the spirit, and we shall soon meet again. The time will soon arrive when the trumpet shall sound. When we depart, we shall hail our mothers, fathers, friends, and all whom we love, who have fallen asleep in Jesus. There will be no fear of mobs, persecutions, or malicious lawsuits and arrests; but it will be an eternity of felicity.

A question may be asked—"Will mothers have their children in eternity?" Yes! Yes! Mothers, you shall have your children; for they shall have eternal life, for their debt is paid. There is no damnation awaiting them for they are in the spirit. But as the child dies, so shall it rise from the dead, and be for ever living in the learning of God. It will never grow [in the grave]; it will still be the child, in the same precise form [when it rises] as it appeared before it died out of its mother's arms, but possessing all the intelligence of a God. Children dwell in the mansions of glory and exercise power, but appear in the same form as when on earth. Eternity is full of thrones, upon which dwell thousands of children, reigning on thrones of glory, with not one cubit added to their stature.

I will leave this subject here, and make a few remarks on the subject of baptism. The baptism of water, without the baptism of fire and the Holy Ghost attending it, is of no use; they are necessarily and inseparably connected. An individual must be born of water and the spirit in order to get into the kingdom of God. In the German, the text bears me out the same as the revelations which I have given and taught for the past fourteen years on that subject. I have the testimony to put in their teeth. My testimony has been true all the time. You will find it in the declaration of John the Baptist. (Reads from the German.) John says, "I baptize you with water, but when Jesus comes, who has the power (or keys) He shall administer the baptism of fire and the Holy Ghost." Great God! Where is now all the sectarian world? And if this testimony is true, they are all damned as clearly as anathema can do it. I know the text is true. I call upon all you Germans who know that it is true to say, Eye. (Loud shouts of "Aye.")

Alexander Campbell, how are you going to save people with water alone? For John said his baptism was good for nothing without the baptism of Jesus Christ. "Therefore, not leaving the principles of the doctrine of Christ, let us go on unto perfection; not laying again the foundation of repentance from dead works, and of faith towards God, of the doctrine of baptism, and of laying on of hands, and of resurrection of the dead, and of eternal judgment. And this will we do, if God permit." (Heb. 6:1-3).

There is one God, one Father, one Jesus, one hope of our calling, one baptism. All these three baptisms only make one. Many talk of baptism not being essential to salvation; but this kind of teaching would lay the foundation of their damnation. I have the truth, and am at the defiance of the world to contradict me, if they can.

I have now preached a little Latin, a little Hebrew, Greek, and German; and I have fulfilled all. I am not so big a fool as many have taken me to be. The Germans know that I read the German correctly.

The Second Death
Hear it, all ye ends of the earth—all ye priests, all ye sinners, and all men. Repent! Repent! Obey the gospel. Turn to God; for your religion won't save you, and you will be damned. I do not say how long. There have been remarks made concerning all men being redeemed from hell; but I say that those who sin against the Holy Ghost cannot be forgiven in this world or in the world to come; they shall die the second death. Those who commit the unpardonable sin are doomed to Gnolom—to dwell in hell, worlds without end. As they concocted scenes of bloodshed in this world, so they shall rise to that resurrection which is as the lake of fire and brimstone. Some shall rise to the everlasting burnings of God; for God dwells in everlasting burnings and some shall rise to the damnation of their own filthiness, which is as exquisite a torment as the lake of fire and brimstone.

I have intended my remarks for all, both rich and poor, bond and free, great and small. I have no enmity against any man. I love you all; but I hate some of your deeds. I am your best friend, and if persons miss their mark it is their own fault. If I reprove a man, and he hates me, he is a fool; for I love all men, especially these my brethren and sisters.

I rejoice in hearing the testimony of my aged friends. You don't know me; you never knew my heart. No man knows my history. I cannot tell it: I shall never undertake it. I don't blame any one for not believing my history. If I had not experienced what I have, I would not have believed it myself. I never did harm any man since I was born in the world. My voice is always for peace. I cannot lie down until all my work is finished. I never think any evil, nor do anything to the harm of my fellow-man. When I am called by the trump of the archangel and weighed in the balance, you will all know me then. I add no more. God bless you all. Amen.

Chapter Forty-Five
Podcast 045 Baptism of Fire, Precursor to Second Comforter

The information originally given in this podcast was according to Mike's learning and understanding at the time. As he received further knowledge and understanding, he amended and corrected some of this information. In this chapter, efforts have been made to correct these misunderstandings.

Amendments from podcast 053—*The Tip of the Spear*
    I have received some information this week about the *baptism of fire and the Holy Ghost*. I previously mentioned that the *baptism of fire and the Holy Ghost*, according to the scriptural pattern, is always accompanied by angels and fire. Now, that's not the fire we relate to; that's a telestial fire. This fire could be called *the glory of God*. In some cases it's *cloven tongues of fire*. I talked to a man who had his *baptism of fire and the Holy Ghost*, and he saw the angels that were ministering to him and others that were with him, and also cloven tongues of fire that he described as little flames that were spinning around above each person who was receiving this ordinance. They all saw that. Now, I talked to another man who'd had his *baptism of fire and the Holy Ghost*, and as I was talking to him, he said he didn't see any fire, and he didn't have any angels administer to him. So, when he listened to podcast 045, he went to the Father, in the

name of Christ, and asked why there hadn't been any fire or angels during his *baptism of fire and the Holy Ghost* episode. The Lord said that there was. He opened up a vision to him where he saw his experience of receiving the *baptism of fire and the Holy Ghost*, and in the vision, he could see the angels and the fire that was there. But, he did not see them when it actually happened to him. I thought that was really interesting too!

Another thing I've learned from some of my mentors who have gone before us and have obtained these things, is this: I have a tendency when I teach these things out of the scriptures, to lay them out pattern-wise and in a step-by-step process. There is nothing wrong with that, other than the fact that the Father and the Son can do their work any way They want to. I have a tendency to say, "According to the scriptures, according to my experience, I've heard and read this is what's going to happen, and that is what's going to happen, etc." As I was talking to this man who has had the *baptism of fire and the Holy Ghost*, who has had the *calling and election made sure through the more sure word of prophecy*, who has received the *Second Comforter*, and has visited many times with the Lord, he said "Mike, all of those things can happen at once, and at the same time." I had believed it could only happen in a certain order and I thought, "Wow! That is so wonderful."

So, as I've mentioned before, I'm like the rest of you who have not received this, pressing forward, and these men and women who are sharing their experiences, give us information that you just can't find anywhere in the scriptures, and that you can't find in the history the Church. These are contemporary accounts of people who are among us that have had, and continue to have, these interactions with heaven and obtain these blessed gifts. So, as they share them with me, I ask if it's okay if I can share these things on the podcast and they say, "Yes." One of them told me that the day has come for these things to be talked about openly. I thought that was interesting because as I look back on my own experience and can see that over the last decade, this has started to open up where people, at first very guarded and very selectively, would talk about it. But, this past week I have read about or talked to several men and women, who have obtained these blessings and received permission to share with me, and I received permission from them to share it with you. I'm so excited! I would never have these experiences if it weren't for these podcasts that people are listening to. I thank my Heavenly Father and our friends who are sharing their sacred experiences with us, so that we can have the confidence to rise up and claim and obtain these same blessings for us. That's the way it works. Romans chapter 10 says that "faith comes by hearing the word of God." That's what's happening. We're hearing about these experiences and, as we do, it is an interesting thing that the process of people obtaining these blessings increases. There are more and more, at a quicker pace, that are obtaining these blessings, and so I'm grateful for that. Praise the Lord for His kindness and mercy to me.

****

Well, good evening brothers and sisters, and Merry Christmas to you. I hope you had a great Christmas holiday and that family and friends were brought together in love and harmony. This past week I had an opportunity to go to Holbrook, Arizona and witness the baptism of a little eight-year-old girl. Her father is familiar with the baptismal ordinance, the proper doctrine affiliated with that baptismal ordinance, and he gave a marvelous talk to the people that were there. The bishop was on hand and I was watching the bishop's face to see how he would respond to this information that is not well understood by the members of the Church. The bishop sat there and nodded his head in agreement, as this father talked about the baptismal ordinance which has three different parts to it. Number one is the baptism of water by authorized mortals. Number two is the laying on of hands to receive the gift of the Holy Ghost. And number three that he mentioned in his talk is *the baptism of fire and the Holy Ghost*. Now, the way that the *baptism of fire and the Holy Ghost* is understood throughout the Church is that when you have your hands laid upon your head during the confirmation part of the baptismal ordinance, and the person officiating says, "Receive the Holy Ghost," the majority of the membership of the Church think that is fullness of receiving the Holy Ghost, or the *baptism of fire and the Holy Ghost* at that point. They think that is a command by the person who is officiating in the ordinance, that the Holy Ghost now becomes the constant companion of the recipient upon whose head these hands are laid. The Brethren in the Church, especially Elder Bednar, are seeking to turn that around. And we've talked about that in some detail, so I won't go into that tonight. You can look that up in *Highly Favored of the Lord,* vol. 1, ch. 8. We laid it out there according to doctrine and according to Elder Bednar's quotes there.

What I have always taught is that the *baptism of fire and the Holy Ghost* is the precursor to receiving the *Second Comforter* and that no one is going to receive the *Second Comforter* until they have had their *baptism of fire and the Holy Ghost.* Most of the time, I believe that is true but I have discovered that those two things can also happen together. I want to make that clarification. Now, another thing that is taught throughout the Church is that the *baptism of fire and the Holy Ghost* is a process. And when I was giving that talk in New Jersey, people that were there in authority were quick to point out to the missionaries that this is a process and not an event. What I would like to say to you tonight is that that is not completely true. The *baptism of fire and the Holy Ghost* is a process that ends with an event, and it is recorded in scripture as such. Now, like everything else in the gospel, everything proceeds from portions to fullnesses. So, you could liken the *baptism of fire and the Holy Ghost* to a physical birth. Physical birth has a process of nine months that ends in an event: birth. The same is true with *baptism of fire and the Holy Ghost.* There is a process of sanctification, of justification, of being cleansed step-by-step through the process of repentance and the power of the atonement of Christ, but it has to end in an event. And what's more, it's a baptism. The very word of baptism, in and of itself, means *to immerse.* The baptism of water is a pattern of *the baptism of fire and the Holy Ghost*, as you are totally immersed in water, so, in order for this to be a baptism you have to be totally immersed in heavenly fire. There is no such thing as a partial water baptism, and so, likewise, there is no such thing as a partial *baptism of fire and the Holy Ghost.* If you don't get the *baptism of fire and the Holy Ghost* you are not prepared to enter into a terrestrial realm; it's a prerequisite. The *baptism of fire and the Holy Ghost* cleanses and renews and quickens your spirit. The *baptism of fire* also has a renewing capability on the physical body, but it quickens the spirit. After the *baptism of fire and the Holy Ghost,* your spirit is changed. The whole thing is a process to help prepare you and transform you to come into the presence of the Lord Jesus Christ, which means that you're going to need to step up now and be prepared to go into a terrestrial world. Keep in mind, the Holy Ghost is the *First Comforter*, and the Holy Ghost is that God or *Comforter,* of the telestial world, and His purpose is to change, transform, cleanse, and purify you so that you can now become a terrestrial being. That's what happens when you have the *baptism of fire and the Holy Ghost.* You are now preparing to become a terrestrial being and to have an encounter with the Lord Jesus Christ on a terrestrial level.

The Lord Jesus Christ is the *Second Comforter,* and His job, His purpose is to transform, further transform, and prepare you to enter into the presence of the *Third Comforter* in the celestial realms of glory, and that is the Father. <u>And I believe</u> that there is even another *comforter* after that, and that is the *Fourth Comforter,* and <u>I believe</u> that that can be our Heavenly Mother. Now the *Third and Fourth Comforters* are not referred to anywhere in the scriptures, nor to my knowledge, anywhere in the writings of the Latter-day Saints. But, I don't think that anybody is going to have an encounter with Heavenly Mother unless they have been changed, transformed and prepared by the Father Himself to meet our Heavenly Mother. So, this is just a movement from one place to another place, each Being at each level and at each state, preparing you to enter into the next realm. So, this *baptism of fire and the Holy Ghost* is recognizable in the scriptures.

I want to take you to 3 Nephi 9 and just show you a couple of things here. This is during the three days of darkness and Christ is speaking to the Nephites after His death and resurrection. Go down to verse 20. Here, the Savior has said that He is going to do away with sacrifices and burnt offerings and in verse 20, the new sacrifice will be:

> *And ye shall offer for a sacrifice unto me a broken heart and a contrite spirit. And whoso cometh unto me with a broken heart and a contrite spirit, him will I* [Christ] *baptize with fire and with the Holy Ghost, even as the Lamanites,*

> *because of their faith in me at the time of their conversion, were baptized with fire and with the Holy Ghost,* **and they knew it not**.

This is the scripture that people use to point to the fact that you can have the *baptism of fire* in a process that you don't even know it's happened to you. So, when it says these Lamanites *"knew it not,"* the interpretation of that is that they knew that something had happened because they could see that, but they didn't know what to call it. They didn't have the words to explain it. It's not like you and I talking about something called the *baptism of fire and the Holy Ghost*. We know there is such a thing. Our problem is that we haven't been taught to recognize it because we think we already received it. We aren't looking for it so we don't know when we receive it. We might feel something but don't know what. We know it not! If you are actively working on receiving the *baptism of fire and the Holy Ghost* you will notice things.

Now, the nine months leading up to the mortal birth may be subtle, but you'll notice that as we get to the end of the nine months process of pregnancy that things began to happen. There is a pattern for that. Everything intensifies and speeds up towards the end of this process of this birth and ends with an event and that is the birth of the baby. It's the same thing with the *baptism of fire*. You can have things happening to you through the gift of the Holy Ghost and through the transforming power and sanctifying power of the Holy Ghost, a step at a time, but as you draw near to this event, you're going to see things starting to speed up in your life. Many of you who are listening to this podcast are in that speeding up place. Now, if you can recognize what is happening to you, then you can look forward with faith and anticipation to the blessed event. Isn't that called the birth of the baby? When you have your *baptism of fire and the Holy Ghost* you're going to be a newborn babe. Something is going to happen to you. You're going to go from a fallen, lost, and hopeless adult state in a telestial world, to a newborn child in Christ where He becomes your Father. You are a child. I want you to notice that one of the absolute criteria of having your *Second Comforter* blessing is to become as a little child. The *baptism of fire and the Holy Ghost* makes you childlike; not childish, but childlike. You come out of that with attributes that have reversed the natural man, falling tendencies and placed you in a situation where you become a newborn child in Christ and He is now your Father.

In Helaman chapter 5, if you read closely, we can see keys in this story here, in this account that can tell us what to expect. You need to ask yourself the question knowing that this is critical. All of you already have received the baptism of water. I don't think there are very many people listening to this podcast that have not been baptized by someone having authority, Aaronic Priesthood authority, to baptize you by water. And you've had hands laid upon your head, you been confirmed a member of the Church of Jesus Christ, and have been given the priesthood injunction (an injunction is a command) to go forth and receive the *gift of the Holy Ghost*. I want you to put those two terms together because they mean the same. So, when you say, "Receive the Holy Ghost," what you're really doing is telling that person now, to go forth and obtain the *baptism of fire and the Holy Ghost*. It's the same thing. Can it happen at baptism? Yes, but a person may be baptized at age eight and live most of their life and not have experienced the *baptism of fire* until later on in their life, at an older age. They may also be baptized at any time in their lifetime and die and never experience the *baptism of fire and the Holy Ghost*. That is my concern. You will never experience this unless you understand it and seek for it with every fiber of desire that you possess. This is not something that is going to automatically happen to you because mortals have laid their hands upon your head and said to receive something. It's not going to happen. That's the problem we have right now in the Church. We have a misunderstanding. We think that's what that means and so when we've been confirmed, we think the whole baptism ordinance is complete and that we now have the Holy Ghost with us all of the time. Many members of the Church are laboring under the illusion that their baptismal ordinance is complete, when in reality it's only halfway there. Remember that statement by Joseph:

> *You might as well baptize a bag of sand as a man, if not done in view of the remission of sins and getting of the Holy Ghost. Baptism by water is but*

> *half a baptism, and is good for nothing without the other half—that is,* **the baptism of the Holy Ghost**.

As we've talked about that before, the *baptism of fire and the Holy Ghost* is not performed by institutions. It is not performed by mortals. It comes under the direction and/or by the Lord Jesus Christ Himself. Notice what He said over there in chapter 9, *"I will baptize you with fire and with the Holy Ghost."* So, we need to ask ourselves the question, brothers and sisters, "Have I received the *baptism of fire and the Holy Ghost*?" And how are you going to know that?

How do you know if you've had the *baptism of fire and the Holy Ghost*? It's simple. You go to the Lord, and you ask Him. Do you think you're going to go to another mortal somewhere and say, "Hey, can you tell me if I've had the *baptism of fire and the Holy Ghost*?" I have seen where some people have said to others, "You have received the *baptism of fire and the Holy Ghost*." Now, how do you know that? You may be under the cleansing influence of that Spirit, and it may be progressing you forward like the nine months of a pregnancy, but unless it ends in the event, you haven't had it. And again, 99% of the people are going to teach that it is a process and not an event. Do you know why they're teaching that? It's because it's upsetting for them to think that if it's an event and they haven't had it, then they are in jeopardy. And so, we call it a process, never mentioning that it's also an event because that salves our concerns and makes us feel like, "I'm okay; I'm in the process." Well, how long does a pregnancy last? You had better get to the birth, folks, and have the event. You can tell when you're getting close because, here's the pattern again: when you're nearing the birth of a baby, everything is escalating. There is more pain. There are signs along the way that that birth is imminent: water breaking, pains that are paced at so much time apart, labor pains. I mean, it is a great symbol. So, let me just say that you need to ask the Lord, "Have I had the *baptism of fire and the Holy Ghost*?" And how important is this? Again, I'll say it is the precursor to the *Second Comforter* and making your *calling and election sure*. You're not going to have your *calling and election made sure,* and have a *Second Comforter* experience unless the baptismal ordinance is completed with fire, in an event.

Let's go over to Helaman chapter 5. This is the story of Lehi and Nephi, Helaman's sons, and this is the Helaman of the 2,000 stripping warriors, one of the sons of Alma the younger. You can look at the whole story in the background: Nephi and Lehi were great missionaries; Nephi gave up the judgment seat to Cezoram, and he and his brethren went out and started preaching the gospel to the Nephites. And in verse 17 it says they went among those who were dissenters among the Nephites, and they had some great success and those that were converted:

> *returned to the [Nephite population] to endeavor*
> *to repair the wrongs that they had done.*

And then verse 18 they go to the Lamanites. I want you to notice that in verse 18, at the bottom it says that when they preach they:

> *preach... with such great power and authority,*

because they preached what was given to them by the Spirit. That is called the gift of tongues. The gift of tongues doesn't always mean that you're speaking in a foreign language or speaking the Adamic language although it can be. As a missionary when I went to Germany, Boyd K. Packer laid his hands upon my head and promised me the gift of tongues. We had language training missions there, and within six months I was reading, writing, and speaking German fluently. So, that certainly is a manifestation of the gift of tongues. And you can also be endowed with the gift of tongues where you speak in an unknown language, and there is an interpreter there that will interpret it, and it's always a message from God. It's something that edifies and lifts the two persons who are involved, the speaker and the translator, and everyone else who's in the room. If there is no edification, if there is no instruction, you can check that as coming from the wrong source. If there's a person speaking in tongues, but there's no interpreter or translator, you can check that as coming from the wrong source. But, another way that you can speak in tongues is that you speak as moved upon by the Holy Ghost. You *"...speak with the tongue of angels... wherefore [you] speak the words of Christ."* So, if you've ever had given to you, either in a talk, a lesson, or in your prayers, the words that you should speak before you spoke them, then you're speaking in tongues. That is a manifestation of the gift of tongues.

Now, as a result of this preaching in verse 19, there were 8,000 Lamanites who were baptized and convinced of the wickedness of the traditions of their fathers. They were having such success that Nephi and Lehi were taken and thrown into prison. The prison they were in was the same prison that Ammon and his brethren were cast into by the servants of Limhi. Verse 22 says that after:

> ...*many days without food, behold they went forth into the prison that they might slay them.*
> *[23] And it came to pass that Nephi and Lehi were encircled about as if by fire,*

Look at the bottom of verse 23:

> *and they were as standing in the midst of fire and were not burned.*
> *[24] And when they saw that they were encircled about with a pillar of fire, and that it burned them not, their hearts did take courage.*

Nephi and Lehi had not had this experience before. This is the first time that they have seen themselves standing in the midst of fire, and you can gather from verse 24, that it was astonishing and disconcerting. And after a few minutes when they see that they are not consumed, then their hearts take courage. Now, along with this you have got the earth shaking and the prison shaking. Go down to verse 27. Here is your key to understanding why you can be *"baptized with fire and with the Holy Ghost, and [know] it not,"* as it says over in 3 Nephi 9. The Lamanites who came in to kill them are standing dumbfounded and struck with fear because everything around them is moving and shaking and they're afraid they're going to be crushed to death. But there are 300 Nephites and Lamanites there. Look at the bottom of verse 27:

> *And behold, they that were in the prison were Lamanites and Nephites,* **who were dissenters**.

Now, what does that mean? That means that these are baptized members of the Church who, for one reason or another, have walked away from activity in the Church. Do we have anything like that today? These are people who have already been baptized by water. These are people who have already had hands laid upon their heads for the conferral of the gift of the Holy Ghost—the invitation—and for some reason have walked away from that. It is key to understand that these people already had a foundation and had made covenants with the Lord. And I would venture to say that, at one time or another, they had felt the Spirit of the Lord, and before their dissension were in a process, at least to one degree or another, of moving upward and they got sidetracked, which happens in our day. In verse 29, a cloud overshadows:

> *And it came to pass that there came a voice as if it were above the cloud of darkness, saying: Repent ye, repent ye, and seek no more to destroy my servants whom I have sent unto you to declare good tidings.*

What are the good tidings to these people? Notice that Nephi and Lehi are sent to the dissenters. In verse 17 it says:

> *And it came to pass that they did preach with great power, insomuch that they did confound many of those **dissenters***

You see? They were out like our MLS missionaries today. If you get called out on and MLS mission your job is to go out and reclaim what they call in the mission field "low hanging fruit." The "low hanging fruit" means you're going to go out and talk too disenfranchised, dissenting members of the Church, who have left the Church for one reason or another. It's not like you're working with total strangers who have no foundation. That's the low hanging fruit; you don't have to work as hard. You don't have to get a ladder to climb up into the top of the tree to pick the fruit because you've already got fruit on the lower branches. That means they've already been baptized, they've made covenants, they have felt the Spirit. And so, what we do as MLS missionaries is, we go out there and hopefully, get them to where they feel the Spirit of the Lord again. The good tidings that they're sent to declare are: let us teach you what it means to complete the rest of the baptismal ordinance. You are operating under misunderstood doctrine. I'll bet you there is no difference with these people then than there are now. I'll bet you that many members of the Church who left the Church, did not understand the doctrine of the completed baptismal ordinance. They lacked the knowledge of the *baptism of fire*. I honestly believe that that's the reason why we have so many people leaving the Church today. They think they have already obtained something and they don't feel anything. You'll see that the *baptism of fire and the Holy Ghost* is full of feeling. Let's go to verse 30:

> *And it came to pass when they heard this voice, and beheld that it was not a voice of thunder, neither was it a voice of a great tumultuous noise,*

Now, this is interesting because all around they've got thunder and tumultuous noise, earthquakes, prison walls shaking, but in the midst of all this:

> *behold, it was a still voice of perfect mildness, as if it had been a whisper, and it did pierce even to the very soul—*
>
> *[31] And notwithstanding the mildness of the voice, behold the earth shook exceedingly, and the walls of the prison trembled again...and behold the cloud of darkness, which had overshadowed them, did not disperse—*

In verse 32, it happens again, the second time. It happens three times:

> *[32] And behold the voice came again, saying: Repent ye, repent ye, for* **the kingdom of heaven is at hand**; *and seek no more to destroy my servants.*

What do you think it means "*The kingdom of heaven is at hand*"? When you've obtained *baptism of fire and the Holy Ghost* you have now stepped up into *the kingdom of heaven*. The *kingdom of heaven* is terrestrial. The Church of Jesus Christ of Latter-day Saints is not *the kingdom of heaven*. It's not even the *kingdom of God* that we teach. *The kingdom of God* is a political kingdom that Joseph Smith was going to establish with something called the Council of Fifty. It was disqualified when the last member of the Council of Fifty died in 1949, and that was Heber J. Grant. We have not built that up yet. So, when it comes out and says, the second time, "*for the kingdom of heaven is at hand,*" that means you have the *baptism of fire and the Holy Ghost*. You're going to enter into a newness of life and be what the *Book of Mormon* calls *"alive in Christ."* That's the good news, the good tidings that Nephi and Lehi are bringing all these people. Do you want to know what they're preaching over in verse 18 when they had 8,000 people join the Church? That's what they were preaching, and they were given what they should say. Verse 33:

> *And also again the third time the voice came, and did speak unto them marvelous words which cannot be uttered by man;*

See this right here, brothers and sisters? Those who were listening to these words are now in the final stages of the nine-month pregnancy. They are about to give birth, and they are hearing the words that are leading to it. Do you sense in this experience that there's an escalation of things? I want to look at one more in verse 36. This is also one of the keys of *baptism of fire and the Holy Ghost*. Not only are they hearing this voice but look at 36:

> *And it came to pass that he turned him about, and behold, he saw through the cloud of darkness the faces of Nephi and Lehi; and behold, they did shine exceedingly, even as the faces of angels.*
>
> *And he beheld that they did lift their eyes to heaven; and they were in the attitude as if talking or lifting their voice to some being whom they held.*

Now, the Lamanites asked the question in verse 38:

> *...and who is it with whom these men do converse?*

And Aminadab, who is a dissenter, says:

> *[39] ...They do converse with the angels of God.*

And I believe that and I know that because you're going to see angels here in just a minute. Angels always accompany the *baptism of fire and the Holy Ghost*. If you look up in verse 36, it says, *"they were in the attitude as if talking or lifting their voice to some being whom they beheld."* And I think that is the truth; I think what they're doing is talking with God. And there are angels present, but Nephi and Lehi now, even though their physical bodies are in that prison, they aren't there. They are in another place. And the person that they are speaking to is Christ.

And they are now into a terrestrial realm. All these people in the telestial world are observing this, but they have not yet had the same experience. Verse 40 they say:

> *What shall we do, that this cloud of darkness may be removed from overshadowing us?*

And brothers and sisters, that is the question that I, all of us, should be asking. If you still think this is only a process and not an event, you are overshadowed with a cloud of unbelief. And you need to be asking the same question that these 300 Lamanites and Nephites ask, *"What shall we do, that this cloud of darkness may be removed from overshadowing us?"* And Aminadab gives the answer, verse 41:

> *And Aminadab said unto them: You must repent, and cry unto the voice, even until ye shall have faith in Christ, **who was taught unto** you by Alma, and Amulek, and Zeezrom;*

You see, these folks have a foundation. They all heard those three men. They were also witnesses to Zeezrom's conversion. Verse 42:

> *And it came to pass that they did all begin to **cry** unto the voice of him who had shaken the earth; yea, they did **cry** even until the cloud of darkness was dispersed.*

It lifted. These are the 300 Nephites and Lamanites, and in verse 43, when the cloud is up, they look at themselves, they look at each other, and at the bottom of verse 43:

> *...they saw that they were encircled about, yea every soul, by a pillar of fire.*
> *encircled about, yea **every soul**, by a pillar of fire.*
> *[44] ...yea, they were encircled about; yea, they were as if in the midst of a flaming fire, yet it did harm them not, neither did it take hold upon the walls of the prison; and they were filled with that joy which is **unspeakable**...*

There is one thing. Put your finger there and go over to section 121 in the *Doctrine and Covenants*. Now, you may start to get a feel. In verse 26, the keyword is *unspeakable*:

> *God shall give unto you knowledge by his Holy Spirit, yea, by the **unspeakable gift of the Holy Ghost**,*

Put right in there, *baptism of fire and the Holy Ghost* because that's what it is:

> *that has not been revealed since the world was until now;*

Notice what else they had in Helaman 5:44, not only *"joy which is unspeakable,"* but they are now:

> *...full of glory.*

These 300 men are now prepared to have a *Second Comforter* experience. I don't know how many of them have it because just because you have *the baptism of fire* doesn't mean you're going to seek for the *Second Comforter*. I would venture to say that there is a good percentage of these 300 men that never saw the *Second Comforter* experience because they didn't know the doctrine. Brothers and sisters, if you have the *baptism of fire and the Holy Ghost*, you are knocking on the veil and the *Second Comforter* experience is not far away. Why? Because you need to have this experience to stand in the presence of the Lord Jesus Christ, you need to be transformed so that you can abide His presence in the world of glory. Otherwise, you wouldn't survive; it would kill you. No unclean thing can dwell in the presence of God. The purpose of the *baptism of fire* is to transform. What I want you to know is it not only changes you physically, but it also quickens your spirit. Your spirit is not the same.

Here is another thing: after you have had the *Second Comforter* experience, the Lord wants you to come to Him frequently. This isn't a one-time thing. He wants you to come to Him frequently, and every time you come to Him, you will experience the *baptism of fire and the Holy Ghost*. You are living in the telestial world. You can't be here and not being spotted, to a degree. So, every time you have this experience, this encounter, and come back into the world where you pay your bills, and you attend school, and you work at your career, and you feel the tugs and pulls of the telestial world, before you can enter back into His presence you are going to need to have that cleansing again. No unclean thing: *"The Lord cannot look upon sin with the least degree of allowance."* So, you need to be cleansed every time you go through. And as you return to Him, after you have had your first encounter with Him, the *Second Comforter,* you'll know things that you didn't know before. So, it becomes more readily available to you, with His permission, but it's my feeling that once you come once, He wants you to come often. And every time that you come, you will need to be transformed from this telestial world that has its effect on you; you can't be here for an hour and not have some effect. So, every time you go into His presence you are going to have this experience, the *baptism of fire and the Holy Ghost.* It's the precursor to your encounter with the Lord. Go back to Helaman 5, verse 45:

> *And behold, the Holy Spirit of God did come down from heaven, and did enter into their hearts, and they were filled as it were with fire, and they could speak forth marvelous words.*

Conversing with the Lord through the veil:

> *[46] And it came to pass that there came a voice unto them, yea, a pleasant voice, as if it were a whisper, saying:*
>
> *[47] Peace, peace be unto you, because of your faith in my Well Beloved, who was from the foundation of the world.*
>
> *[48] And now, when they heard this they cast up their eyes as if to behold from whence the voice came; and behold, they saw the heavens open; and angels came down out of heaven and ministered unto them.*

Now, there is your event.

> *[49] And there were about three hundred souls who saw and heard these things; and they were bidden to go forth and marvel not, neither should they doubt.*

You can let the world pull you back away from this. If you do not stay on this path and press forward, it's possible for you to go backward and lose this experience and begin to **doubt** what's happened to you. You wouldn't think that that would happen, but I've seen it. I've seen people who have had marvelous experiences, and they let doubt get in the way. The word used in the *Book of Mormon* is, "It's not *reasonable* that such thing should happen." See, you live in a scientific world that says, "I won't believe it until I see it." You can take these choice spiritual experiences, and because of the "reasonableness" of the telestial world, you can lose it all through doubt.

[50] And it came to pass that they did go forth,
Remember, when you have these experiences are you supposed to talk about them? If you have the *baptism of fire and the Holy Ghost* are you supposed to talk about it? Have you ever been told that we don't talk about these things because they are sacred? Of course, it's sacred. We've talked about "casting your pearls;" you just don't do it before pigs. Here's another example of that:

> *and did minister unto the people,* **declaring throughout all the regions round about all the things which they had heard and seen**,

There is your example: testify! And here is why you testify of this:

> *insomuch that the more part of the Lamanites were convinced of them, because of the greatness of the evidences which they had received.*

See you testify of these things. If you have your *Second Comforter* experience and you entertain an angel, then you testify of that. At this point, when you have had this experience, the *baptism of fire and the Holy Ghost,* you become what Moroni calls, *"the chosen vessels of the Lord."* And then you go out and testify, to what Moroni calls in Moroni chapter 7, *"the residue."* See, you have two groups, *the chosen vessels,* and *the residue. The residue* are those who haven't had this experience, and you testify what has happened to you with such power that the evidence of your testimony convinces them. Then look what happens in verse 51:

> *And as many as were convinced did lay down their weapons of war,*

Now, what are the weapons of war today? Somebody hurt your feelings; somebody offended you, so your weapon of war is you're going to hold a grudge. "Why, as long as that man is the bishop, I'll never go back to church," and on and on. Another weapon of war is that you don't tell people that you love them, and another is you don't say, "I was wrong," or you don't say the words, "Can you forgive me?" These are the weapons of war, and because the evidence of those who have had the *baptism of fire and the Holy Ghost* is so powerful it touches the hearts of *the residue*, and they lay down their weapons war and also their hatred and the traditions of their fathers:

> *[52] And it came to pass that they did **yield** up unto the Nephites the lands of their possession.*

Yield is the key word because yielding is the final step in your spiritual progression. Go over to Helaman chapter 3 and let me show you that word *yielding*. *Yielding* now ties in with what we call the *law of consecration*. Let's go to Helaman 3:34. Do you remember what these people did? They *yielded* up everything they had; they *yielded* up their possessions to the Nephites and their lands they had—probably stolen and taken in warfare, but nonetheless—they tried to repair the things they had done when they had the *baptism of fire*. Verse 34:

> *And they were lifted up in pride, even to the persecution of many of their brethren. Now this was a great evil, which did cause the more humble part of the people to suffer great persecutions, and to wade through much affliction.*
>
> *[35] **Nevertheless** [meaning in spite of the persecution and the much affliction] they did fast and pray oft,*

Do you want some keys on how to obtain the *baptism of fire*? Here are some. Fasting once a month, by the way, is not fasting oft. And praying once a day, now-a-days, is not praying oft. You'd better be praying at least three times a day, as the scriptures indicate. And then your prayers better move from foundational, primary prayers, on up to mighty prayer, and then even something holier and higher than that:

> *and did wax stronger and stronger in their humility, and firmer and firmer in the faith of Christ,*

These are the results of fasting and praying often in the midst of persecution and great affliction.

> *unto the filling their souls with joy and consolation,*

Remember what it said back there? They were filled with *"joy which is unspeakable"*:

> *yea, even to the purifying and the sanctification of their hearts, which sanctification cometh because of their **yielding their hearts unto God.***

Triple underline that! That's the key.

So, let me give you some things, just some things you can look for so you can recognize some characteristics of the *baptism by fire*. You may not see anything but you will likely "feel" something. Characteristic number one, you are encircled by fire or a pillar of fire. The person who's writing this says like a column of light or plasma that surrounds them. I like that. It's not a literal telestial fire, it's a heavenly fire, and the reason that it is encircling them is that, in order for it to be called a baptism, it has to be a total immersion or there is no baptism. There are no partial baptisms here. It's all immersed, one in water and the other in fire. Number two, the presence and ministration of angels. Number three, you're going to obtain a remission of sins. We've talked about a remission being different than forgiveness. A remission is a total transformation that involves not only the physical body but also the spirit, and all the effects of sin are removed. There is a healing and a wholeness that comes with the remission of sins that doesn't have to come with the forgiveness of sins. Number four, purification of the heart by fire. All that the Savior wants from us, brothers and sisters, is your heart; He doesn't want your mind, He wants your heart.

There's a man that had his *Second Comforter* experience, and he stood before the Savior. After he had witnessed the wounds in His hands and His feet, the Savior reached down and picked him up, faced him face-to-face, and He asked him one question. The one question was, "Where is your heart?" He called him by name, "Ralph, where is your heart?" And Ralph said he couldn't answer the question. Well, Ralph would have never had that encounter if he hadn't, had the *baptism of fire and the Holy Ghost*. So, I think Ralph had a lot to learn even though his heart had to be right, to a certain degree, to have this experience.

Five, speaking with a new tongue and speaking with the word of angels by the power of the Holy Ghost. Number six, sanctification. You become holy by being filled with the Holy

Ghost. The Holy Ghost is a sanctifier. Sanctification, according to Moroni 10:33, is:

...that ye become holy, without spot.

That has to happen in order for you to come into the presence of the Lord.

Let's go over to 3 Nephi chapter 19, and quickly look at one more. This has been on my mind this week because of the baptism of this little girl that I saw, and I was reminded by the talk that the father gave. He understood the complete ordinance. He gave a talk on the Holy Ghost, and told his little eight-year-old daughter, "Now, sweetheart, the Holy Ghost is waiting for you, to be your constant friend, the closest friend that you've ever had. He's waiting for you, but you have to go find him." I thought, "Good for you, Dad! You're teaching that eight-year-old."

Now, you know the story in 3 Nephi. We have the 2,500 people there the first day, and then they spend all night going out to tell everyone about it. In chapter 19 we have the beginning of the second day, and there must've been thousands of people here. We have a tendency to think that what we're reading about here is happening to everybody. But if you look closely, it is not. What you're reading about here in 3 Nephi 19 is talking about the Twelve. I know for years as I read about this I thought that everybody was having this experience, but they're not. It's the Twelve that are having this experience. Now, let's go up and look at that in verse 11:

> *And it came to pass that Nephi went down into the water and was baptized.*
>
> *[12] And he came up out of the water and began to baptize. And he baptized all those whom Jesus had chosen* [that's the Twelve].
>
> *[13] And it came to pass when they were all baptized* [the Twelve] *and had come up out of the water,*

I want you to know, brothers and sisters, that these disciples have already been baptized. This is not their first baptism; this is a re-baptism. It was authorized by the Spirit of the Lord, and they are re-baptizing. The purpose of their re-baptism is that there was a

new covenant that they were entering into, and to a new commitment to serve Christ all the days of their lives. Verse 13:
> *the Holy Ghost did fall upon them, and they were filled with the Holy Ghost **and with fire**.*

Who? The Twelve. So here you have how many thousands of people who are standing by witnessing this? They are seeing an example of the *baptism of fire and the Holy Ghost;* it's not happening to them. I'm not going to say it didn't happen to others that were there in these days, but you have 2,500 people that had an eyewitness account where they did see, hear, and handle the Savior. The people that came weren't there the first day, but came on the second day didn't have that experience. But they are witnessing this. Verse 14:
> *And behold, they were encircled about as if it were by fire; and it came down from heaven, and the multitude did witness it, and did bear record;*

You see that is everybody else looking at the Twelve:
> *and **angels** did come down out of heaven and did minister unto them.*
>
> *[15] And it came to pass that while the angels were ministering unto the disciples, behold, Jesus came and stood in the midst and ministered unto them.*

Now, let's go over to another page. You can look at all this, but it is important to understand that we are talking about the disciples here, and the multitude is witnessing it. Let's go down to verse 24. Jesus prayed, and then the Twelve were praying, and after He prays a little bit, He comes to them and in verse 24:
> *And it came to pass that when Jesus had thus prayed unto the Father, he came unto his disciples* [the Twelve],

See, you have just got to get a picture of this. Here is Jesus interacting with the Twelve, and you've got thousands of people standing around that are witnessing this manifestation. They see it, but they are not involved. They are not involved as the Twelve are:
> *and behold, they did still continue, without ceasing, to pray unto him;*

That is a definition of mighty prayer:

> *and they did not multiply many words, for it was given unto them what they should pray, and they were filled with desire.*

Do you want to know what the next step is above fundamental, foundational, primary prayer? There it is. And by the way, in this prayer they are ***crying*** unto the Lord. This is your precursor to the *baptism of fire*:

> *[25] And it came to pass that Jesus blessed them as they did pray unto him; and his countenance did smile upon them, and the light of his countenance did shine upon them, and behold they* [the Twelve] *were as white as the countenance and also the garments of Jesus; and behold the whiteness thereof did exceed all the whiteness, yea, even there could be nothing upon the earth so white as the whiteness thereof.*

That is the *baptism of fire and the Holy Ghost*. Look a little bit further, He goes a little ways off, He prays to the Father, and He says this. Do you want to know what the *baptism of fire and the Holy Ghost* does? Watch:

> *[28] Father, I thank thee that thou hast purified those whom I have chosen* [the Twelve], *because of their faith, and I pray for them, and also for them who shall believe on their words,*

That's *the residue*. The Twelve are *chosen vessels*. The residue are now going to witness and have a testimony given to them:

> *that they may be purified in me,*

Who? *The residue,*

> *through faith on their words,*

Whose words? The Twelve.

> *even as they* [the Twelve] *are purified in me.*

This is a plan set up between *chosen vessels* and *the residue*. *Chosen vessels* are ministered to by angels and have the *baptism of fire and the Holy Ghost:*

> *[29] Father, I pray not for the world, but for those whom thou hast given me out of the world,*

Who's that? The Twelve. What does it mean to be out of the world? It means you have been lifted from a telestial to a terrestrial plane, where Jesus Christ is now your Father and your

God, and you are now being ministered by the *Second Comforter*:

> *because of their faith, that they may be purified in me, that I may be in them as thou, Father, art in me, that we may be one, that I may be glorified in them.*

We talked about that, being made perfect in Christ:

> *[30] And when Jesus had spoken these words he came again unto his disciples; behold they did pray steadfastly, without ceasing, unto him;*

Why? Why to Him? Because He is now their God. Does that mean that they will never pray to the Father again? No. That just means that He is there and something has happened because of His ministration and He is the center focus of everything that has happened in their life. How appropriate that they should pray to Him. And even the Savior says to the Father in verse 22:

> *...they pray unto me; and they pray unto me because I am with them.*

That's appropriate. There is nothing wrong with that. It doesn't take anything away from the Father. Do you think Heavenly Father and Heavenly Mother are displeased because they see these Twelve praying unto Their Beloved Son? Why, I think they would rejoice! Verse 30:

> *And when Jesus had spoken these words he came again unto his disciples...and behold they were white, even as Jesus.*
>
> *[32] And tongue cannot speak the words which he prayed, neither can be written by man the words which he prayed.*

And I will tell you that whatever those Twelve were saying is the same thing; you couldn't write it down, and you couldn't testify of it because those are the same words which Jesus would speak. Look at verse 33:

> *And the multitude did hear and do bear record; and their hearts were open and they did understand in their hearts the words which he prayed.*

> *[34] Nevertheless, so great and marvelous were the words which he prayed that they cannot be written, neither can they be uttered by man.*
>
> *[35] And it came to pass that when Jesus had made an end of praying he came again to the disciples, and said unto them:*

Look at this. It is so amazing:

> *So great faith have I never seen among **all the Jews**;*

That includes the Twelve and the First Presidency. That includes Peter, James, and John and the Twelve, or the eleven at that point:

> *wherefore I could not show unto them so great miracles, because of their unbelief.*

What these Nephites are witnessing right here, at the temple area around Bountiful, has never been witnessed, nor heard, nor recorded in all of the house of Israel. Look at verse 36:

> *Verily I say unto you, there are none of them* [the Jews] *that have seen so great things as ye have seen; neither have they heard so great things as ye have heard.*

Here's a question. Did Peter, James, and John have the *baptism of fire* before Jesus left? Did they have the *baptism of fire*? The answer is no. When did they get it? You can read about it over in Acts 2 and 3, and that is after the forty-day ministry of Christ. So, when He says "I've never seen anything like this in all of my ministry among all of the Jews on the Eastern continent, as what I've seen here among you," is it any wonder that these people, the Nephites, were obliterated from the face of the earth?

Brothers and sisters, you have a record in your hands of the people who have obtained something through the gospel of Jesus Christ and priesthood power that no other society or people had ever obtained on the earth. Christ has ministered to lots of people in different societies. They have their records. There are records that will come forth of other societies and people in other lands where He went and ministered unto them because He is the God of the whole earth, and His sheep are on the whole earth, and He has been there. But never did you have such a society, from Adam up to today that obtained what these Nephites did. I testify to you, there are many records on parchments and plates that are still hidden up in the earth in caves and hidden places that will come forth that we don't have. And isn't it marvelous that of all of the records the Lord brought forth, He brought the record of one people who obtained something that no other people had obtained. What a tender mercy that is for us. Especially for us in this day who are seeking the face of the Lord, to have the *baptism of fire*, to make our *calling and election sure*, and to have an encounter in the presence of Christ while still alive in the flesh. What other record do you think would help you obtain that more than the *Book of Mormon*? No wonder the Church is under condemnation. *Doctrine and Covenants* 84:

> *[54] And your minds in times past have been darkened because of unbelief, and because you have treated lightly the things you have received—*
> *[55] Which vanity and unbelief have brought the whole church under **condemnation**.*
> *[56] And this **condemnation** resteth upon the children of Zion, even all.*
> *[57] And they shall remain under this **condemnation** until they repent and remember the new covenant, even the Book of Mormon and the former commandments which I have given them, not only to say, but to do according to that which I have written—*

This is a whole society that obtained life in Christ. Go with me to Alma 9 and let's learn about the people whose record we are reading. I hope that after tonight you have a new appreciation of the *Book of Mormon* and that you take the *Book of Mormon* to be your handbook on how you enter into the presence of the Lord Jesus Christ and have your *Second Comforter* experience, and that you press forward boldly for this. Verse 18:

> *But behold, I say unto you that if ye persist in your wickedness that your days shall not be prolonged in the land, for the Lamanites shall be sent upon you;*

Which they were. Now, go down a couple of lines:

> *...and ye shall be visited with utter destruction...*

> *[19] For he will not suffer you that ye shall live in your iniquities, to destroy this people. I say unto you, Nay; he would rather suffer that the Lamanites might destroy all his people* [which they did] *who are called the people of Nephi, if it were possible that they could fall into sins and transgressions,*

See, it's better that an enlightened people be taken out rather than continue to bring in generation after generation of God's children into a ripened, fallen society where they have no chance because of the wickedness of their fathers. It's better to take them all out. Remember where *"much is given much is required; and he who sins against the greater light, shall receive the greater condemnation."* These Nephites were wiped out. And look what it says at the bottom of verse 19:

> *after having had so much light and so much knowledge given unto them of their Lord their God;*
>
> *[20] Yea, after having been such a* **highly favored people of the Lord;**

We've talked about that.

> *yea, after having been favored* **above every other nation, kindred, tongue, or people;**

There you go. That was from Adam up to the present; look at your date. What is the date here? What are we looking at? 82 BC. So, from 4,000 BC to 82 BC there had never been another people who had been as favored as this. And I'll tell you that there has never been another people since then that have been so favored, including the Latter-day Saints.

> *after having had all things made known unto them, according to their desires, and their faith, and prayers, of that which has been, which is, in which is to come;*

See, they had Urim and Thummim. They also had priesthood signs in which they could inquire concerning the past, present, and future:

> *[21] Having been visited by the Spirit of God; having conversed with angels,*

The reason they can do that is because of the *baptism of fire*:

> *and having been spoken unto by the voice of the Lord;*

That is the *more sure word of prophecy*:

> *and having the spirit of prophecy, and the spirit of revelation, and also many gifts, the gift of speaking with tongues, and the gift of preaching, and the gift of the Holy Ghost, and the gift of translation;*

That's another door that is opened with the *baptism of fire and the Holy Ghost*, brothers and sisters. Do you want to be numbered among the house of Israel? Do you want to be that small little remnant of the Gentiles who repent of their sins and are numbered among the house of Israel? When we move from the day of the Gentile to the day of Israel and start to see Melchizedek Priesthood, patriarchal priesthood power poured out upon the earth, one of the gifts of that is translation. We are on the cusp of the ordinance and gift of translation being restored among those who have paid the price. I will tell you what; nobody is going to have access to the gift of translation and that ordinance, who has not had the *baptism of fire and the Holy Ghost*. Absolutely not:

> *[22] Yea, and after having been delivered of God out of the land of Jerusalem,*

Etc., etc., etc. Skip down to 23:

> *And now behold I say unto you, that if this people, who have received so many blessings from the hand of the Lord, should transgress* **contrary to the light and knowledge which they do have**, *I say unto you that if this be the case, that if they should fall into transgression, it would be far more tolerable for the Lamanites than for them.*

Skip over to Mormon 5:16 and let me show you another one that is fantastic. You see, brothers and sisters, Christ is the God of the terrestrial world; Father is the God of the celestial world. You can access the Father while you are here in this telestial world. There are people who are visiting with the Father and the Son, and with Mother. Now, go with me to verse 16:

> *For behold, the Spirit of the Lord hath already ceased to strive with their fathers;*

That means the God of the celestial world was known by these people. This is Cumorah. This is what is happening:
> *and they are without Christ and God in the world;*
> *and they are driven about as chaff before the wind.*

This is the fulfillment of Alma 9 when it says that if they get to that point of degeneracy, then they're wiped out. *"For of him unto whom much is given much is required; and he who sins against the greater light shall receive the greater condemnation."*

What kind of light did these people have? Look at verse 17:
> *They were once a delightsome people, and they had Christ for their shepherd;*

You can take that literally now; that's the *Second Comforter*:
> *yea, they were led even by God the father.*

And they were taken through the processes that we've talked about tonight, from the Holy Ghost and angels into the presence of the Son, who took them into the presence of the Mother and Father in Heaven. And they knew them:

> *[18] But now,* [here is the sad part] *behold, they are led about by Satan, even as chaff is driven before the wind, or as a vessel is tossed about upon the waves, without sail or anchor, or without anything wherewith to steer her; and even as she is, so are they.*

Look at this:
> *[19] And behold, the Lord has **reserved their blessings**, which they might have received in the land, **for the Gentiles who shall possess the land.***

That is our day. That started with Joseph Smith and is now about ready to end. How have we done? We have these blessings here that they are talking about, the blessings of this Nephite society who were alive in Christ and sinned against it; those blessings were reserved for us. How have we done? How have we done as the Gentile? Think members of the Church of Jesus Christ of Latter-day Saints. Don't think of people outside the Church. The Gentiles:

> *[22] And then, O ye Gentiles, how can ye stand before the power of God, except ye shall repent and turn from your evil ways?*

[23] Know ye not that ye are in the hands of God?
This is to us. This is not speaking to non-members. This is to members of the Church of Jesus Christ of Latter-day Saints. We've talked about this:
> *Know ye not that he hath all power, and at his great command the earth shall be rolled together as a scroll?*

That is pre-millennial:
> *[24] Therefore, repent ye* [to us], *and humble yourselves before him, lest he shall come out in justice against you—lest a remnant of the seed of Jacob shall go forth among you as a lion, and tear you in pieces, and there is none to deliver.*

How are you going to escape the remnant of Jacob, how are you going to do that? And they are in our midst right now. I'll tell you how you're going to do that. Tonight, you ask Heavenly Father, "Have I received the *baptism of fire and the Holy Ghost?*" I've given you scriptural examples. If the answer to your prayer is no, then you press forward, and you go for that with all you're worth because that is the way that you will survive *the lion*. If you don't have the *baptism of fire and the Holy Ghost*, and if you're not foreordained for other purposes, you won't survive. There will be nonmembers that will come through, but the Gentiles, meaning the members of the Church, know better. We know better! Now, we have been believing false doctrine; we have accepted false traditions. It isn't taught on purpose. There is no conspiracy at a Church level to deceive the Saints. It's just that we have had a difficult time preserving the truth that was restored from heaven. No fault finding, no finger pointing, it's just the way it is. Now, you and I that know differently can make a difference. We can seek for this and obtain, individually, that which may be more difficult institutionally. God bless us to seek for this *"unspeakable gift of the Holy Ghost,"* which is the door through which we enter into the presence of the Lord and receive all of the blessings. God bless us to do that I pray, in the name of Jesus Christ, the Holy Messiah, amen.

Resources:
3 Nephi 9:20

Joseph Smith, *History of the Church*, 5:499 from a discourse given by Joseph Smith on July 9, 1843, in Nauvoo, Ill.Helaman 5:17

2 Nephi 32:2-3 *"...speak with the tongue of angels..., wherefore [you] speak the words of Christ."*

Helaman 5:19

Mosiah 21:23 Ammon and his brethren cast into prison by King Limhi

Helaman 5:22-24, 27, 29-33, 36, 38-52

2 Nephi 25:25 "...we are made alive in Christ..."

D&C 121:26

Alma 45:16 *"...the Lord cannot look upon sin with the least degree of allowance."*

Helaman 16:18 *"That it is not **reasonable** that such a being as a Christ shall come;"*

Moroni 7:31 *"...the chosen vessels of the Lord..."*

Moroni 7:32 *"...the residue..."*

Helaman 3:34-35

Moroni 10:33

3 Nephi 19:11-15, 22, 24-25, 28-30, 32-36

D&C 84:54-57 *"condemnation"*

Alma 9:18-23

D&C 82:3 *"...much is given much is required..."*

Mormon 5:16-24

An Easiness and Willingness to Believe
Michael T. Ringwood
Of the First Quorum of the Seventy
October 2009 General Conference

We learn about the cause of this change during a most remarkable year. During the 62nd year of the reign of the judges, 8,000 Lamanites in Zarahemla were converted as Nephi and Lehi taught with power and authority and had what they should teach given unto them (see Helaman 5:18–19). Three hundred others were converted through a miraculous experience in which they heard a voice that did pierce them to the very soul (see Helaman 5:30). **These 300 had gone forth to kill Nephi and Lehi as they sat in prison, but the 300 found themselves calling upon God when Aminadab, who was a former Nephite and dissenter from the Church, remembered** and knew they should pray till they had faith in Christ (see Helaman 5:35–41). Many more Lamanites were converted through the testimony of the 300 as they ministered unto the people, declaring what they had seen and heard (see Helaman 5:49–50).

Chapter Forty-Six
Podcast 046 Atonement: The Law of the Celestial Kingdom

Good afternoon, brothers and sister, and happy New Year to you! I'm happy to be with you again today. I pray that 2017 will be the year for *the remnant*. Because of my experience with the podcasts, I'm in a position to see, hear, observe, and experience things that maybe some of you are not in a position to see and observe. Let me share with you some things that I see that are very exciting. Compared to the population of the Church, there is a small number of Latter-day Saint men and women where there is definitely a movement, a spiritual endowment, that is being poured down upon them. Most of the time, they know not why they are being moved upon by the Spirit to do things, to say things, to make decisions and movements affecting themselves. They are finding themselves doing things as directed by the Spirit that they could not imagine only months or weeks, or, in some cases, a few years before. But, it seems to be a movement that is accelerating and growing stronger and stronger each day. For those brothers and sisters who have felt the Spirit move upon them to become particular and separate and have a great desire to remove themselves from Babylon and the world, I feel that 2017 is going to be a significant banner/ensign year. I count myself blessed to be among that group and to have felt that call.

You can know a lot about a man or woman by observing their enemies. This week, I have again read the accounts of the persecution of the Savior and the latter days of His ministry where He was arrested, scourged, and crucified. I looked at the people that had such a deep hatred for Him and who opposed Him. By studying His enemies, you can obtain a spiritual witness of His divine calling and His ministry and mission. There's a pattern I think we need to look at. I've been observing what's taken place since November 8th, when all of the rules and past political history were set aside, and a new history was made. Something that has moved the whole world is that the American population stood up and brought in an outsider to be the next President of the United States. All along, I watched with interest, the opposition to President-Elect Trump and I continue to watch that, even up to the latest, where the Tabernacle Choir is now under fire as a result of President-Elect Trump's success, and the opposition that he faces. I can't help but think that the United States of America has been given a reprieve. I've thought a lot about that and that we've been given an opportunity to see what we'll do, as American citizens, with a reprieve, and how we'll use that time to benefit us in a future day. I, like you, have read the signs of the times and I know that eventually, as has been prophesied by Joseph Smith and other prophets, that the United States of America, as we know it, will cease to exist. I understand that. Like you, I have read the signs and understand the prophecies and look around me and see what's going on. I wonder if the Lord hasn't given us a little time frame and a window where the catastrophes and the calamities that are foretold by the prophets and in the scriptures have been forestalled for a period of time. If yes, for what reason? I've pondered that, and I've heard commentary by other Latter-day Saints and by general authorities and priesthood leaders who say that we have been given a reprieve and the purpose for that is to further advance the work of the temples and the missionary work throughout the world. I believe that! I believe that there are many yet, kept from the knowledge of the truth because they simply don't know where to find it. We need to have some semblance of organization, some lack of chaos so that the Church can move forward and fulfill that part of its ministry, which is to proclaim the gospel and redeem the dead and to perfect the Saints.

Today, as I was pondering that, a thought came to me about *the remnant*. There may be a higher and nobler purpose for a reprieve that's not talked about generally, and that is so those people who are seeking for the highest blessings that can be obtained in mortality, can have the time they need to come up and lay claim on those blessings. What if the Lord, in His kindness, also has in mind, that *remnant* of Latter-day Saint men and women who are seeking, asking, knocking, sacrificing, who are taking time to be holy? What if this reprieve is for them, in order to come up and finish their preparations? It's like the Savior said, *"I...finished my preparations unto the children of men."* These are preparations that need to be finished by *the remnant* before we have a societal breakdown and an economic collapse, before we go into World War III, before thermonuclear devices start to go off in the United States and throughout the rest of the world, and before we are invaded by China and Russia and other allies. You can see that our President-Elect is really stirring up a lot of dirt in the bottom of the pond. I loved what he said this last week about the UN. It has a lot of potential, but when was the last time you ever saw the UN solve any problems? They don't solve problems. They create problems. Never have we had a president say things like that. So, I'm wondering if 2017 will be a banner year and if we're being given some time for some peace and prosperity in order for *the remnant* to come up and claim and obtain these tremendous blessings. When the world devolves into chaos and anarchy, these blessings will be necessary in order to provide the service for trapped Latter-day Saints and other good people throughout the world. Good men and women—members and nonmembers—will be trapped with no hope of escape or deliverance. *The remnant* will then step forward, having received the *baptism of fire and the Holy Ghost*, having their *"Father's name on their foreheads"* (which means having their *calling and election made sure*), and having received the blessed experience of a personal encounter with their Lord and Savior, Jesus Christ, the *Second Comforter*. All of this takes time. Joseph Smith said:

The things of God are of deep import; and time, and experience, and careful and ponderous and solemn thoughts can only find them out.

I wonder if *the remnant* hasn't been given some more time in order to finish preparations so that they can move forward in power and in the might of the Lord without the restrictions of time and space, and be able to move through Godly portals on missions. These missions will be to rescue those who are otherwise in hopeless situations with no chance of deliverance. They will be able to move through masses and mobs and anarchy, and through cataclysmic events that have never before been seen in the history of the world, i.e., thermonuclear war, radiation fall-out, earthquakes, and tsunamis. *The remnant* will move forward as translated men and women to rescue those and bring them *"to Zion singing with songs of everlasting joy."* Is that what has happened to us? Have we been given a reprieve? I know that America doesn't stand a chance politically and if she does not, and her people do not embrace the God of the land, who is Jesus Christ, and repent and change their ways, then destruction is inevitable! But, I just can't help believe that we've been given a reprieve. How long? I don't know. But I think that it behooves all of us who have felt the call to Zion and may become emissaries and rescuers for the Lord Jesus Christ, in a day of chaos and disintegration, to now move forward with more faith and trust in the Lord Jesus Christ than we ever have before.

Go with me over to Moroni. Let's look at a scripture for a minute. This is a scripture that we've talked about before, and I just want to hit it again. In Moroni 7, he talks about the ministration of angels. Moroni is quoting his father's sermon here, and he divides up the groups of the Lord's servants into two categories. One, a group he calls *"the chosen vessels of the Lord."* I think, my friends, my brothers and sisters, that you and I should strive, starting today, to become a *"chosen vessel of the Lord"* in this year. The rest of the group are called *"the residue."* *"Chosen vessels of the Lord"* are they who behold angels. Go with me to Moroni 7:30. This is talking about the ministering of angels:

> *For behold, they* [angels] *are subject unto him* [Christ], *to minister according to the word of his command,* **showing themselves**

Now, that's a gift that Moroni mentions in chapter 10. It's called, *"the gift of beholding of angels"* or spirits of the just. That is a gift. So, they show themselves:

> *unto them of strong faith and a firm mind in every form of godliness.*

We should seek to behold angels because it's in the beholding of them that you qualify for verse 31:

> *And the office of their ministry is to call men unto repentance, and to fulfil and to do the work of the covenants of the Father,*

Well, some of *"the covenants of the Father"* have to do with the establishment of Zion and the events leading up to it:

> *which he hath made unto the children of men, to prepare the way among the children of men, by declaring the word of Christ unto* **the chosen vessels of the Lord**,

Chosen vessels are they who have beheld angels, who are of a strong faith and a firm mind in every form of Godliness. Their job is to be direct instruments in the Father and the Son's hands to fulfill the covenants that pertain to our day, and once they have these experiences:

> *that they may bear testimony of him.*
> *[32] And by so doing, the Lord God prepareth the way that* **the residue** *of men*

The residue is everybody else who has not come up to this level:

> *may have faith in Christ; that the Holy Ghost may have place in their hearts, according to the power thereof; and after this manner bringeth to pass the Father, the covenants which he hath made unto the children of men.*

We are baptized, immersed in fire, that then leads to, and you are on the threshold of having your *calling and election made sure* and receiving the *Second Comforter*. When we get to that position, then we are taught from on high.

I'm periodically asked throughout the week about what books I would recommend for people to study. "What kind of books do you study?" As I have mentioned before, I stay away from that. I don't buy books anymore. Every once in awhile, the Lord will guide me to a document on the internet that comes to me as an answer to my individual prayers and what I'm seeking to obtain. But I look at that as information that comes from angels who are ministering to me unaware, and it's a part of the process to bring me up so that I can be prepared to minister in the day of chaos to those men and women who are trapped. So, brothers and sisters, let's make up our minds today; I know I have. In the spirit of fasting and prayer, I've looked into my life and seen where the vestiges of unbelief are, where the barriers are, that are keeping me from beholding the face of my Savior and being sanctified and made holy. So, when I stand in His presence and He asks me; "What is wanted? Before I go to the Father and leave you, Mike, is there anything that I can grant? Do you have a request for me?" I already know what that request will be. I've already passed that threshold of unbelief, wondering if such a thing could ever happen to me. I know what can happen. I expect it to happen. I claim my right to that privilege and promise. When I stand before my Savior, and he asks me; "Is there anything I can grant unto you before I leave?"

"My desire is to remain on the earth as long as the earth stands and bring souls unto thee, Dear Lord. That is my desire."

Now, I need to remove the last vestiges of unbelief and come up and be a man of strong faith and a firm mind in every form of Godliness. I am looking for messengers from my Father to teach me. I know that they will teach me in the ways of life and salvation.

So, brothers and sisters, starting today and looking at 2017 being the glorious day of rebirth, fire, glory, and the day to be clothed with a garment of light, let's introspect into our lives right now, and ask, "What is keeping me from this?" The Lord has said, *"It is your privilege and a promise I give unto you."* If we are not accessing that and if we're not sensing that we're moving forward in transformation and holiness, we need to ask ourselves what is keeping us from it.

We have family visiting over the holidays and Margie and I sit and watch them. I see that they all have a smartphone in front of them, both thumbs on the keypad, and eyes six inches away from the screen, beholding the image of the beast. They are so caught into that and sucked into that vortex of distraction and sleep and chains of hell. Margie even said, "Put those things away and let's talk!" To see them struggle with putting away that distraction and do something as simple as have a family conversation tells me how far down the track we've gone. What we have is only a small window of time given to us by the grace of Christ, who has raised up an outsider to block the New World Order and the coming Babylon with her anti-Christ and false prophet, for America to repent and turn to her God. I'm sorry to say that I don't believe she will because *Doctrine and Covenants* 29:17 gives a prophecy concerning America and concerning the Gentiles of the latter-days. It comes out and says:

For they will not repent.

Usually, when the Lord talks about people being able to turn around, it's always "if **they** will, then **I** will." Section 29 talks about thermonuclear war, disease, plagues, famine and pestilence, sword, blood, death, and horror, but the Lord comes out and says that they will not repent. So, I'm not hopeful that we are going to see a rebirth of America. In one way, I'm happy for that because the rebirth of America is not the establishment of Zion. What we are looking for is the establishment of Zion and her cause. That's where you and I come into play.

So, with that, let's look at what's blocking us. Do you need to stop watching movies that offend the spirit? Are you put to sleep in the things that entertain you? Are you distracted and do you block the Spirit by what you allow to enter in through your eyes and your ears? Do we need to take a look at media and make some serious changes? Do we need to cancel Netflix? Do we need to seriously limit our Facebook time? Do we need to be more careful about how much time we spend on YouTube? Do we need to rise earlier in the morning? Do we need to spend time meditating and seeking to enter through that secret, sacred door? As President McKay said:

Meditation is one of the most secret, most sacred doors through which we pass into the presence of the Lord.

Do we need to visualize more? Do we need practice seeing with the eye of faith? Do we need to ask the Lord to bless us with the gifts of the Spirit, which are common among those who've been born of Christ and have become His sons and daughters? The gift of tongues? The gift of healing? The gift of beholding spirits? The gift of faith? The gift of teaching? Do we need to ask for these things? If you take the first letters of ask, seek, and knock and write them in order, it spells out the word *ask*. Is the Lord trying to teach us something here? Are we remaining and perishing in the dark because we don't ask? Therefore, we are left in the dark. Is that what's going on? Have we been so put to sleep by Babylon, even *the remnant*? Does *the remnant* have a remnant of distractions that we need to get rid of? What is it that's keeping us? Time is running out. We don't have years and years to access these doctrines with their equivalent blessings and promises. Wilford Woodruff used to talk about the things that we talked about in these podcasts and said, "It's old men's doctrine," because it usually took you living your whole life to come to a point where you could even begin to understand these higher doctrines, let alone access them and attain them. We don't have that time. I'm talking to young men and young women who are asking questions about *calling and election*, the ministration of angels, the doctrines of Godliness, the mysteries of the kingdom. This is not limited anymore to older people. There's a younger generation, not many, but there's a younger generation who are coming up, that instinctively know and are seeking for these privileges and blessings. So, 2017, let that be the year to obtain.

 I have a couple of thoughts I would like to share with you that I've been pondering. Go with me to *Doctrine and Covenants* 105. Sections 101, 103, and 105 are great sections that have to do with Zion, her cause, and the establishment of a Zion Society. These sections were given at a time when Latter-day Saints were being driven from pillar to post. They were being driven out of their inheritance lands that they purchased with money; out of Jackson County, and were driven into Clay County and Daviess County, Caldwell County, all the way up to Far West. Eventually, they were driven out of Far West, right out of Missouri, and back across the river into Illinois. These sections have to do with the doctrine of establishing Zion. I was thinking about that today. Go with me over to section 105 and let's just look at verse 1 for a minute. The Lord says:

> *Verily I say unto you who have assembled yourselves together that you may learn my will concerning the redemption of mine afflicted people—*
>
> *[2] Behold, I say unto you, were it not for the transgressions of my people, speaking concerning the church and not individuals, they might have been redeemed even now.*
>
> *[3] But behold, they have not learned to be obedient to the things which I required at their hands, but are full of all manner of evil, and do not impart of their substance, as becometh saints, to the poor and afflicted among them;*

You can see some of the problems, the barriers, that kept them from coming up and obtaining these blessings and establishing Zion. Remember, we've talked about how Zion begins one man and one woman at a time. You have to become a Zion person before you'll ever begin to see anything to do with establishing a society. So, do you see the barriers that they were talking about? It says that they were full of all manner of evil. I have a friend who is a stake president over in Snowflake, and I had a chance to chat with him. His time is almost completely consumed with dealing with sexual immorality and apostasy among the Latter-day Saints. He looked at me, and he said, "Mike you have no idea."

I said, "President I have no illusions. I'm old enough and know what's going on." You can find every manner of sin. I mean, **every** manner of sin among the membership of the Church. Even back here in section 105, we're looking at 1834, the Lord comes out and says the saints *"are full of all manner of evil."* Then look at this part. This is always a huge barrier. This is one that we can think about. How can we individually not become tainted with this last one? He says that they *"do not impart of their substance, as becometh saints, to the poor and afflicted among them."*

There's something we ought to take a look at in this year of 2017, as we strive to come up and obtain. What are some of the barriers? What are some of the stumbling blocks to Zion? Here's some of them. For those who should be considered saints and the things that becometh saints: you need to take care of the poor and afflicted among you. I think it's interesting. We'll come back to this in a minute. Go over with me to Mosiah 4 in the *Book of Mormon*. Once you obtain a remission of your sins, which comes through the *baptism of fire and Holy Ghost*, you can lose that if you are not careful. Once you obtain it, the secret then is how do you **re**tain it. King Benjamin gives us the key to retaining all of these beautiful, higher blessings. Look at Mosiah 4:26. King Benjamin says this:

> *And now, for the sake of these things which I have spoken unto you—that is, **for the sake of retaining a remission of your sins** from day to day, that ye may walk guiltless before God—*

Now, without looking any further, if you were to stop right there and ask yourself a question, "What is the one thing that the angel taught King Benjamin that is the requirement to retain a remission of your sins?" To retain that ability to walk with God, look what he says:

> *I would that ye should impart of your substance to the poor, every man according to that which he hath, such as feeding the hungry, clothing the naked, visiting the sick and administering to their relief, both spiritually and temporally, according to their wants.*

That's the key! Do you want to know how to retain what you've obtained? The secret is you're dealing with the poor, the sick, and the afflicted.

Go back to section 105. Now that brings me to verse 4. Verse 4 is what I want to chat with you about and share some feelings and thoughts about:

> *[4] And are not **united** according to the **union** required by the law of the celestial kingdom;*

Let's stop there for just a minute. Because of those things mentioned in 2 and 3, people are in a state of separation. See, in verse 4, it says the opposite of the state they find themselves in verse 3. The opposite is where they need to be, and in verse 4 that is to be *"**united** according to the **union** required by the **law** *of the celestial kingdom."* You should triple underline that. What is that? It doesn't say the laws; it says **the law** of the Celestial Kingdom. Let's look at a couple of other verses, and then I want to bring you back to some thoughts that we can work on a little bit:

> *[5] And Zion cannot be built up unless it is by the principles of* **the law of the celestial kingdom***;*

We better find out what that law is because there is no Zion without that law. He says at the bottom of verse 5:

> *otherwise* [unless we do this] *I cannot receive her* [Zion] *unto myself.*

Zion begins with an individual. You see? "To be received unto the Lord Himself," is having had the *Second Comforter* experience! Don't put that off into some future estate. Don't think of a society because it begins with individuals. If you want to make your *calling and election sure* through that encounter and be cleansed and purified and made holy by the *baptism of fire and by the Holy Ghost*, you need to be living the *law of the Celestial Kingdom*. Otherwise, none of that is going to happen. So, I come back to the question, "What is this law?" Verse 6:

> *And my people must needs be chastened until they learn obedience, if it must needs be, by the things which they suffer.*

Let's come back to verse 4 because I think that it holds the key to what the *law of the Celestial Kingdom* is. Let's circle a couple of words in verse 4, *united* and *union*.

> *[4] And are not* **united** *according to the* **union** *required by the law of the celestial kingdom.*

I wonder if the *law of the Celestial Kingdom* is *atonement*. Not *the* Atonement; drop the "the" off and just put *atonement*. I wonder if that's the law. What got me thinking about this was that in some of the statements by the prophet Joseph Smith, he says that Jesus is treading in the footsteps of His Father and that the Father had been a Savior on an older world. We can assume that His Father was also, and His Father, and the Grandfathers. Go with me to Revelations in the *Bible*. Let me show you how the whole King Follett Discourse came from one scripture in the Book of Revelation. That whole doctrinal discourse on the character of God and His nature, given in April of 1844, just two months before Joseph Smith was shot to death, originated from the first chapter of Revelation. The first four verses are a salutation to the seven churches that were in Asia, which John had stewardship over at the time. This whole thing is being delivered to him by an angel sent by God with this message. So, in verse 4 it comes out, and it says:

> *John to the seven churches which are in Asia: Grace be unto you, and peace, from him which is, and which was, and which is to come; and from the seven Spirits which are before his throne.*

Now, watch verse 5. Follow this:

> *And from Jesus Christ,*

So, now we're talking about the Savior. You have to read this carefully, or you will miss it:

> *who is the faithful witness, and the first begotten of the dead, and the prince of the kings of the earth. Unto him* [Christ] *that loved us, and washed us from our sins in his own blood,*

That whole verse 5 is talking about Christ. Now continuing to talk about Christ:

> *[6] And* [Christ] *hath made us kings and priests unto God* [that's the Father] *and his Father* [that's the Grandfather]; *to him be glory and dominion for ever and ever. Amen.*

Did you catch that? Joseph Smith taught the principle in the King Follett Discourse and other places:

> *Where was there ever a son without a father? And where was there ever a father without first being a son?*

So, my mind is thinking about these things and also about what we read last week when Jesus was talking about His Father;

> *I do the things I saw my father do.*
> *Jesus, what are you going to do?*
> *I lay down my life as my Father did, and take it up again.*

See, the Father performed **an** atonement and His Son, Jesus, performed **an** atonement. I believe that the Grandfather performed **an** atonement.

I'm wondering if, in section 105, the *law of the Celestial Kingdom* isn't atonement. I'm wording this specifically: *atonement*— a concept, like Zion; an eternal concept like Israel. The words Zion and Israel don't originate on this earth as it began with Adam and Eve. These are eternal concepts that exist everywhere in eternity. Israel, Zion, and I think, *atonement* is also an eternal principle. Look at the word atonement. You've' broken this down all of your life. At-one-ment—we've heard that all the time in the Church. What's the *atonement* seeking to do? It's seeking to bring separated parties into a state of oneness. Look back at verse 4. What are the two words you circled in verse 4, section 105? The *law of the Celestial Kingdom* has to do with *unity* and *union*, being *united*. What does the *atonement* do? It unites and brings into **one**ness. Things prior to that were separated. So, I wonder if the *atonement* is much more than what we think that it is and that it is the very *law of the Celestial Kingdom*. In section 132, verse 7, Joseph Smith says:

> *And verily I say unto you, that the conditions of this law are these: All covenants, contracts, bonds, obligations, oaths, vows, performances, connections, associations, or expectations,*

I think that all other laws and covenants, ordinances, and all the things that he listed are appendages to the *law of the Celestial Kingdom,* which is what? *Atonement*. It's that power that exists, always has existed, and always will exist that brings unity, order, and oneness in an otherwise divisive, chaotic place.

Go over to Alma 34. These are just some ideas that have been on my mind this last week. Then, **an** *atonement* that is worked out by **an** atoning one, **an** anointed one, would be a mission fulfilled in the overall concept and *law of the Celestial Kingdom* that's required in order to bring people up and let them live in a society that's governed by *atonement*. *Atonement* is always a principle of sacrifice. How did the Mothers in Heaven and the Fathers in Heaven atone? What's Their life like? Their life is based on sacrifice. Exalted Beings sacrificed themselves for the benefit, welfare, and blessing of lesser beings, or beings who are in a more inferior state of progression than they are. Only They bring them up. There's only one way that the Fathers and Mothers can bring Their children into the life They enjoy, and that's by sacrificing Themselves. They do that through condescension, through ascending and descending, through entering and leaving, going in and going out until They *"go no more out,"* and they sit with all the Holy Fathers in the Kingdom of God to *"go no more out."* I'm putting all this together in my mind and thinking that *atonement* is a mission, a ministry, an atoning ministry by an Anointed One, chosen by the Elohim for the benefit of others who are striving to come up to where They are. Is *atonement* the *law of the Celestial Kingdom*, the law that keeps everything unified and in order? Atonement—being *at one*? Not *the* Atonement because I'm not trying to identify one single event that portrays itself from a person's age, 30 to 34. I'm not taking anything away from that. Isn't it interesting that when we come into a telestial world, we become divided? It's the great kidnapping scenario. When the Father sends His children into a telestial world, for all intents and purposes, He has lost them. They are truly in a lost and fallen state, and unless there is a rescue effort to redeem and to pay a ransom for lost children, kidnapped, taken by force from their parents, never to come back into the family circle unless there is a price paid—a ransom. If you don't pay the ransom, the kidnapper says; "Your child will die. You pay the ransom, or I'll kill your child." You see the great symbolism involved here? Here's a family that's split up; it's separated. It is in every state but *unity* and *union*. Something has to happen to reconcile these different, divided conditions. So, we have One sent on a mission who is not only willing but able. And it appears that there is only One per system who can do that. Father was One in His system, and I'll bet you that Grandfather was One in His system. And Yeshua is One in our system. The Jewish word for Jesus, the Hebrew word is *Yeshua Hamashiach*: Jesus the Messiah, the Anointed One, the Chosen One. He is the One who, under celestial law, was chosen, willing, and able because of Him proving Himself from the beginning of this system to where it comes time in the meridian, to atone and make it possible for reconciliation of God's children to their Heavenly Parents. He is prepared from before the foundation of the world, meaning that through age and experience, unbelievable accumulation of knowledge and wisdom and intelligence and light and truth, He is the Lamb chosen from before the foundation of the world to atone, to reconcile, to rescue, to redeem. You ought to look up the word *redemption*. It means *to repurchase at a price, something that you previously owned.* That's redemption. The price was blood, sweat, agony, and tears.

So, do the Elohim sit enthroned in a celestial world that is governed by a law that they call *atonement*? Is that the *law of the celestial world*? Go with me to Alma 34. This is Alma's missionary companion, Amulek, who was teaching us some things about the atonement:

> *[8] And now, behold, I will testify unto you of myself that these things are true. Behold, I say unto you, that I do know that Christ shall come among the children of men, to take upon him the transgressions of his people, and that he shall atone for the sins of the world; for the Lord God hath spoken it.*

So, what's the purpose of atonement? It is reconciling separated family members to their Parents. It is bringing separated family members, separated by force, back into the circle of the family and making them one:

> *[9] For it is expedient that* **an** *atonement should be made; for according to the great plan of the Eternal God there must be* **an** *atonement made, or else all mankind must unavoidably perish;*

The kidnappers got us, the ransom note has been written, the demands have been made, and if there is no payment, the children die:

> *yea, all are hardened; yea, all are fallen and are lost, and must perish except it be through* **the** *atonement which it is expedient should be made.*

I want you to notice; these are some words that got me thinking along this line. If Amulek is speaking by the power of the Holy Ghost, and I know that he is, then these words we need to pay attention to. Notice that in verse 9 it talks about *"**an** atonement"* and at the bottom of verse 9 it talks about *"**the** atonement."* Is that significant? Is that talking about a mission by an Atoning One, an Anointed One, to come into this system and to perform a mission for which He was foreordained and prepared from the foundation of the world to accomplish? Remember, He wasn't only willing. There may have been many of God's children who were willing, but there was only One who was able. Go down to verse 10:

> *For it is expedient that there should be a great and last sacrifice; yea, not a sacrifice of man, neither of beast, neither of any manner of fowl; for it shall not be a human sacrifice;*

It's the sacrifice of a God. And it's His blood, under those circumstances, that has to be shed in order for a reconciliation, a rescue. And conditions are to be set so that man can be redeemed and come back into the presence of his Father and Mother:

> *but it must be an infinite and eternal sacrifice.*

Well, brothers and sisters, just some thoughts I have that had on my mind as I think about the Elohim who sit enthroned in the highest estate. I believe in multiple estates. I believe that there are different levels of progression. I believe that the temple hints towards that and if we are in tune, we can receive revelation for ourselves on just how many estates there are. I believe that the scriptures give an introduction into the estates in Abraham chapter 3, by talking about the first and second estates. But, as we have talked about before, I believe there are multiple estates of probation, and if we follow the estates of probation, we can enter into estates of progression. The Lord can teach us about these things. I believe that these are the doctrines that will be taught in the day of Israel when the day of the Gentile is over. I believe that we are on the edge of that day. Hence, *the remnant* are being moved upon in a mighty way to come up, to shake off the chains and shackles, to have the scales removed from our eyes, to obtain the privileges and promises that God has given us, and to do it now because we are running out of time. If you and I don't do it, here's the promise: God will *"raise up"* somebody who will. Joseph was told that. No one is indispensable. You have a foreordained mission. You have a glorious destiny. We don't want to die in our sins and wake up in the resurrection only to learn that it is too late and that we forfeited our foreordained, divine destiny and mission. <u>I believe</u> that destiny is to establish Zion and to be translated through the doctrine and ordinance of translation, which <u>I believe</u> is about to be restored to the earth. <u>I believe</u> it will be restored by emissaries from the city of Enoch. <u>I believe</u> that much of this is going to be done outside of the confines of the membership of the Church. <u>I don't believe</u> that the general membership of the Church is going to access this. <u>I believe</u> that the Brethren are inspired in their General Conference addresses and doing all that they can, within limits that have been placed by the Lord, to wake the people up. You know the parable of the Ten Virgins as well as I do. At least 50% and <u>I believe</u> that's generous, will awaken. Hence, the purpose of these podcasts is to help us learn the doctrine, seek for the revelations and confirmations of the Holy Ghost, and become perfected in receiving personal revelation so that the Lord can guide us individually and collectively when the time comes, to fulfill His mighty purposes. In that day, He will gather His people, gather His jewels, and perform His strange act.

This is the year, brothers and sisters. Is there anything in the coming days, weeks, and months, to keep us from rending the veil of unbelief and having the power and knowledge and glory of heaven poured down upon us while still in the flesh? I pray that we'll seek these things. Ask, seek, and knock. In the name of Jesus, amen.

Resources:
D&C 19:19 *"I...have finished my preparations unto the children of men."*
D&C 133:18 *"...Father's name on their foreheads."*
Teachings of Presidents of the Church: Joseph Smith, (2011), 261–70
D&C 45:71 *"...shall come to Zion, singing with songs of everlasting joy."*
Sermon in the Grove, June 16, 1844
Moroni 7:30-32
Moroni 10:14 *"...the gift of beholding of angels..."*
D&C 67:10 *"...it is your privilege and a promise I give unto you..."*
D&C 29:17
D&C 105:1-6
Mosiah 4:26
Revelation 1:4-6
King Follett Sermon
D&C 132:7
Alma 7:25 *"...go no more out."*
Alma 34:8-10

Chapter Forty-Seven

Podcast 047 Within the Veil

Good afternoon brothers and sisters. It is good to be with you again. I hope that you have a great Sabbath afternoon since this is being recorded on the Sabbath day. What a great day to discuss the gospel of Jesus Christ and the mysteries of the Kingdom of God. I don't think it's by chance that this year's scriptural theme for young women and young men, interestingly enough, is James 1:5-6. It's the scripture that opened the heavens and allowed the *dispensation of the fulness of times* to dawn after the long night of apostate darkness. I know God always does things with a purpose, and his purpose is to exalt his children. I think that this scripture coming around to us at this point completes a full circle. I've been thinking about that today, so let's look at that scripture in James 1:5:

If any of you lack wisdom,

Even when so much has been restored and given to us through the restoration, there still seems to be a huge lack of wisdom among the Latter-day Saints, the interpretation of *wisdom* being "the proper use of knowledge." In Babylonish, *proper use* is interpreted as "Godly." So, *"If any of you lack wisdom…"*

let him ask of God,

There it is! It's hidden in plain sight. Again, *"ask of God."* We've talked about this on other podcasts. We just spend way too much time, brothers and sisters, seeking verification and validation from other fallible and flawed mortals; and it's a lot. I put myself in this same category. I'm learning with you. What does it take for us to finally approach the Father, in the name of Christ, and drink from that fountain in its purity, instead of wallowing around here in this telestial world continually seeking for validation, information, and additional witnesses from people who are struggling like you and me? For the most part, they know no more than you and I, and in many cases, they lack more wisdom than we do. What's it going to take?

> *[5] If any of you lack of wisdom, let him ask of God, that giveth to all men liberally,*

Look at that. Isn't that interesting? Does it apply to us now? I see our Father in Heaven, Jesus, and the Holy Ghost in my mind's eye, especially the Holy Ghost, who ministers to us in this world, standing off to the side, watching what we do, with His arms folded, His head kind of cocked to one side, and tapping His foot saying, "When is it my turn?" And, here we are, gathering all of this information from books,—and books are okay because the Lord says in *Doctrine and Covenants* 88 that you should gather wisdom from the best of books. But, Joseph came out and said that if *"you gaze into heaven five minutes, you would know more than you would by reading all that ever was written on the subject."* I think that books, book learning, libraries, and gospel libraries all have their part. But I have come to a point where I don't buy books anymore. I have a library in here that is stacked from the floor to the ceiling. I've read those, and they are important, **but once you get through that phase**, it's important that we stop relying on the things of this world and go to the source:

> *that giveth to all men liberally, and upbraideth not; and it shall be given him.*

Look at that. See upbraid? That's been one of my favorite scriptures as I've sought to delve into the mysteries of Godliness and have asked the question, "Should I do this? Or shouldn't I do that? Is this appropriate or not appropriate?" I placed too much value on the opinions and instructions of other people. I had to pass that barrier and get beyond what other people were saying in this world. God doesn't upbraid. In fact, in our day, if you want to seek His face, it's going to require you to step way outside of where you have been comfortable up to this point—way outside. As I have mentioned in other podcasts, you're going to find yourself faced with contradiction and paradox. But I want you to know that if you lack wisdom, ask Him. So, if there is something you are asking, "Should I do this or should I not," even if people around you are saying that you should not do it, go to Him; trust in Him. I can promise you that in your path to seeing the face of the Lord, you will be required to do things that will take you way outside of your comfort zone, and it will be hard for you to do.

There is a biography about Neal A. Maxwell, written by Bruce C. Hafen, that's called *The Disciple's Life*. It's a great big book, 512 pages long. I am sure some of you have read it. On the back of the dust cover is a little one-sentence statement that sums up the whole meaning of the book. It says this:

If we are serious about our discipleship, Jesus will eventually request each of us to do those very things which are most difficult for us to do.

I've heard some comments this week, and people have asked if the Abrahamic test and the trial of our faith mentioned in Ether 12, are the same thing. First of all, the phrase "Abrahamic test" is not scriptural. It is true that Abraham was asked to perform a test, but it is not a scriptural phrase. But *"the trial of your faith"* is. Notice that the scripture says that you will receive no witness until after *"the trial of your faith."* That witness is to see the Lord Jesus Christ, face to face, and have Him minister to you face to face. That's the witness. If you want that witness, you're going to be hit with a trial that is equal to the blessings of that witness. That's just the way it is. We need to be practicing now, sacrificing things that are difficult for us. Put your will aside, stop doing everything you want to do, start seeking His will, and align yourself with it.

Now, the second verse in James is:

*[6] But let him ask in faith, **nothing wavering**.*

See, that applies when you get into that area of praying to see the face of God in this life. I want you to remember that the first principle of the gospel is not faith in the Lord Jesus Christ. Faith in the Lord Jesus Christ was part of Article of Faith number 4.

But, in the *King Follet Discourse,* given two months before Joseph's death, he told us what the first principle of the gospel is, and it was not faith in the Lord Jesus Christ. It is as Joseph says:

> *It is the first principle of the gospel to know for a certainty the character of God, and to know that we may converse with Him as one man converses with another, and that He was once a man like us;*

That's the first principle. Imagine that! The first principle of the gospel is the *Second Comforter.* Boy, have we gone way astray. But that's all right. There's an awakening taking place, and that's part of what I want to talk to you about tonight.

> *[6] But let him ask in faith, nothing wavering. For he that wavereth is like a wave of the sea driven with the wind and tossed.*

Don't be afraid to step outside and do something. You're going to have to be somewhat creative. You're going to have to start doing some unique things that you've never done before if you want these kinds of blessings and privileges that the Lord has in store for you. This is not for the faint-hearted. You go forth in courage, knowing that the Lord would never ever lead you to a place in your progression that you are not prepared to pass what's there, to learn the experience that's there, and gain the wisdom from it. He wouldn't put you there if you weren't capable of fully and sufficiently handling any challenge that's associated with that encounter. You can do it, so don't be afraid. And know that he's not going to chew you out for trying. Joseph said that he never knew of God being displeased with anybody for wanting more knowledge. He wants you to move out. He wants us to seek for more and not be satisfied. Remember, it's okay to be where you are; it's not okay to stay there. As you press forward, upstream, always moving upstream, remember that water flows down. Everything in this world, this telestial schoolhouse, is designed to take you down. If you want to just relax and stay in one place, you'll find yourself downstream. There is no such thing as relaxing and staying in one place. You may be protected on a plateau for a few minutes, but there is no growth sitting on a park bench in the sunshine; it's always upstream. That's why the Lord uses the words, *press forward.* That illustrates an effort against some form of resistance or opposition. That's the way it is. You can bet that the greater the blessing you seek, the greater the opposition will be. We talked about that to some degree. So, remember that part: He doesn't upbraid.

Some of you have shared with me some great experiences, and I thank you for casting your pearls to me. I am so honored that you trust me. We've not met face to face. It's not me and the words that I speak, and it's not any charismatic dialogue on a recording; it's the Spirit. It's Spirit speaking to spirit. If I speak and teach by the Spirit, and you hear by the Spirit, then you will feel comfortable when the Lord tells you to share with me some things; and you have. And I have to tell you that your pearls strengthen my faith and build my confidence, for me personally, to press forward and pierce that veil. Remember, the veil was never meant to be a wall. It was always meant to be rent.

I have learned some things about spiritual dimensions. I want to share with you an experience I had in New Jersey. I pray the Holy Ghost will give me utterance and the Holy Spirit will direct and guide. When we were in New Jersey, Margie and I used to take exercise walks in a little park early in the morning. It was across the street from the apartment where we lived and was a beautiful place. We were in a place called Parsippany, New Jersey. It was just gorgeous. I've never seen such beautiful forests. I live in forests; I'm a half mile from the largest virgin Ponderosa Pine forest in the world. But this was a different kind of forest, and it was hardwood, beautiful, green, and just gorgeous. They had an asphalt path that would wind in and out of this beautiful park and we'd go over there in the mornings after all the other people had taken their walks and gone to work. So, late morning we would walk around in there, and I had some wonderful experiences in there. It was one of those places where I was walking that I practiced praying with uplifted hands, as the scriptures teach us to pray. As I walked down this path and I looked ahead of me, I saw a shaft of sunlight that was coming down through this beautiful green canopy. It was just a pillar of light. I looked around myself and made sure that nobody was going to come up on me, you know, conscious to make sure I was alone. I went and stood in that pillar of light, faced the sun, closed my eyes and let that sun beat down on my face and warm my whole body. I reached my hands heavenward, and I just prayed and talked to my Father in Heaven in the name of His Son. I had a marvelous experience there, just filled with the Spirit. But I got nervous because I was afraid someone would walk up behind me and see this man standing in this shaft of sunlight with his arms stretched out. Anyway, I became self-conscious; otherwise I would have stayed there much longer than I did. As I brought my arms down, opened up my eyes and continued my walk, I was just filled with the Spirit of the Lord. I walked around the corner and there was a huge boulder about half the size of a Volkswagen car sitting on the right, off the path, back in the trees. My attention was drawn to this rock, and the Spirit guided me and said, "Go over to that rock." It was just a feeling. I didn't hear any voices that uttered sentences; it was just a feeling. It said, "Go over to that rock." It was about forty feet off the path, back into the trees, kind of dark and shaded, no sunlight coming through that particular place. As I walked back there and got close to that rock, the Spirit again seemed to say inside, in a thought, "Place your hands on that rock." This was an old rock. I guess all rocks are old, but I had the feeling that this one had been there a long time. So, in obedience, I laid my hands on that rock, and I sensed it was alive. I could feel its life. I just stood there with both hands on that rock, my eyes closed, and I knew that this was a living thing. The feeling that I got was that it was very old and, dare I say, **extremely wise**. Ha-ha! That's the feeling I got. I've never had anything happen like that before, and I've never had anything quite like that since. But what it did was teach me that everything around us is alive. There is nothing in this world that is not alive. Everything is a soul and has life in it. It has a physical, outward, telestial body, if you will, and an inward, alive spirit. The definition of a soul is the body and the spirit together. That's in *Doctrine and Covenants* 88. Through that, I learned that things that seem to be inanimate are very much alive and aware. There is an awareness there. That's the word I would use to describe that. To one degree or another—not all at the same levels of awareness and intelligence—there is an awareness and a life there. The Lord gave me that experience to know that everything He creates praises Him. As I had my hands on that old, big rock, I sensed that it was praising the Lord. The

Lord took me over there and had me put my hands on it so I could feel what this living thing was doing. It was old, it was wise, and in its way, was praising the Creator. I thought, "That fulfills the measure of its creation," as does every living thing. God's children, who are at the top of that spectrum of awareness, can have an interaction with the rest of His creations that can teach us something. What that taught me was this: if I want to, at some future day, as a Zion man, exercise power over the elements of the earth, I need to be doing something now to practice that. The ability to call down the powers of heaven and to control the elements isn't something that's going to be given all at once. That isn't the pattern. That isn't the way the Lord works. He works from lesser to greater, from portions to fullnesses, from small to large. That's the way He works.

So, that experience taught me and prepared me so that when I came home from my mission, I could do some things that are way outside the mainstream. If I have a sick animal, or if I have a horse that's foundered, I can anoint that horse's forehead with oil. And, while somebody's holding the halter rope, I can place my hands on that horse's forehead and bless that horse by the authority of the Melchizedek Priesthood, in the name of Jesus Christ, and **know** that the horse will respond to the blessing and will be made whole and healthy and be healed. I know that! I have now done those things. I can lay hands on living things whose job it is to fulfill the measure of their creation and, in another case, bring forth fruit. I can lay hands on those living creations, whether they are trees, grape vines, or berry bushes, and in the name of Jesus Christ, through the channel and the medium of the priesthood, give those things blessings to fulfill the measure of their creation and combat the downward pull and destructive forces of the telestial world. And because I am exercising faith and power and love in behalf of God's other creations, and because I am at the top of that spectrum in my ability to reason and to visualize and commune with God the Eternal Father in a unique way that lesser creations can't, I can bless their lives. And I better be doing that and getting some practice at it now and not wait until the need arises and it becomes a life and death situation.

So, *"He gives...liberally and upbraideth not."* Don't be afraid. Think outside the box. If you have a question whether something is appropriate or whether it should or should not be done, go to the Lord. Ask God, who giveth liberally; ask Him. Are you going to go ask another human being, another mortal, to do something that they haven't done and find out from them if it is okay? Do something different, and you will find that you have results that are much, much, different.

I've been thinking about the *Second Comforter,* and some of you have shared with me your *Second Comforter* experiences. I hold those sacred, and I've asked you if I could share those with Margie and you've given me permission. I won't talk about that here, but I will talk about some general things that I'm observing. I have an advantage, which maybe you don't at this point, because of these podcasts. We did not plan on these podcasts becoming what they are right now. I could not imagine when we started giving these little lessons to a few friends that we've served missions with in various places, that it would go to the point where it has and reached so many people. But it gives me the unique perspective that I have, and maybe I can share some things with you.

Let's go over to section 88 in the *Doctrine and Covenants*. I've had some things on my mind I want to share with you. Section 88 illustrates some principles and some patterns. What I'm learning from the exposure across the board to so many people is that men and women are attaining and obtaining these blessings. It is happening, and it's happening at an accelerating rate. Until about ten years ago, you couldn't have any real dialogue or obtain any information about these sacred things, i.e., *calling and election made sure,* the *Second Comforter,* the doctrine of translation, the *baptism of fire and the Holy Ghost,* the ministration of angels, etc. Even though these kinds of things are scriptural, and you could read about them, you would be hard-pressed to find a modern account of these things happening to someone here and now in our day. We always assumed that they were happening, but for you to come across an actual account of this happening to somebody other than a prophet, an apostle, or somebody in a general authority position, was really difficult.

One of my mentors was Hyrum L. Andrus. Some of you will know brother Andrus who was a BYU professor. I devoured all of Brother Andrus' material, which was from the *Pearl of Great Price* textbook that he used teaching the class at BYU. I took one of his classes. Brother Andrus was way ahead of his time, and it got him in trouble. He was severely censored by authorities for teaching some of the things he did in an open forum. He came under intense persecution from his peers at BYU, as did Glen Pace and a few others. They were just ahead of their time. They shared personal experiences that were as close as you could get at that time to what we are talking about here tonight. So, I just hung on every word and feasted on what Brother Andrus taught. Margie and I had an opportunity to go to his house and have Brother Andrus give us each personal blessings, which I hold sacred. This was ten years ago, and we discussed these same things. I will just tell you that in the blessing that Brother Andrus gave me, he mentioned three times that when talking about these things, I should "use wisdom and prudence." Those are the two words he used throughout the blessing. That was from a person who had been beaten up, persecuted by his peers, from members of his own church on talking about things that were part of the Restoration doctrines that the Lord revealed to the prophet Joseph Smith but had somehow become secretized. The old saying that those that have had those experiences don't talk about them and those that haven't had these experiences do is false doctrine. I am so happy that we have come away from that. What I want to tell you is, in 2016, these experiences of seeing the Lord and conversing with Him are now becoming more and more prevalent among Latter-day Saint men and women.

I want you to go to *Doctrine and Covenants* 88:83:

*He that seeketh me **early** shall find me,*

I want to come back to that in just a minute. Go back a few verses and go to verse 62. We're going to compare verses 62, 63, and 83 together.

[62] And again, verily I say unto you, my friends,

These are the six men who were meeting with Joseph in the School of the Prophets: Lyman Wright, Sidney Rigdon, and others that were mentioned as being assembled in section 88 verse 1:

> *I leave these sayings with you to ponder in your hearts, with this **commandment***

You should triple underline that word *commandment*:

> *which I give unto you,* [Here it is] *that ye shall call upon me **while I am near**—*

You ought to circle those four words, *"while I am near."* Those words indicate that He is not always near. But at this point, when section 88 is given here in 1832, the commandment was that you call on Him while He is near. I want to testify to you that He is **near** now, in 2016! I believe that He is closer and that the fulfillment of verse 62 is more relevant right now as I'm speaking than ever before since the day of the Restoration. A *"**commandment** which I give unto you, that ye shall call upon me while I am near—"* Then look:

> [63] *Draw near unto me and I will draw near unto you;*

That requires you to make the first move. If you're sitting back and waiting for Him, you will wait and die in your waiting, without an encounter. **You** must act and step out. *"Draw near unto me and* [then] *I will draw near unto you,"* but you have to make the first move. And depending on what you want, that first move is more likely than not, going to be very unorthodox.

Now, go back down to verse 83:

> *He that seeketh me **early** shall find me,*

The 1828 *Noah Webster Dictionary* says that the root word of **early** means *to advance* or *to shoot up*. The definition says, *in advance of something else; forward; as in early fruit, that is fruit that comes to maturity before other fruit; early growth* or *first*. Go down to footnote 83b for the word **early**. It says *Procrastination,* and if you look in the Topical Guide under *Procrastination,* you will see the words *apathy, idleness, and slothful*. Procrastination is *to intentionally put off the doing of something that should be done* and is the opposite of what the Lord wants us to do. The feeling of these two verses (62 and 83) is that there is a time to act, and not procrastinate. There comes a time when He withdraws and is not **near,** and it is too late. When The Holy Spirit prompts us to seek His face, we need to cast away unbelief, take a step of faith into the dark, and move forward, trusting in Him. This all ties into the statement made by

Joseph that the time will come when we will realize that which we could have and should have done, but it will be TOO LATE! We must ***draw near*** to the Lord ***early***, and in verse 63 He says:

> *seek me diligently*

In all those other references it says, *"ask...and knock,"* and at this point, it usually says, *"seek and ye shall find."* This one says:

> *seek **me** diligently and ye shall find **me**;*

The key is to *seek diligently*. There's that implication of an uphill, pressing against resistance and opposition struggle. This is not the nice little picture of Jesus standing on the outside of the door of your heart, knocking on the door with no doorknob, and you have to open it from the inside. To even get Him to come to that door is going to require you to do something that is unorthodox, that is different. And again, we need to seek Him *early* before the days of our *"probation are past,"* as it says in Helaman 13:38:

> *Ye have **procrastinated** the day of your salvation until it is everlastingly too late, and your destruction is made sure;*

I listened to testimonies in testimony meeting today, and I've gotten past the point where Fast and Testimony meeting used to be a pet peeve. It just always bothered me that we would come to that meeting fasting and praying and in the spirit of fasting and prayer, and people would take it upon themselves to use that time to give a lesson or give a talk. We would get lesson-monies and travel-monies, but we wouldn't get **test**imonies. We wouldn't get what Alma calls, *"pure testimony."* There we are in fasting and prayer, prepared, and we get up and talk about Sunday School lessons, and we talk about visits to relatives, etc., etc. I have since learned that everybody is at a different place in their progression and that I shouldn't find fault and I shouldn't accuse, but I should sit there and just enjoy the association and the society of the saints and do what I can within my own little circle to help things move upstream:

> *[63]...**seek** me diligently and ye shall find me; **ask**, and ye shall receive; **knock**, and it shall be opened unto you.*

> *[64] Whatsoever ye ask the Father in my name it shall be given unto you,* **that is expedient for you***.*

That's the part right there: *expedient*. I can tell you that *expedient* is this: the Lord wants you to pierce the veil. It's *expedient* that you do that. What's not *expedient* is that you have unbelief, doubts, and fear that will keep you from coming unto Him. What's *expedient* is, *"If any of you...[will] ask of God, that giveth...liberally and upbraideth not; and it shall be given him."* That's *expedient!* Look at verse 67:

> *And if your eye be single to my glory, your whole bodies shall be filled with light...*
>
> *[68] Therefore, sanctify yourselves that your minds become single to God, and the days will come* ***that you shall see him****; for he will unveil his face unto you, and it shall be in his own time, and in his own way, and according to his own will.*

That's the *Second Comforter*. That's what the Lord wants. And can I tell you, there are more people, men and women, that are obtaining this than you think! You, in all probability, in your associations with the members in your stakes and in your wards, have shaken hands with and know Latter-day Saint men and women who have obtained the presence of the Lord. They're not in positions of high profile. They're not necessarily in church leadership. They are the quiet ones. They are the "STP's," the same ten people who do everything quietly within their wards and their branches and their stakes. In quiet, sacred moments, when moved upon by the Spirit, they may testify to you of things that eye hath not seen, neither the ear heard, nor hath entered into the hearts of men the things which the Lord has in reserve for those who love Him and keep His commandments, *the chosen vessels*. More and more, they are casting their pearls and testifying. The day will come in the second half of *the dispensation of the fullness of times, the Day of Israel*, when these things that are now spoken carefully, but are spoken, will be spoken openly and testified of. That's the day that is coming.

Let's go over to section 67 for just a minute, brothers and sisters. Let me show you some other things that I have had on my mind. This is so wonderful! Again, I'm in such a position that my confidence is so high, and my trust in the Lord is so deep and complete. I am ridding myself of the vestiges of unbelief, and I'm doing it, to a large portion, because of you. What you share with me rips that unbelief away. I hear your testimonies, I hear your voice, and I read your words, and my confidence waxes strong in the presence of the Lord. I can move forward, and I know I can obtain. Section 67 verse 10:

> *And again, verily I say unto you that it is your **privilege**, and a **promise** I give unto you that have been ordained unto this ministry, that inasmuch as you strip yourselves from jealousies and fears, and humble yourselves before me, for ye are not sufficiently humble, the veil shall be rent and you shall see me and know that I am—*

This part ties in with my lesson today because I want to talk to you about the veil. You will see Him and know that He is:

> *not with the carnal neither natural mind, but with the spiritual.*

In order for you to have this experience and access this privilege and promise, you are going to have to step out of this world. We're in the carnal, temporal, natural world and it is enmity against God. This whole world is counter to God and who He is. We're going to have to step out:

> *[11] For no man has seen God at any time **in the flesh*** [that's the *Second Comforter*], *except quickened by the Spirit of God.*

You are going to have to see Him with the spiritual mind, not with the carnal or with the natural. You're going to have to be *quickened* by the Spirit of God to do it! Look at 12:

> *Neither can any natural man abide the presence of God, neither after the carnal mind.*

You have to tie that back to verse 10. You're not going to see Him with the carnal or natural. You're not going to see Him in the carnal or natural world. There has to be a change. And look at verse 13:

> *Ye are not able to abide the presence of God now, neither the ministering of angels; wherefore, continue in patience until ye are perfected.*

And I love this part:

[14] Let not your minds turn back;
Once you've started this journey, don't go back. Don't let Lucifer (Satan) rob you of your privilege and promise that God Almighty gives you, to **see His face in the flesh**:

> *and when ye are worthy, in mine own due time, ye shall see and know that which was conferred upon you by the hands of my servant Joseph Smith, Jun. Amen.*

What Joseph conferred upon them were the keys that open the veil and place you in the presence of God. That was restored to him.

Let's go to another place here. Let's go to section 84 and let me show you one other thing I saw this week. Section 84, verses 17-25 talk about the failure of the house of Israel in the days of Moses to obtain the *Second Comforter*. We've talked about this so we won't go into it in any detail. Prior to verse 17, it talks about priesthood and how it's been used upon earth from Adam on up to Moses and gives some interesting and powerful information. Verse 19 says:

> *And this greater priesthood administereth the gospel and holdeth the key of the mysteries of the kingdom, even the key of the knowledge of God.*

Now, remember that Jesus is, *"the author and finisher of our faith."* What we're striving to do here is to enter into His presence while in the flesh and obtain what's reserved for us there. *Priesthood* is the channel in which the keys are revealed on how to enter into the presence of God and have your faith finished. *"Jesus [is] the author and the finisher of [your] faith."* He is the plan. He is the way. He has given us the knowledge of how we do this. In his book, *Following the Light of Christ into His Presence*, John Pontius teaches the formula for how we can go step by step, one at a time until we are in the presence of God. Then, like Abraham, we can say, *"Thy servant has sought thee earnestly; now I have found thee."*

It's interesting to me that those verses talk about the rejection, and so in verse 25 the Lord takes:

> *....Moses out of their midst, and the Holy Priesthood also;*

Then let's go on over here to verse 54. Here's the tie-in I have. There are lots of different things in this section—*the oath and covenant of the priesthood*, and in verses 43-49 lots of information on *the light of truth* and *the Spirit of Christ*. Then in verses 50-52, it talks about coming unto the Father and escaping *"the bondage of sin."* Verse 54:

> *And your minds in times past have been darkened because of unbelief,*
>
> *[55] Which vanity and unbelief have brought the whole church under condemnation.*

Unbelief about what? What is the unbelief that has condemned the church?

> *[56] And this condemnation resteth upon the children of Zion, even all.*
>
> *[57] And they shall remain under this condemnation until they repent and remember the new covenant, even the Book of Mormon and the former commandments which I have given them, not only to say, but to do according to that which I have written—*
>
> *[58] That they may bring forth fruit meet for their Father's kingdom; otherwise there remaineth a scourge and judgment to be poured out upon the children of Zion.*

That scourge is to bring us to a state of humility where we can re-enter and re-commit to the covenant that we take lightly because of unbelief, which covenant has to do with the *Book of Mormon* and treating lightly the things which God has given us. <u>I believe</u> that it is not by coincidence that the story of the Children of Israel rejecting their *Second Comforter* invitation is only a few verses removed from the verses that talk about the latter-day church being condemned. I believe we are under condemnation because we treat lightly, or not at all, this whole doctrine of obtaining the face of the Lord in the flesh and having a *Second Comforter* experience. I believe that is what we treat lightly. Brothers and sisters, we have all but removed this doctrine from our doctrinal discourse in the Church. It's all but gone. And if that isn't treating something powerful and monumental lightly, then I don't know what is. That could bring us to condemnation.

What is interesting to me is that the *Book of Mormon* is a record, from beginning to end, that teaches us, step by step, how to obtain the *Second Comforter*. If you want to know what the main message of the *Book of Mormon* is, it's how to come unto *"this Jesus"* that Moroni talks about. He says, *"...he hath talked with me face to face, and...he told me in plain humility."* If the *Book of Mormon,* from 1 Nephi chapter 1, verse 1, which talks about being *"highly favored of the Lord,"* and ends with Moroni discussing coming unto *"this Jesus"* face to face and speaking with Him in plain humility, isn't a volume that teaches you how to obtain this lofty encounter, then I don't know what is. Is that what we're talking about with the condemnation because we have left the doctrine of the *Second Comforter*? We have left the doctrine of *calling and election made sure*? We've left the doctrine of the *baptism by fire and the Holy Ghost*?

Go with me to 3 Nephi 11, to the appearance of Christ in America. What's the first thing that He talks about after He introduces Himself and they have a mass *Second Comforter* experience? That goes through verse 17, then the next thing He talks about is the ordinance of baptism. He spends the whole rest of the chapter talking about the ordinance of baptism. In verse 32, He says;

> *And this is my doctrine,*

And what's the doctrine? Go to the bottom of verse 32:

> *...the Father commandeth all men, everywhere, to repent and believe in me.*
> *[33] And whoso believeth in me, and is baptized, the same shall be saved;*

Verse 35:

> *Verily, verily, I say unto you, that* **this is my doctrine** [repent and be baptized],

Now, I want to skip down to verse 37:

> *And again*

Here we go, *"again,"* reiteration, one thing after another. What's the doctrine of Christ? What's the Father commanding us to do? "The Father commands everybody to repent, come unto Me, the Lord Jesus Christ, and be baptized in My name and you shall be saved."

> *[37] And **again** I say unto you, ye must repent, and become as a little child, and be baptized in my name, or ye can in nowise receive these things.*
> *[38] And **again** I say unto you, ye must repent, and be baptized in my name, and become as a little child, or ye can in nowise inherit the kingdom of God.*
> *[39] Verily, verily, I say unto you, that **this is my doctrine**,*

So, what's the doctrine? Repent, become as a little child, be baptized, and you shall be saved:

> *and whoso buildeth upon this buildeth upon my rock, and the gates of hell shall not prevail against them.*

The gates of hell are the gates that are in a wall that surrounds those people in hell. When you enter into those gates and become a part of that hellish society, to get out of there is difficult because they *"prevail against [you]."* They are locked and secured. You don't want to enter those gates or enter that society because once you're in there, it is difficult and, in some cases, impossible to be delivered. You don't want to even get close to those gates. Look at verse 40:

> *And whoso shall declare more or less than this,*

More or less than what? To repent, become as a little child, and be baptized:

> *and establish it for my doctrine, the same cometh of evil, and is not built upon my rock;*

So, brothers and sisters, what is the one attribute of a little child? You could say they are innocent, but I'll tell you that one of the characteristics of a little child is they ask a lot of questions. What's the Lord telling us? Repent and ask a lot of questions. Don't be afraid. There is no such thing as a bad question. There are only unasked questions. That's bad! I've had people come to me as a teacher and say this kind of thing, "This may be a dumb question..." The only dumb question is the one that is not asked. If you want the *Second Comforter*, you must ask questions. Ask, ask, ask! You take it to the Lord. You go to the source. That's what a little child is. They ask questions, and they **believe** when the person they're asking gives them the answer! They don't second guess the answer. **Ask,** and ye shall receive.

Well, those are the things that have been on my mind lately. We are on the edge. Another thing I thought about this week is that you can see indicators that you know that the Lord is near and that He's striving for people to come up and behold His face while in the flesh. It is a mighty striving. It is a downward reaching from heaven, and there must be an upward reaching from earth. If you take that downward reaching and put a base to it, it forms a pyramid. You take that upward reaching, and you put a ceiling to it, it's a pyramid. If you overlap those two pyramids together, you have the seal of Solomon, which is called the Star of David, which is the Savior Star. There are different stars that belong to the members of the Godhead. The Star of the Elohim is the Melchizedek Star. There's a five-sided star, a six-sided star, a seven-sided star, and there's an eight-sided star. The eight-sided star is two squares overlapping at an angle that creates eight points. That is the Seal of Melchizedek and is the Star of the Elohim. We need to be reaching up because I promise you, He is reaching down and waiting for you to make the first move.

I want to go over to Ether 3 and talk to you these remaining few minutes about the veil here. There is probably more than one veil. I'm not going to say there's only one because I don't know. I have learned some things, and the Spirit has taught me some things this week that I want to share with you that I believe I am interpreting correctly. Ether 3 is the story of Mahonrimoriancumur. Let's go to verse 19. I want you to look at the wording here:

> *[19] And because of the knowledge of this man he could not be kept **from beholding within the veil**;*

Notice that wording, *"from beholding within the veil."* In other words, as long as you are kept within the veil, you can't behold. What he did brought him into a position outside the veil. Look at the bottom of verse 19:

> *and he had faith no longer, for he knew, nothing doubting.*

Now, verse 20, here we go again:

> *Wherefore, having this perfect knowledge of God,*
> *he could not be kept from within the veil;*

It seems like the brother of Jared finds himself **within** a veil. Not behind one or not on the other side, but the word is **within**. And in order for him to see the things that he sees, he has to come without. I was thinking about that peculiar wording, *"could not be kept from...within the veil."* Our physical body that is made up of the elements of the natural world: is that the veil? I've pondered that, and I'll come back to that in just a minute.

Go over to Ether 12:21:

> *And after the brother of Jared had beheld the finger of the Lord, because of the promise which the brother of Jared had obtained by faith, the Lord could not withhold anything from his sight; wherefore he showed him all things, for he* [the brother of Jared] *could no longer be kept without the veil.*

In other words, there was something restricting him from coming to the other side, but because of promises and faith, he was able to make that escape and see something outside. I pondered that and isn't it interesting that every time people have these so-called near-death experiences, they see things in the spiritual realm. I never did like the term near death because it wasn't **near** death; they died. I think of Spencer's experiences in *Visions of Glory* and what he saw and beheld all came when he was dead, and his spirit left that body. It was outside the body. Is the body the veil? Once you step outside of that veil, do you behold? We'll go back to section 67 where it says:

> *[10] ...the veil shall be rent and you shall see me and know that I am— not with the carnal, neither natural mind, but with the spiritual.*

You see, everything that is carnal, everything that's physical, everything that's temporal, everything that's natural, is a barrier to things which are spiritual. The *Second Comforter* experience is certainly a spiritual experience.

We have a tendency to think that the things of the spirit are not the **real** things. In our convoluted, natural-man thinking, we think that the things in this world are the real things and that anything outside of this world is not necessarily real. The older I get, the more I feel that this world is illusionary and that the real world is what's **outside** of the natural world. Some of you have shared *Second Comforter* experiences, and because you're like me, you feel that when Jesus comes to you, He comes in this world, He comes into this world. I'm not going to say that He can't, frankly, because I don't know at this point. When Joseph sees the Father and the Son, nine times in the account he calls it a vision. Nowhere does he call it a visitation. How many times do we hear of people having the *Second Comforter* experience, where they see God face to face, and they say something like this, "Whether in the body or out of the body, I know not." How many times have you read that? This is what got me thinking about this, where Moroni says the brother of Jared, *"could not be kept from within the veil,"* whether in the body or out of the body. And then, we talk about out of body experiences. Almost always, all of those out of body experiences are encounters with the spiritual side of things where you see other people. You see whole congregations and societies; you see God and angels and all kinds of things, but it doesn't happen until you are out of the body.

So, I guess what I want to say to all of us today is that maybe we need to look at this not necessarily differently. But in addition to what we are thinking, maybe we need to be looking for that appearance of Christ as not so much **Him** walking into my room and saying, "Here I am, come up and handle me," as much as **something happening to you**. *Doctrine and Covenants* 67 says you're not going to have this experience until you are *"quickened by the Spirit of God."* Quickened means *to be made alive*, and that may be your *Second Comforter* experience. Doesn't change the fact that you see Him, that He calls you by name, that He invites you to come up and witness for yourself the wounds in his hands and feet and side, that He embraces you and you feel the warmth of His body, that He kisses you on the cheek, and that He lays hands on your head. It doesn't change the fact that that can all happen and probably will, **outside of the natural world**. Some of you have called up and shared with me and said, "I've had this experience," and you go on to share an experience. "Brother Stroud, I don't think it was in this world. I don't know, but I don't think it was in this world. But I found

Him. I saw Him, He spoke to me. He embraced me. I felt His body." That can all happen. It can happen in the spiritual realm. You don't have to be in the physical body to have that experience is what I'm saying. I'm not going to say that it can't because obviously in 3 Nephi 11 the Lord Jesus Christ appeared in this world and 2,500 people went up and had an encounter while they were in this world. But, I think we need to broaden our thinking on this and not limit this to when you look for the Savior to come, you look for Him to walk into your bedroom, or for Him to meet you on a mountaintop, or in a solitary desert place. It may be that you are in those places and taken out and encounter Him, in His own way, in His own time, and according to His own will.

Let's broaden our horizons, my dear brothers and sisters. The important point is that you have that encounter. Think about what it is you want to sacrifice because *"[you] receive no witness until after the trial of your faith."* I'll just share this, and I don't suppose Margie would mind. We fast once a week as a part of our sacrifice. Then we thought about what else we could give up that would be difficult, a sacrifice. Both of us decided that we were going to give up cookies, candies, chocolate, and dessert. No small thing in this world, especially in a Mormon society where everything is red punch and cookies. That's a part of the things we decided we wanted to do. Another thing is, we attend the temple weekly and say our prayers three times a day. In my fasting, I ask the Lord to help me visualize and *"[see] with [the] eye of faith."* I know that before I see my beloved Savior and have a *Second Comforter* experience, I'll need to have seen that experience in my mind, envisioning it through *"the eye of faith"* before the actual encounter takes place and I find myself, as Ether says, *"glad."*

Well, brothers and sister, I love the Gospel. I'm so excited about what's happening here. I'm excited for you! I'm excited about what is happening to you! Not that I am the fount of all knowledge, I am not. I am humbled that you even listen to this. Margie and I really are quite amazed that anybody is even listening. We're humbled and grateful that you are because through that there's an exchange, and we are the beneficiaries.

God bless you. I testify that you are on the right track. Don't let anything take you away! **Don't turn back!** In the name of Jesus Christ, amen.

Resources:
James 1:5-6
D&C 88:118 *"...seek ye out of the best books words of wisdom..."*
Teachings of Joseph Smith, Chapter 36, *"if you gaze into heaven five minutes..."*
Biography of Neal A. Maxwell, *The Disciple's Life* by Bruce C. Hafen
Articles of Faith 1:4
King Follet Sermon, "It is the first principle of the gospel to know for a certainty the character of God..."
Teaching of Presidents of the Church: Joseph Smith Chapter 22 pages 201-270
D&C 88: 62-68, 82-83 also Proverbs 8:17 *and **those** that **seek me early shall find me.***
Helaman 13:38
Matthew 7:7 *"...seek and ye shall find..."*
Alma 4:19 *"...pure testimony..."*
Moroni 7:31 *"...the chosen vessels..."*
D&C 67: 10-14
D&C 84:17-25, 43-49, 50-52, 54-57
Hebrews 12:2 *"...Jesus the author and finisher of our faith..."*
Following the Light of Christ into His Presence by John Pontius
Abraham 2:12 *"Thy servant has sought thee earnestly; now I have found thee."*
Ether 12:41 *"...this Jesus..."*
Ether 12:39 *"...he hath talked with me face to face, and that he told me in plain humility..."*
1 Nephi 1:1 *"...highly favored of the Lord..."*
3 Nephi 11:32-40
Ether 3:19-20
Ether 12:21
Visions of Glory by John Pontius
D&C 67:10-12
Ether 12:6 *"...ye receive no witness until after the trial of your faith."*
Ether 12:19 *"...beheld with an eye of faith, and they were glad."*

ABOUT THE AUTHOR

 Mike Stroud was born March 1944 to Walt and Eileen Stroud in Salt Lake City, Utah. He attended BYU and received a BA and MA degree.

He is trained in Outdoor Survival and Primitive Living. He has spent a lifetime in the outdoors as a hunter, tracker, and outdoorsman.

Mike enjoys training horses and has spent many years exploring wild places on horseback. He is a western history lover and re-enacts the mountain man era, and the old west.

He served a mission to Bavaria, Germany, and he and Margie have served missions together in Mongolia, Central Philippines, and in New Jersey.

Mike has spent his lifetime as a teacher, working 27 years in The Church of Jesus Christ of Latter-day Saints Church Education System. He retired from CES in 2006.

Mike and Margie reside in Eagar, Arizona. He is the father of 12 children, 29 grandchildren, and 7 great-grandchildren.

Made in the USA
San Bernardino, CA
14 April 2018